Social Work and Mental Health in Scotland

Transforming Social Work Practice – titles in the series

To order, please contact our distributor: BEBC Distribution, Albion Close, Parkstone, Poole, BH12 3LL. Telephone: 0845 230 9000, email: learningmatters@bebc.co.uk. You can also find more information on each of these titles and our other learning resources at www.learningmatters.co.uk.

Social Work and Mental Health in Scotland

STEVE HOTHERSALL
MIKE MAAS-LOWIT
MALCOLM GOLIGHTLEY

Series Editors: Jonathan Parker and Greta Bradley

First published in 2008 by Learning Matters Ltd.

All rights reserved. No part of this publication may be reproduced, stored in a retrieval system, or transmitted in any form by any means, electronic, mechanical, photocopying, recording, or otherwise, without prior permission in writing from Learning Matters.

© 2008 Steve Hothersall, Mike Maas-Lowit and Malcolm Golightley

British Library Cataloguing in Publication Data
A CIP record for this book is available from the British Library.

ISBN: 978 1 84445 130 2

The rights of Steve Hothersall, Mike Maas-Lowit and Malcolm Golightley to be identified as the Authors of this Work have been asserted by them in accordance with the Copyright, Designs and Patents Act 1988.

Cover and text design by Code 5 Design Associates Ltd
Project management by Deer Park Productions, Tavistock, Devon
Typeset by Pantek Arts Ltd, Maidstone, Kent
Printed and bound in Great Britain by Ashford Colour Press Ltd

Learning Matters Ltd
33 Southernhay East
Exeter EX1 1NX
Tel: 01392 215560
info@learningmatters.co.uk
www.learningmatters.co.uk

Contents

v

List of abbreviations

ACVO	Aberdeen Council of Voluntary Organisations
AMP	approved medical practitioner
BASW	British Association of Social Workers
BMA	British Medical Association
BPS	British Psychological Society
CAMHS	child and adolescent mental health services
CBT	cognitive behavioural therapy
CFI	Camberwell Family Interview
CIPFA	Chartered Institute of Public Finance and Accountancy
CORO	compulsion order with a restriction order
CPA	Care Programme Approach
CPN	community psychiatric nurse
CSIP	Care Services Improvement Partnership
CSWO	Chief Social Work Officer
CTO	compulsory treatment order
DES	Dissociative Experiences Scale
DID	dissociative identity disorder
DoH	Department of Health
EC	European Commission
ECT	electroconvulsive therapy
EE	expressed emotion
EMCDDA	European Monitoring Centre for Drugs and Drug Addiction
EU	European Union
EVOC	Edinburgh Voluntary Organisations Council
GDS	Geriatric Depression Scale
GHQ	General Health Questionnaire
GIRFEC	'Getting It Right for Every Child'
GP	general practitioner
GTCS	General Teaching Council for Scotland
HMIe	Her Majesty's Inspectorate of Education
HMSO	Her Majesty's Stationery Office
HUG	Highland Users Group
IAF	Integrated Assessment Framework

ICP	individual care pathway
IPT	interpersonal therapy
MAPPA	multi-agency public protection arrangements
MDO	mentally disordered offender
MHO	mental health officer
MHTS	Mental Health Tribunal for Scotland
MWC	Mental Welfare Commission
NES	NHS Scotland Education
NHS	National Health Service
NICE	National Institute for Clinical Excellence
NIMHE	National Institute of Mental Health for England
NMC	Nursing and Midwifery Council
ONS	Office for National Statistics
OPCS	Office of Population, Censuses and Surveys
OPG	Office of the Public Guardian
OPM	Office of Public Management
OT	occupational therapist
PHCT	primary health care team
PHIS	Public Health Institute of Scotland
QoL	quality of life
RMA	Risk Management Authority
RMO	responsible medical officer
SACAM	Scottish Advisory Committee on Alcohol Misuse
SACDM	Scottish Advisory Committee on Drug Misuse
SAMH	Scottish Association for Mental Health
SCID-D	Structured Clinical Interview
ScotPHO	Scottish Public Health Observatory
SiSWE	Standards in Social Work Education
SPDN	Scottish Personality Disorder Network
SSRI	selective seratonin reuptake inhibitor
SSSC	Scottish Social Services Council
SWSI	Social Work Services Inspectorate
TMS	transcranial magnetic stimulation
VNS	vagus nerve stimulation
WHO	World Health Organisation

Introduction

This book is a text for students of mental health social work and for those in related professions. We know of no other such exclusively Scottish text at this level and, as such, it appears to be unique. It may be used as a beginner's guide to mental health law and policy in Scotland and it may, therefore, be of value to practitioners of greater experience who come anew to the mental health arena. For example, practitioners contemplating taking the step up to Mental Health Officer training will find it very useful as an introductory orientation before beginning their MHO studies.

The book is a completely new edition of *Social work and mental health* (Golightley, 2006) which has been substantially revised to accommodate the Scottish mental health scene.

The question a reader might ask at this point is *exactly how much revision was needed to shift the perspective from England/Wales to Scotland*?

The answer is that since the inception of the Scottish Parliament in 1999, mental health law, policy, practice and ethos have changed so dramatically as to represent a quantum shift from what is happening south of the border. There were always some marked differences between Scottish and English/Welsh law and policy, but the advent of the Scottish Parliament in 1999 coincided with the movement for change in mental health service provision in Scotland gaining critical mass and it is possible that no other aspect of civil life in Scotland has been so dramatically overhauled since devolution.

It was therefore not just a case of changing all the references to law and policy in this book, substantial though that exercise was in itself. The very tone of much of the text has had to be changed to take account of what is now a very *Scottish* perspective. Some of this is reflected in the policy drivers to include *recovery* in all aspects of a person's journey through mental health services, the notion that everybody is entitled to find an individual personal solution to their mental health problems and to walk a path towards their own recovery. Some of the difference is found in the relatively different ethnic mix of modern Scotland as well as the fact that Scotland, while not free of racism and ethnic tensions, has so far not felt the impact of some of the major incidents like *Clunis* (Ritchie et al., 1994) and *Bennett*, which indicate large-scale problems in how mental health services are delivered to the black community. Some of the difference is also found in the institutions of the Scottish Parliament and the Scottish Government which diverge widely from aspects of Westminster.

Much of the crucial difference is, however, to be found in the rapidly changed law around mental health in Scotland which has necessitated making three new chapters out of the original one relating to the law in the original Golightley edition. Some of the tone of the original text has been altered because the close working relationship between health and social work partners in Scotland, while not devoid of tensions, make the old conflict between medical and social models of mental health and illness seem out of date.

However, the most subtle and all-pervasive difference is in the shift in thinking about mental health which, early on in the book, causes the authors to have to explain the use of terms like *mental health, mental disorder, mental illness* and *mental well-being*.

The reader might now ask the question *what has been retained from the original book?* This book has kept the original text where it has not had to be revised by the above. It has retained the original structure and the focus upon social work, mental disorder, the medical perspective, the orientation to service users' perspectives and to ethics, values and anti-discriminatory practice but reoriented these towards the uniquely Scottish developments referred to above.

It is hoped that this book conveys a flavour of the optimism surrounding mental health in Scotland despite the strange mix of prejudicial attitudes to people who struggle to maintain good mental health and the chronic and endemic poor mental health felt by vast numbers of the population (a strange mix because it is surely counter to self-interest for us to be prejudiced against something which is very likely to impact upon ourselves). Scotland is a relatively small place of about 5 million people. That means that much can be achieved on a manageable scale. However, this book is not merely an explanation of the wonderful steps towards improving the mental well-being of the population as it is also critical of the process and very open about discussing the huge problems faced.

Chapter outline

Chapter 1 introduces the concepts of mental health, mental illness and mental disorder. It discusses social work practice in relation to these concepts by way of introducing a discourse on values and an ethical base for practice. It gives illustration of this with recourse to race and ethnicity, disability and other attributes which amplify the problems experienced by service users. The chapter also introduces some different ways of understanding mental health and mental illness. Most notably it discusses the medical framework for understanding, diagnosing and treating mental disorder and the social orientation to understanding its impact upon individuals.

Chapter 2 discusses civil law in Scotland as it relates to mental disorder, with a central focus on the Mental Health (Care and Treatment) (Scotland) Act 2003 and the sources of human rights law.

Chapter 3 introduces the concepts of capacity and incapacity and relates them to the protective suite of legislation (Adults with Incapacity (Scotland) Act 2000 and Adult Support and Protection (Scotland) Act 2007.

Chapter 4 completes the introduction to what is often called 'mental health law'. It focuses on criminal law aspects of the Mental Health (Care and Treatment) (Scotland) Act 2003 and the Criminal Procedures (Scotland) Act 1995. The chapter also focuses on risk assessment and management strategies and policy for mentally disordered offenders.

Chapter 5 discusses the policy and practice relating to child and adolescent services in Scotland.

Chapter 6 expands the discussion of practice-related issues by examining provision for people who receive short-term assistance. It centres on support for depression and prevention of suicide.

Chapter 7 continues the theme of practice in relation to the provision of longer-term assistance and service users with longitudinal needs. It focuses upon the case study of a man with schizophrenia.

Chapter 8 provides a focus on inter-professional working. It introduces wider issues relating to the *dynamics* of collaboration, examining some of the influences such as the legal and policy frameworks which facilitate effective partnerships.

Chapter 1

Perspectives, ethics and values in mental health social work

ACHIEVING A SOCIAL WORK DEGREE

This chapter will help you to begin to meet the following (Scottish) Standards in Social Work Education (SiSWE) (Scottish Executive, 2003a), available at: www.scotland.gov.uk/library5/social/ffsw.pdf.

Key Role 1: Prepare for, and work with, individuals, families, carers, groups and communities to assess their needs and circumstances.

Learning Focus:

1.1 Preparing for social work contact and involvement.

1.2 Working with individuals, families, carers, groups and communities so they can make informed decisions.

1.3 Assessing needs and options in order to recommend a course of action.

Key Role 2: Plan, carry out, review and evaluate social work practice with individuals, families, carers, groups, communities and other professionals.

Learning Focus:

2.2 Working with individuals, families, carers, groups and communities to achieve change, promote dignity, realise potential and improve life opportunities.

2.5 Working with groups to promote choice and independent living.

Key Role 3: Assess and manage risk to individuals, families, carers, groups, communities, self and colleagues.

Learning Focus:

3.1 Assessing and managing risks to individuals, families, carers, groups and communities.

3.2 Assessing and managing risk to self and colleagues.

Key Role 4: Demonstrate professional competence in social work practice.

Learning Focus:

4.1 Evaluating and using up-to-date knowledge of, and research into, social work practice.

4.2 Working within agreed standards of social work practice.

4.3 Understanding and managing complex ethical issues, dilemmas and conflicts.

4.4 Promoting best social work practice, adapting positively to change.

Key Role 6: Support individuals to represent and manage their needs, views and circumstances.

Learning Focus:

6.1 Representing, in partnership with, and on behalf of, individuals, families, carers, groups and communities to help them achieve and maintain greater independence.

Introduction

Bud Powell, one of the great jazz piano players of the twentieth century, spent periods of his life in mental hospitals in Paris and New York. When asked by his friend and carer Francis Paudras about the source of his problems, he answered: *I hope that your spirit will always be in accord with your being and installed in a strong and well balanced body* (Paudras, 1998).

This chapter examines the relationship between values and contemporary social work practice in mental health services provision. This has a crucial role in relation to the people of Scotland who, in comparison to most Western countries, experience relatively poor mental health. For example, one study found it to rate 23rd out of 29 Western countries (WHO, 1998). This is manifested in a very high suicide rate, high recorded instances of deliberate self-harm and high prescription rates for anti-depressant medication (Scottish Executive, 2007a, 2007g). Out of an awareness of this, mental health services in Scotland have been in a process of major transition since the inception of the Scottish Parliament in 1999 in an attempt to produce a service that is appropriate and responsive to service user needs. This theme of change is introduced in this chapter and followed through in the rest of the book.

The chapter also deals with what is meant by mental illness and mental health and the importance of understanding what various diagnoses mean, and the implications of adopting medical models is assessed. A complementary perspective that incorporates the impact and relevance of factors such as gender, ethnicity and age is also explored. Overlaid onto these are discussions surrounding broader social and structural factors which often manifest through social exclusion and isolation. These are also themes that will be developed throughout the book.

Values and ethics are at the heart of culturally competent and ethically sound professional practice. This means that social workers should be able to value and understand their own culture and be able to work in a sensitive manner with people from other cultures. To become culturally competent requires empathy, understanding and accepting of differences (Patel et al., 2003; Walker, 2003b).

According to the Scottish Government,[1] drawing on data from the European Commission (EC, 2005), approximately one person in four will experience mental health problems at some time in their life and many of them will seek help from a professional. It is usually the family doctor who is the 'first port of call'. With more severe cases, they in turn refer people on to the various agencies whose remit is to provide specialised mental health services. These services include health, social care and social work agencies that are trying to work together to provide a seamless service for the user. Some GP practices have social workers attached to them and this often means that these workers will be doing direct work with service users, working in the community alongside other mental health professionals. Social workers also work in psychiatric hospitals and in specialist community mental health teams, some of which may have a specialist remit for children. Social workers outside the mental health setting also come across mental health problems in addition to the *presenting problem* that led to referral in the first place. Furthermore, there is a wide range of social workers in various voluntary services from social support services to residential and supported accommodation services.

Within this book we shall guide you through the various levels of service organisation and delivery.

What is meant by mental health?

The World Heath Organisation describes mental health as:

> *a state of well-being in which the individual realizes his or her abilities, can cope with the normal stresses of life, can work productively and fruitfully, and is able to make a contribution to his or her community.* (WHO, 2001, p11)

A strategy for the mental health of the European Union

In January 2005 the World Health Organisation held a conference for European Ministers to start a process of drawing up a framework for comprehensive action and political commitment to mental health. This led to a Green Paper which is intended to stimulate debate within Europe and to engage a broad range of institutions, health and social care professionals, the research community and service users in discussions about how best to improve public mental health.

The Green Paper outlines three areas for improvement:

- *Mental ill health affects every fourth citizen and can lead to suicide, a cause of too many deaths.*

- *Mental ill health causes significant losses and burdens to the economic, social, educational as well as criminal and justice systems.*

- *Stigmatisation, discrimination and non-respect for the human rights and the dignity of mentally ill and disabled people still exist, challenging core European values.*

The Paper goes on to describe how mental health is a growing challenge to the EU and supports the WHO view that, by 2020, depression will be the highest-ranking cause of disease in the developed world (WHO, 2001). Other statistics include the statement that:

> *Currently, in the EU, some 58,000 citizens die from suicide every year; more than from the annual deaths from road accidents, homicide or HIV/AIDS.* (EC, 2005, p4)

Clearly there are significant inequalities within member states and the Paper proposes that a strategy would be focused upon the prevention of mental ill health, the improvement of the quality of life for people with mental health problems and the development of a mental health information and research system for the EU.

A word about terminology

There are different terms currently used to describe the same thing. You will hear terms such as mental distress, mental illness, mental disorder, mental health problems and mental ill health all used by professionals and policy-makers. In this book the following terms are used.

Mental disorder

This is the specific term used in mental health legislation as discussed and it has a precise meaning:

> *... mental disorder means any–*

- mental illness;

- personality disorder; or

- learning disability,

> *however caused or manifested; and cognate expressions shall be construed accordingly.*
> 'S 328 (1) Mental Health (Care and Treatment) (Scotland) Act 2003'

Mental illness

We will discuss mental illness in detail below. Suffice to say here that it is a medical concept which embodies the notion that the mind has a normal range of functioning which can be upset by illness, much as the working of the heart can be damaged or disrupted by heart disease. The mind can be described as the brain in action. It is the process of thought, memory, emotions, sensations, dreaming and so on that constitute the brain's daily activity. The relationship between *mind* and *brain* can be better understood if we think of it in relation to any physical activity of the body. We have already mentioned the *heart.* The brain is an organ, as is the heart. The heart beats to pump blood around the body. When we say that *the mind* is *the brain* in action, we can also say that *the heart beat* is the *heart* in action. There are diseases of the heart that are manifested in irregular heart beats (tachycardia, for example). Similarly, in the theory of mental illness, there are diseases of the mind, as the brain in action (schizophrenia, for example) as opposed to diseases of the brain itself (brain tumours, for example).

Personality disorder

It is outside the scope of this book to say much about personality disorder. Personality is a set of identifiable characteristics contained in a person's psychological make-up. You could think of it as the face of the psyche, the outwardly recognisable border between the person's inner world and other people. How it may be *disordered* or what may *disorder* it are subjects of great debate. For our purposes here, it is best to consider that we all have dysfunctional aspects of our personalities and therefore, some would argue, we all sit on the spectrum of personality disorder. However, personality disorder only becomes a serious issue when its maladaptiveness to relationships with others, with society and/or with the law attains a threshold worthy of clinical diagnosis. In diagnostic terms, there are many types of personality disorder such as anti-social, borderline and psychopathic personality disorders. Broad characteristics include things like difficulty in learning social rules and a seemingly selfish preoccupation with oneself, sometimes to the extent of only being able to relate to others for what personal gain can be extracted from the relationship.

We will briefly mention personality disorder in Chapter 4, in reference to mentally disordered people who break the law by committing criminal offences. There is a central issue around the diagnosis of personality disorder which has been problematic for those suffering from it and those who offer them services. This issue is that personality disorder is often considered, by even relatively well-informed practitioners, to be untreatable. To respond positively to this debate, the Scottish Executive gave funding to set up the Scottish Personality Disorder Network (SPDN) in 2004 (see websites at the end of this chapter for more information).

The SPDN contributes to the process of re-examining what may prove to be a myth of untreatability, by using research, discussion and information sharing. When we discuss integrated care pathways below and in Chapter 7, bear in mind that the NHS in Scotland is designing a care pathway for people with personality disorder. This is an attempt to get health care providers to address the treatment need of this group of people better. SPDN has set up a research programme and workshops where attendees are actively able to feedback on the work to date of the group looking at treatment pathways for borderline personality disorder. Encouragingly, the process of the SPDN draws on service user involvement and it is already clear that certain basic things do positively affect treatment outcomes, such as clear and consistent approaches to service users and openness, honesty and non-confusing communication with them. It may even come to pass that, in a few decades' time, we come to critically view how we treat people with personality disorder today, much as we look back upon the treatment of people affected by schizophrenia in the 1950s.

Learning disability (formerly known as mental deficiency, mental subnormality and mental handicap)

With learning disability, the individual's rate of development and progress is slower than for most and there is no treatment or cure as this is a long-term, permanent condition. Responses aim to provide an environment in which the individual can achieve their fullest potential.

Of the three components of mental disorder, our main preoccupation in this book is with mental illness.

Mental health and mental illness

We have already fallen into the common error of using terms imprecisely and therefore contributing to the general confusion. Do not be alarmed to read this. We did so knowingly because we had to say some very general things before taking you to the point where differentiating the terms would be meaningful. However, if you look back, you will note that we were reliant upon the term 'mental ill health' when we largely meant mental illness. We derived the term from a very reputable source in the European Green Paper (EC, 2005). It might also be more comfortable to use such a term when some people are offended by the notion that their own mental experiences are equated with an 'illness'. The word is loaded with connotations of power and the sometimes uncomfortable history of psychiatry (Foucault, 1964; Szasz, 1972).

In order to acknowledge these issues, we shall start to differentiate concepts by considering the more or less traditional way of conceiving of these things. Most commonly we can think of the range from being in a state of good mental health to being mentally ill (Figure 1.1).

Figure 1.1: Range of mental illness

The problem with this is that it is possible to be mentally unhealthy without being mentally ill and vice versa. To explain this further, let us set the word 'mental' aside for a moment. A person may be physically healthy and ill at the same time. Think of a very fit and sporty person who has diabetes for example. A person may also be unhealthy but not ill. Think of someone who takes no exercise, drinks five pints of beer every night and smokes forty cigarettes a day. There is an undeniable relationship between unhealthiness and illness because this person is likely to become ill sooner than people who take good care of their bodies, but the relationships are not so simple as in Figure 1.1.

Let us reintroduce the word *mental* now. Mental means 'relating to the mind'. As already discussed, the mind can be described as the brain in action. It is the process of thought, memory, emotions, sensations, dreaming and so on that constitute the brain's daily activity. The idea that one can experience mental health and, more importantly, one can take care of one's own mental health is very important in Scotland. As we will discuss below, there is an entire set of government policies targeted upon this idea out of a concern that as a nation we are at a point of crisis in our national mental health. The policies aim to address mental health and well-being. Well-being is an even broader term to describe a subjective state of feeling comfortable in, and well-adjusted to, the world.

In this conception, mental health has a separate but related range from good to poor, distinct from that of mental illness (Figure 1.2).

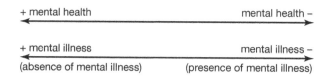

Figure 1.2: Range of mental health (see Tudor, 1996; Bromley and Curtis, 2003)

To further quantify mental health, good mental health would include a sense of being well adjusted to and attuned with the environment. While most human beings would seem to want to be happy most of the time, this does not equate with happiness. For example, it is mentally healthy to be sad when someone we love dies. Because human beings are social animals, good mental health extends to our relationships with others. Isolation, loneliness, lack of belongingness, social exclusion, being subject to hate or racism are all attributes of or contributors to poor mental health. The concept leans very heavily towards the 'Belongingness and Love' and 'Esteem' layers of Abraham Maslow's Hierarchy of Need (Maslow, 1987). If you are not familiar with this very useful way of conceiving of human needs, an excellent summary of it can be found at www.businessballs.com/maslow.htm.

In this book, as we progressively discuss the discrimination and social exclusion often experienced by people affected by mental illness, you will see how it is common that mental illness and poor mental health go hand in hand. However, by the simple analysis at Figure 1.2, it is possible to think in terms of taking steps to improve the mental health of mentally ill people by helping them to have more control over their lives, by breaking down barriers and confronting stigma and discrimination and by facilitating social inclusion and belongingness.

Having thus sorted out mental health from mental illness, you should be aware of the ways the terms are used from now on in the book. Also have an eye to the less focused way in which the term 'mental health' is used, even by very official sources, sometimes to great confusion. Why, for example, should 'mental health law', which is principally about mental illness and generally about mental disorder, be named after 'mental health'?

The strategy for Scotland

Health is one of the policy areas where powers are devolved to the Scottish Parliament. Therefore the planning and implementation of health policy is the remit of government in Edinburgh and its Civil Service, *the Scottish Government* (which was called *the Scottish Executive* until September 2007). The government has set about improving mental health care in general. Key policy documents are *Delivering for health* (Scottish Executive, 2005n) and *Delivering for mental health* (Scottish Executive, 2006c). One of the key tasks for the reformed services is to combat the effects of social exclusion and to provide a service that is user-focused. The idea is that through a combination of policy initiatives and good practice, people will have a greater awareness of their own responsibility to maintain good mental health and services will form new partnerships between the providers and recipients of these. Thus various initiatives have been put in place to meet the needs of specific populations such as people who are deaf, people who experience depression and children and young people. The policy has two distinct strands: one seeks to raise public awareness of the importance of mental well-being and the destructive impact negative attitudes towards mental health can have. There is an anti-stigma campaign (*See Me Scotland*) and the wider public campaign includes open access services such as a national suicide helpline (*Breathing Space*) and self-help strategies (such as *Doing Well by People with Depression*). The other strand is targeted upon modernising service delivery for those who experience more serious problems.

This more inclusive approach has a focus on developing and refining community-based services which has been a trend over the last two decades. Prior to this, care was provided largely through admission to hospitals, many of which were based on the outskirts of cities and towns. As patients were transferred from hospital to community, the danger was that services would become more fragmented. With decentralised and community-based structures there is a need to establish general standards against which these community services can be judged. The Mental Health Delivery Plan charges NHS Education Scotland (or NES, the NHS's education division) with the responsibility for drafting and implementing *individual care pathways* (ICPs), which will provide quality-assured standards for the provision of care for people with specific disorders. For example, there will be an ICP which will determine basic standards of service for people with schizophrenia, one for people with depression, one for people with personality disorder and so on. It is recognised that the hospital orientation of services in the past has left Scotland weak in terms of community-based crisis provision, necessitating the development of National Standards for Crisis Services (Scottish Executive, 2006j).

The Mental Health Delivery Plan is target focused. In other words, it contains specific targets which it expects health boards and their partner services such as local authority social work services to meet. For example, it contains specific targets that health boards will reduce their prescription of anti-depressant medication by being more focused upon giving it to only those who need it according to clinical guidance. Therefore it can no longer be used as a 'quick-fix' for hard-pressed GPs who meet high levels of demand from patients with low-level mental health problems. It follows from this that there must be increases in provision of talking therapies and self-help and support groups (Scottish Executive, 2007e).

Similarly, there is a target to reduce hospital re-admission rates by 10 per cent by 2009. The National Standards for Crisis Services is one strand of the provision to meet this target. Yet another facet of the Delivery Plan, and one which cannot be rendered into a target, is the requirement that *recovery* be built into all aspects of service-delivery. Recovery is a service-user oriented concept which expresses the right of those who experience mental illness to expect that they can recover from their difficulties. It is significant in the context of the history of mental health services in which the majority of people often remained the passive recipients (often for life) of services.

Recovery in this sense is an empowering concept. Recovery is in the eyes of the beholder and not necessarily that about which your doctor knows best. For example, recovery may be about finding personal solutions to living with the experience of hearing voices rather than having your voice-hearing 'medicalised' as a symptom which your doctor can treat. As a social worker you may be working with service users and communities as well as other professionals to plan, implement and evaluate mental health services. The emphasis on user empowerment, community development and non-discriminatory services are all part of the tool-kit that you will be expected to develop.

But before you can begin to consider yourself an effective mental health social worker, you need to understand the values that underpin professional practice and how they are reflected in agency policy and practice and endorsed in governmental policies. You need to understand the part that you will play as a social worker/social care worker in the modernising agenda. It is important that as a developing professional your practice demonstrates commitment to promoting equality and respecting diversity. And in the area of mental illness and mental health, these concepts take on a very different meaning.

The importance of values

Social work is fundamentally a moral activity. Social workers often refer to values; indeed Clark (2000) suggests that these are the staple diet of social workers although the word is often used indiscriminately when 'principles' or 'ethics' would be more accurate. Clark suggests that there are four core values:

1. The worth and uniqueness of each individual.

2. The entitlement to justice.

3. The essentiality of community.

4. The claim to freedom.

These values are given statutory force through the Scottish mental health legislation (see Chapter 2), which provides binding principles guiding its use. The principles stress not only the importance of these values, but they require services and practitioners to uphold them. There is a crucial link between the principles, the values of social work and the recovery movement.

All social workers and students of social work are now required to register with the Scottish Social Services Council. This process will allow external confirmation that a member of staff is registered and suitably qualified. This process regulates who can and who cannot enter the profession. It is considered necessary in order to drive up the standards of social work and social care practice (Banks, 2006).

The need for a Code of Professional Practice becomes apparent when you begin to learn about the role that social workers have alongside other professionals who deliver mental health services. They need to be assured that nationally agreed standards of service delivery are being adhered to and that the service provider can be held accountable when services fall short.

How are you going to be guided by values and ethics? The Code of Practice for Social Services Workers (SSSC, 2005) sets out the responsibilities for both employers and employees as follows. Social service workers must:

- protect the rights and promote the interests of service users and carers;
- strive to establish and maintain the trust and confidence of service users and carers;
- promote the independence of service users while protecting them as far as possible from danger and harm;
- respect the rights of service users while seeking to ensure that their behaviour does not harm themselves or other people;
- uphold public trust and confidence in social services;
- be accountable for the quality of their work and take responsibility for maintaining and improving their knowledge and skills.

ACTIVITY *1.1*

Look at your copy of the Code of Practice for Social Services Workers which sets out the kind of professional conduct and practice that is required (SSSC, 2005). If you are a student of social work or a qualified social worker you should have ready access to a copy of this Code from your registration pack. If you do not have a hard copy, it is available online at: www.sssc.uk.com/NR/rdonlyres/761AD208-BF96-4C71-8EFF-CD61092FB626/0/Codesof Practice21405.pdf or from the Scottish Social Services Council, Compass House, 11 Riverside Drive, Dundee DD1 4NY. E-mail: enquiries@sssc.uk.com.

ACTIVITY *1.1* *continued*

Take a few minutes to read through the Code and give some thought to how it relates to the subject matter of this chapter in terms of ethics and values in working with people who are vulnerable because of mental disorder.

Comment

Focusing on one of the headings which states that you must *respect the rights of service users while seeking to ensure that their behaviour does not harm themselves or other people*, we would like you to bear this in mind as we explore aspects of work with people with mental health problems. It is particularly important because this group of people are vulnerable and have a lengthy history of having their rights ignored or abused. On the other hand, as we will see when we examine mental health law in Chapter 2, people affected by serious mental illness can be a risk to themselves or other people and so rights and restrictions have to be carefully balanced.

Values in action

Implicit in the Code of Practice is the importance of recognising and respecting diversity. This is more than valuing people irrespective of their race, colour or ability. It also involves valuing and respecting that people think and behave differently. People of all ethnic backgrounds and from all countries experience mental disorder, and the service user population is made up of ordinary people from all social classes. While distorted reporting of mental health issues in the popular press may give a different picture, the 'one in four' statistic means that no one can say that they will live out their life without experiencing the trauma of poor mental health.

In the past, medical practice was seen as the dominant partner in relation to social work in this field through its claim to a scientific knowledge base. Advances in medication have reinforced the idea that an individual's mental disorder can be managed and that the key process is diagnosis followed by medical treatment, monitoring and evaluation. While technological developments in psychiatric medicine in the last seventy years have been enormous, there is a danger in this process that the 'treated' become subservient to those who are doing the 'treating'.

Social workers who bring a social perspective to the concept of mental illness need to work with medical and health colleagues to provide an effective and *balanced* service, but they also need to be at the forefront of processes that empower service users. Implicit in this approach are some ordinary but powerful principles.

- The first is that in order to empower someone we need to work with them rather than do things to them. Empowerment means partnership, openness and honesty.

- The second principle is that the service user must have an explanation of their disorder which is meaningful to him or her. This requires an understanding of medical and psychological matters. To convey these, we need to practise active listening, to respect the user's perspective and to mediate it with our technical explanations for his or her experiences.

- The third principle is that service users ought to have the opportunity to engage with professionals on an interpersonal level. This could mean that social workers have to find ways to build up professional relationships that are more person-to-person oriented, as opposed to being expert-to-non-expert (Blackburn and Golightley, 2004).

- The fourth principle (and one that sets the lie to any claim on behalf of professionals to the only form of expertise) is that the service user is the expert in their own mental health problem. This is a principle very much oriented towards the concept of recovery as discussed above. Service users may not know the answers, but they certainly experience the effects of the symptoms and therefore have the questions. They alone have experienced the disintegration of 'normality' as they know it and their explanation should be put alongside the professional view and the two then evaluated against each other. If your world is upside down or inside out it cannot be understood by people who only see things one way up or the right side out. If a service user is hearing voices the social worker must not dismiss these but try to understand what that might feel like and how best these can be managed. This is not to collude with delusional behaviour as this could be unhelpful, but is to recognise the other person's sense of reality, however distorted it may appear because of their illness.

By working with service users to value their experiences, and by seeing the problem through their eyes, the prospect is opened up to work in a manner that is holistic, empowering and honest.

Ethical dilemmas

Health service personnel and social workers manage dilemmas on a daily basis. There are usually two components that help us to think about the nature of these.

- Firstly, there may be competing views about what should be done. How would you respond to a service user when he or she wants to stop taking medication when there is evidence that this would cause a serious relapse into mental illness? As with any ethical dilemma, people might argue strongly for one position or the other, depending on how they balance the risks to health with the right to self-determination.

- The second characteristic is that a dilemma must have a distinct moral component to it, such as the avoidance of lying, the primacy of life, self-determination or issues of confidentiality. These are sometimes referred to as *normative principles*.

Resolving ethical dilemmas takes more than just referring to these normative principles or the various codes of conduct. It requires professional judgements to be formed after weighing up one principle against another. In subsequent chapters we will see that modern mental health legislation offers a number of guiding principles which help us to negotiate our way through these difficulties.

The following activity will help you to think further about the nature of ethical dilemmas.

CASE STUDY

Sanjay is a long-term service user who has recurring bouts of depression which are serious enough to warrant his treatment with anti-depressants. In the past when his mood has been very low he has talked about 'ending it all'. As his social worker you visit regularly and he tells you in confidence that he has stopped his medication and is going to experiment with herbal medicine which is more usual in his culture. He has asked your opinion about this action and told you to keep this conversation confidential.

ACTIVITY **1.2**

Should you respect his wishes? Jot down what your response would be and what the issues are. Now compare your notes with the following paragraphs.

Comment

If anyone wants to stop taking medication then this is their right under common law. In certain circumstances, and providing that they are under compulsion of the Mental Health (Care and Treatment) (Scotland) Act 2003, they can be made to have treatment against their wishes. However, as he does not fulfill the criteria for such compulsion (see Chapter 2), Sanjay can stop his medication. Whether this is a good thing or not is open to debate.

Arguments against keeping Sanjay's confidence derive from differing sources. There is the consideration of paternalism, usually derived from the possession of so-called 'expert knowledge'. In contrast, there is the consideration of autonomy where the person has freedom over his or her own body (and mind) which is essentially a moral principle. This more recovery-oriented view suggests that individuals are experts in their own mental condition and as such, with support, they *can* know best. The resolution of this type of dilemma requires you to balance the strength of one concept against the other. In practice you would probably seek to encourage Sanjay to sit with the others involved in his treatment and to talk through his and your views and try to get to a position where his shift to herbal remedies is informed by evidence, monitored and reviewed. This view might also be strengthened were he to understand that there are sometimes serious physical and psychological consequences to the sudden and uncontrolled withdrawal from many anti-depressant medications.

You would need to take into account a number of other factors including:

- the extent to which Sanjay has capacity to make such a decision;
- the quality of the information on which his views are based;
- if there was any coercion on him when making his decision; and
- the nature of any legal issues that could change the nature of the discussion (see Chapters 2 and 3).

One way that service users can be helped to make good quality decisions is through advocacy services. By using advocates who are independent of the mental health team, but who have expertise in assisting service users to express their views, the quality of service user participation in decisions can be enhanced. The Mental Health (Care and Treatment) (Scotland) Act 2003 (the 2003 Act) places a duty upon local authorities and health boards to make advocacy available to services users such as Sanjay.

A brief review of some of the literature about ethics and values

There are many texts and writings on ethics and values which are of use to social workers and other professionals. We note the following as being of particular value:

Banks, S (2006) Ethics, accountability and the social professions. 3rd edn. Basingstoke: Palgrave Macmillan.

Bisman, C (2004) Social work values: the moral core of the profession. In British Journal of Social Work, *34 (1), 109–23.*

Clark, C (2006) Moral character in social work. British Journal of Social Work, *36, 75–89.*

McBeath, G and Webb, S (2002) Virtue, ethics and social work: being lucky, realistic and not doing one's duty. British Journal of Social Work, *32, 1015–36.*

Reamer, F G (1998) The evolution of social work ethics. Social Work, *43 (6), 488–500.*

Warnock, M (1998) An intelligent person's guide to ethics. *London: Gerald Duckworth.*

Ethnicity and mental health

Racism appears to be growing in Scotland with media attention focused on people seeking asylum. As the then Justice Minister Cathy Jamieson pointed out:

> *Today's figures show that there were over 5,000 racist incidents recorded by the police in 2005–6–with over half carried out against people of Asian origin and predominantly carried out on a Friday and Saturday night by white men aged under 20.* (Scottish Executive News Release, 27 March 2007)

It was in response to this trend, that the then Scottish Executive launched a public advertising campaign featuring the banner headline *No place for racism in Scotland* (www.onescotland.com).

While the smaller population of Scotland means that it has not experienced the same difficulties England has in relation to ethnicity and mental health, it is equally true that north of the border the discrimination that is experienced by people with mental health problems can be intensified if that person happens to be from a black or minority ethnic community. A service user talks about her experience of using mental health services as a black person:

> *Coming to mental health services was like the last straw ... you come to services disempowered already, they strip you of your dignity ... you become the dregs of society.* (Keating and Robertson, 2002, p18)

Fundamental to developing better social work practice is having better quality information about the range of ethnic groupings in your area and using it more effectively and creatively than is evident at present. A starting point is for you to become familiar with population data and information about ethnic minorities, including an appreciation of their culture. Providing mental health services that are responsive to the needs of individuals requires that such services should reflect the rich diversity that makes up our society.

Although these views were commonly held throughout health and social services, social work was one of the few professions that placed special emphasis on training in anti-racist and anti-discriminatory practice in the late 1980s. At the policy level, the Scottish Government's strategy sets out in the *See Me* campaign the need to combat discrimination against individuals and groups with mental health problems and promote their social inclusion. This has built on the legal foundation laid down in the Human Rights Act 1998 and is given extra strength by the introduction of the Race Relations (Amendment) Act 2000.

ACTIVITY **1.3**

Have you seen any of the posters or film and TV advertisements from either the See Me *or the* No Place for Racism in Scotland *campaigns? Try visiting the websites (www.semescotland.com and www.onescotland.com). Why do you think the government would sanction the spending of thousands of pounds on such campaigns? Why, do you think, is there a need to promote diversity in Scotland?*

Comment

Did you answer both these questions by considering that discrimination both against people with mental health problems and against people from different backgrounds must be alive and well in the Scottish consciousness? While, as mentioned above, there appears to be less evidence in Scotland than in England of the impact of culture in the delivery of mental health services, it would be foolishly complacent to think that it is *not* a factor.

As mentioned above and more fully discussed in later chapters, the 2003 Act contains binding principles (section 1) which state that any person discharging any function under the terms of the 2003 Act *shall* have regard to a number of factors including:

> *... the patient's abilities, background and characteristics, including, without prejudice to that generality, the patient's age, sex, sexual orientation, religious persuasion, racial origin, cultural and linguistic background and membership of any ethnic group. (s 1(3)(h))*

This latter point is especially relevant as there is a risk of assuming stereotypes on the grounds of such attributes as sexual orientation or culture, which can not only cause offence but can be widely misleading. In any event, understanding what the 2003 Act refers to as someone's *background characteristics* is only a first step towards anti-oppressive practice.

Are black people and those from minority ethnic groups the only community who get poorer services than the majority population? The answer is a qualified *no*! Other groups include older people, children and adolescents, women and people who are deaf. All these groups are broadly referred to in this book, but working with mental health users who are deaf raises some interesting parallels with working with black and minority ethnic users as well as some challenges for you to face in your practice.

Deaf people and mental health

To further illustrate our case that people with mental illness often face double discrimination, there are limited specialist services available for deaf people who have severe mental illness. This was highlighted by the independent inquiry into the care and treatment of Daniel Joseph (Mischon, 2000), which was commissioned by some of the London health authorities. Daniel was profoundly deaf and was admitted to hospital from the courts having been made subject to a hospital order (under English legislation) with restrictions after pleading guilty to manslaughter on the grounds of diminished responsibility. Concern over his treatment resulted in the Westminster government consulting about services for service users who are deaf, and this has had an impact on Scottish mental health services for people with sensory disabilities, which are currently under review.

People who are deaf report that mental health services are difficult to access and often do not cater for their specific needs. To raise our awareness of the specific needs of minority communities the Scottish Executive consultation work with all Scottish local authorities and health boards (2006) is worth looking at. Developing awareness of specific communities is an important, but only a first, step towards developing appropriate and responsive services (www.scotland.gov.uk/Topics/Health/health/mental-health/servicespolicy/Surveys/sensorylosssurvey/).

Members of the deaf community experience mental health problems just like people from any other community. However, because of the difference in language and culture between those who are assessing deaf service users and the service users themselves, misdiagnosis of mental disorder can result and as a consequence deaf people can receive services and treatment that are inappropriate. Good practice needs to take into consideration the requirements of the Disability Discrimination Act 1999 which makes it clear that mental health services have to take reasonable steps to facilitate the uptake of services by people who are deaf and who have mental health problems. This includes the use of an interpreter at the various stages of assessment and service provision.

Culture is a central feature of a person's identity and that at the very least must be taken into consideration when working with service users from black and minority ethnic communities or when working with service users who are deaf.

Does the relative social exclusion that deaf people experience contribute to their mental health problems? This is reported as being a factor in the relationship between the psychological health of deaf people and their subsequent call upon mental health services. In other words being deaf can increase your vulnerability to mental health problems (Ridgeway, 1997). Later in this chapter explanations are given of the cause and manifestation of mental illness and in particular the role that stress plays in mental health.

Until recently *mental health* services seemed to be based around the assumptions that users were all from a hearing population that is predominantly white British. Both of these assumptions are well off the mark and need to be challenged and changed. In reality, the respect for the person's cultural identity is the predominant value that ought to underpin your practice.

CASE STUDY

Shaz is a deaf person who lives alone and, at the age of 32, has very few connections with the deaf community. She is a fluent user of British Sign Language but since her remand to prison on theft charges, her health has suffered. Over the last ten years or so she has been treated for depression and has taken anti-depressants. The stress of being in prison has caused her more distress to the extent that she would like to see a social worker. However, the prison service does not have a person who can sign and therefore they must seek outside specialist support. By chance the local community mental health team has a member of staff who can sign and she accompanies the social worker to the prison and carries out an assessment with the prison doctor.

Comment

This example shows how services can respond in an effective way. However, having a person who can effectively communicate in the same language as the service user is often a matter of luck and there is a need for more services of this kind. A deaf person who communicates through sign language is likely to find that being in an environment where there are people fluent in sign language is more conducive to their recovery than being in a hearing world. Of course, once the specialist worker leaves the prison, Shaz is left still having to cope with the traumas of prison and an essentially hearing world. This still leaves you having to explore with Shaz and the interpreter what specific needs she might have in respect to her deafness.

Learning disability and mental health

People who have a learning disability can experience a range of mental health problems just like the rest of us. However, the presence of a learning disability may prevent professionals and carers recognising the symptoms of mental health problems as these may be associated with their disability. It is important for carers and professionals to look beyond stereotypes and to seek honest (and sometimes painful) explanations for behaviour that has changed. Finding out what is wrong will call for quality communication and observation skills and working in partnership with carers and service users. There are some informative guides published by the Royal College of Psychiatrists and other specialist organisations such as MENCAP, most of which you can download from their websites.

There are few research and evaluation studies in the field of learning disability and mental health – dual diagnosis, the technical term often used, is discussed in detail below. This tends to maintain this important area as low priority yet policy expounded in the Scottish Executive paper *The same as you? A review of people with learning disability in Scotland* (2001a) focuses on participation and inclusion and urges people with learning difficulties to use local and mainstream NHS services. This of course includes mental health services (see www.scotland.gov.uk/ldsr/docs/tsay-02.asp).

The coexistence of mental health problems alongside learning disability may be one of the explanations for a range of challenging behaviours. Such behaviour may not be a characteristic of a person's learning disability but may be as a result of mental health problems.

This is a theme that Moss et al. pick up in their article in the *British Journal of Psychiatry*, which showed that there was some evidence for a statistical association between challenging behaviour and psychiatric disorder (Moss et al., 2000, p454). They concluded that depression was four times more prevalent in people with learning disability who exhibited challenging behaviour than for people with learning disability itself. This finding, although needing to be treated with some caution, is important as depression is so often overlooked in people with a learning disability.

Working with service users who have this form of dual diagnosis will often mean mobilising community resources to provide support and connection with others in the community. This idea of 'connectedness' is described by Gilbert (2003) who comments that: *Mental distress and mental illness is so often about a disconnection, false connections or an over-concentration on one aspect of our lives* (p22). Like any other service user, you as a social worker will want to access the whole person and how they draw support or otherwise from their families, carers and the community. Facilitating better connections within the community may be the most appropriate intervention that you can make, and in situations where there is a learning disability, the possibilities around coexistent mental illness must not be ignored.

Being able to recognise the impact of structural racism and discrimination

Section 26 of the Mental Health (Care and Treatment) (Scotland) Act 2003 places a duty upon local authorities to create services that actively promote mental well-being. Given what has been said above about the effect upon poor mental health of services that are badly attuned to cultural difference, it is easy to see that services which do not include minority cultures or people with disabilities will fail to meet their s 26 duties.

Perspectives on mental illness

There are numerous perspectives about mental health and illness and you need to get a good understanding of the various *models* that are in current use. This means that you can then evaluate one against the other and, more importantly, begin to put your practice in an appropriate framework. To help your understanding, socially and medically oriented perspectives are described here as being two of the key perspectives that inform work with service users who have a mental disorder.

Firstly, we should consider from where the general public gets information about mental illness. There appears to be an odd process at work here. On the one hand, mental illness is extremely common. Indeed, it would a very unusual person who did not know someone who has been affected by it. On the other hand, by and large the public seems to gain its understanding of mental illness through the media and, in this regard, the media can present a very distorted view. The 'lay perspective', as it might be called, is important and can be influential upon the creation of policy in a democracy. For a study which examines how the media exerts a largely negative influence upon how people conceptualise *mental health* (generally meaning mental illness), see Philo (1996) and for a more promising approach, see Scottish Executive (2005f).

ACTIVITY *1.4*

Messages in the media

Think about the media coverage of mental illness and jot down the 'memorable' words. Can you remember the last time you read an article which used positive adjectives or cele-brated the success of people who experience problems because of mental illness? What terms are most often used to portray mental illness? Does this portrayal vary from media source to media source, from tabloid to serious newspapers?

Comment

You may well have written down terms like 'psycho' or 'looney' which are in common use and have very negative connotations. These are some of the mechanisms by which behav-iours can become associated with certain labels and consequently become self-fulfilling prophecies. What are your views about this? Is calling someone a 'nutter' just a piece of harmless fun or does it bring with it unwanted labels and expectations?

Words that are used by the media, particularly the tabloid press, are often associated with violence and risk. Even though the risk of a stranger who is mentally ill killing you is very small, some of the press coverage suggests that it is a common occurrence.

Finally, you might find it interesting to look at coverage in the press over the next few weeks and compare different newspapers and, if you have the time, think about how you would rewrite the headlines (see Scottish Executive, 2005f).

Explaining mental illness

It is easy to see two major perspectives which inform our understanding about mental illness:

- that which draws from a medical orientation and is essentially a biomedical or disease model; and

- that which draws from an essentially psychosocial perspective and is influenced by refer-ence to social factors.

While the medical perspective still dominates to a large extent, it is no longer helpful to think of the *medical* and the *social* model as being antagonistic, opposite perspectives. Social policy and more enlightened thinking and practice is driving health and social care into ever closer partnerships both functionally and theoretically, so it is more fitting in today's climate to regard these as *complementary* perspectives.

A medical perspective

This is the perspective commonly adopted by doctors, notably psychiatrists. It gives cre-dence to the claim that organic or biomedical causes will eventually be found for all true forms of mental disorder. It postulates that there are detectable processes in the working of the brain, such as the transmission of nerve impulses that make up thoughts and feel-ings by chemical agents known as neurotransmitters, which can malfunction by over- or under-production of one chemical or another, distorting perception and understanding of the world and causing diseases like depression and schizophrenia.

This way of understanding people's experience while they are mentally ill necessitates a framework of diagnosis. A diagnosis will be made by the psychiatrist who will refer to manuals which describe and order the symptoms and thereby allow for a diagnosis to be made. The most commonly used manual by UK psychiatrists is the International Classification of Diseases or ICD-10 (WHO, 1992), available online at www.who.int/classifi-cations/apps/icd/icd10online/. It has an American counterpart, less used in the UK, the DSM-IV (APA, 2005), available online at www.psychiatryonline.com/.

While it is important for social workers to have a working knowledge of diagnoses and the bio-chemical basis of mental illness, their main body of knowledge is drawn from the social implications of mental disorder which relates primarily to the way that manifestations of mental illness are often met within a society highly prejudiced towards some forms of difference.

Assessment

As a social worker you are most likely to be involved in the early stage of assessment and treatment of mental disorder. Campbell (1999) suggests that social workers can only become competent when, as a practitioner, they are able to synthesise interpersonal skills with theories and ideas about the causes of illness. This is the case for all settings and aspects of the work. You may also be involved later in your career as a mental health offi-cer (MHO) with specific responsibilities under legislation and associated regulations and guidance to assess a service user for whom compulsory measures of care and treatment may be necessary. This is covered in some detail in subsequent chapters. An in-depth assessment would need to include some or all of the following:

- previous history of mental problems including any history of diagnosed mental illness;

- significant risks posed by the above to the person and/or others;

- service user self-assessment of their strengths and attributes to overcome difficulties;

- cultural and religious aspects;

- employment status;

- relationship strengths and weaknesses;

- substance use or misuse including drug and alcohol use (Scottish Executive, 2006b).

It is all too easy to become drawn into a deficit model of assessment, which focuses upon *problems* and treats the service user as a problem. The importance of avoiding this approach is to identify what would be considered to be the most effective way of proceeding in partnership with the person. The aim is to work in a manner that the service user would describe as culturally sensitive and which focuses upon their strengths rather than their deficits. People who have experienced difficulties because of mental illness may have also experienced *what works for them* and your task may be one of mobilising resources to help *them* be in a stronger position to deal with their problems in a way that is meaningful to them. This can be described as a *recovery-oriented approach*.

For those service users who are clearly presenting with symptoms and behaviours that are likely to need more specialist services and the possible use of medication, a referral to the GP and then to psychiatric services would be appropriate and even necessary.

Diagnosis

As with physical diseases from measles to melanoma, a diagnosis based upon the identification of a cluster of symptoms is crucial to the successful application of treatment. A diagnosis of mental disorder is always given by a doctor who is usually a psychiatrist. It emerges out of considerable contact between the doctor and the service user. The assessment process as described above will assist in the making of a diagnosis. Psychiatrists are trained to use a phenomenological approach; in other words, they try to establish a pattern of signs and symptoms which helps to distinguish between those people who are eccentric, unusual or who have only occasional symptoms, from those who are unwell and require some form of active intervention. This is an important point to remember as s 328(2) of the 2003 Act states that:

A person is not mentally disordered by reason only of any of the following –

(a) sexual orientation;

(b) sexual deviancy;

(c) transsexualism;

(d) transvestism;

(e) dependence on, or use of, alcohol or drugs;

(f) behaviour that causes, or is likely to cause, harassment, alarm or distress to any other person;

(g) acting as no prudent person would act.

In order to avoid variation in assessment between doctors it is common to use one of a number of psychiatric assessment tools or structured interview schedules. These have all been standardised, a process by which the reliability of these tools is established. They help the psychiatrist to assess the presence of certain symptoms which act as 'signposts' to effective diagnosis. The schedules include the Present State Examination (PSE), which has 40 components to it, or the more commonly used Beck Depression Inventory.

The importance of a diagnosis is that it:

- acts as a pathway to more specialised care and treatment;
- is a process in which most patients have faith (sometimes in spite of evidence to the contrary);
- can mobilise support from other agencies such as housing and income maintenance for those in need;
- should involve other professional views being sought, including those of social workers;
- should occur over a period of time of more than a few days, often weeks or even months.

However, service users seldom report the diagnostic process as being empowering and often complain that their views are seldom sought except as signposts to a diagnosis

(Clark and Rowe, 2006; May, 2006). This is where the skills of the social worker can be very effectively used in order to help people integrate their experiences as effectively as possible, given all the circumstances at that time.

Classification of mental disorders

While the medical framework within which mental disorder is understood by doctors is definitely not above criticism, it is also often misunderstood. The basis of it *is* highly scientific and based upon a system whereby manifestations of illness can be categorised. Classification is an important step in the diagnosis of mental disorder. Mental disorder is broken down into various categories representing groups of symptoms. Thus, if a cluster of symptoms fit into a recognised pattern they can then be classified as, for example, schizophrenia. A diagnosis is a shorthand version of what the psychiatrist believes to be wrong with the person. Such classifications also enable treatment and outcomes to be better predicted. Although as a social worker you will not be using these classificatory tools to make a diagnosis, it is worth familiarising yourself with some of the main features. This will help you to understand the basis of a diagnosis.

The nature of this process is rigorous, and great efforts have been made to try to ensure their validity and reliability. For example, the ICD-10, published in 1992, took nine years to prepare and test and included extensive field trials of the draft text in many countries. Even so these classifications have been the subject of dispute over the years (Menninger, 1963) and it is important to remember that a diagnosis is only as good as the information on which it is based. You might want to think about how such diagnoses may be influenced by social factors, the imposition of values and other attributes.

Although as a social worker you are usually not directly involved with the determination of a diagnosis, you will need to share the ownership of it when working as part of a multidisciplinary team. It is important that you have some understanding of the main characteristics of the above and what the various treatment options are for each. You are also going to be involved in the complex interaction of the service user and their cultural and social background. For example, with disorders like depression, which has a biological component to it, a combination of medication and social intervention is often the most effective treatment.

Treatment

There are different ways of treating users who have some form of mental disorder. The effectiveness of such treatment depends upon its nature and the skills of the people providing the treatment. These treatments are briefly discussed below. Every treatment option must have the risks weighed up alongside the possible benefits, for no treatment is without some cost and risk. Medical practitioners are trained first and foremost to do no harm to their patients. The 2003 Act and its underlying principles (s 1 and 2) are designed to improve safeguards for all patients, but there are some areas of treatment where extra safeguards are required and Part 16 of the 2003 Act makes particular reference to these areas in conjunction with specific regulations. The dominant mode of treatment is medication but the notion of treatment (see s 329 of the 2003 Act) also includes the following.

Psychosurgery

This is little used and then only for those with chronic conditions of obsessional and depressive disorders. It can only be given with the patient's informed consent or, where the person is incapable of giving consent, they do not object to the proposed treatment (s 236). Part 16, s 234 to 236 of the 2003 Act deal with these matters and the provisions and safeguards apply to both informal patients and those subject to compulsory measures under the 2003 Act. This type of treatment is the irreversible removal or destruction of brain tissue. Psychosurgery can only be given in accordance with the provisions of this part of the 2003 Act and as such cannot be regarded as urgent medical treatment as per the terms of s 243.

Electroconvulsive therapy (ECT)

ECT consists of administering an electric shock to patients who are sedated and is usually used when there has been an inadequate response to medication. It can be an effective treatment for depression, especially when this is accompanied by psychotic delusions. Patients are usually given a course of treatment of six to 12 applications. Where a person is subject to compulsory measures under the terms of the 2003 Act, s 237–242 apply. In limited circumstances, ECT can be given as an emergency treatment, providing certain criteria are satisfied (s 243).

Psychological treatments

Psychological treatments are many and varied and may include:

- behavioural therapy which is based on learning theory (classical, operant and social learning theories);

- cognitive therapy which focuses on incorrectly learned behaviours;

- counselling, which has many variants;

- psychotherapy, which also includes many variants; and

- differing forms of systemic and family therapy.

(See Scottish Executive, 2007e)

Complementary therapies and alternatives to medicine

As yet many of the complementary therapies, although popular with service users, are not 'proven' by research. They include hypnotherapy, dance, acupuncture and herbal remedies and these can have a role to play in combination with other forms of treatment. As interest continues to grow, some clinical trials have suggested that for moderate depression, St John's Wort may be effective, and evidence suggests that exercise may also perform a valuable function. The psychological benefit of boosting self-esteem through some of these therapies should never be underestimated (Crone, Smith and Gough, 2005; Saxena et al., 2005).

Medication

Medication has become an important part of the treatment of mental disorder for many service users, but it is not the only way of managing a mental disorder. Medication works by either stopping the release of chemicals in the brain or by increasing the activity of certain parts of the brain. In the 1950s there was a pharmacological revolution with the arrival of new forms of medical treatment including chlorpromazine (Jones, 1993). This changed the lives of many patients with enduring mental illness in long-stay hospitals by giving them the opportunity to be treated in the community.

Today there is a new revolution of atypical anti-psychotic drugs which have far fewer side effects than the previous ones, and are also in many instances more effective. Some of the older medications caused amenorrhoea in women which may have prevented long-term users from having children, whereas the main side effect of the new medication is significant weight gain.

Medication is divided into six types (see Table 1.1).

Table 1.1: The six types of medication

Type	Example	Typical use
Anti-psychotics	Chlorpromazine, risperidone and in schizophrenia treatment-resistant conditions clozapine	
Anti-depressants	Prozac (fluoxetine)	Depression
Mood regulation	Lithium	Bi-polar affective disorder
Anti-epileptic	Carbamazepine	Epilepsy
Anxiolytics	Diazepam	Anxiety states
Hypnotics	Temezepam	Insomnia

RESEARCH SUMMARY

There has been a continuous increase in the prescribing of anti-depressants in Scotland. In 1992/93 there were 1.16 million prescriptions. In 2005/06, this had increased to 3.53 million. On a daily basis, the use of anti-depressants in the population aged 15–90 has grown from 1.9% in 1992/93 to 8.7% in 2005/06. (High Level Summary of Statistics Trends for Health and Community Care, 2006, at www.scotland.gov.uk/Resource/Doc/933/0049813.pdf)

It is important at this point to remind ourselves that the 2003 Act is the first piece of Scottish mental health legislation to make explicit and specific reference to dealing with children who may have a mental disorder. Specific provisions apply along with reference, as required, to the Children (Scotland) Act 1995 (the 1995 Act). In terms of medical treatments, the relevant sections referred to above make special provisions concerning children and s 249 of the 2003 Act offers interpretation in relation to this part of the 2003 Act as does Vol 1 of the 2003 Act Codes of Practice (Scottish Executive, 2005i). It is important to remember that the treatment of mental disorders in children requires that extra attention be paid to the possible impact of medication upon them. Chapter 5 looks specifically at children and young people.

Understanding the major forms of mental disorder

The dilemma facing anyone who works with emotionally vulnerable people is to be able to differentiate between *normal* and *abnormal* behaviour. The unusual behaviour or eccentricities of people are what make life so interesting and we should value such diversity. Clearly though, there is a point beyond which the eccentric becomes markedly disordered and the person is in need of help. The main disorders that you will come across are described below.

Schizophrenia

Schizophrenia is a complex disorder with a number of variants, although the prognosis is well understood by specialists. It is a neuropsychiatric disorder where a number of factors may have impacted upon the central nervous system resulting in a cluster of symptoms that are classified as schizophrenia. It is commonly thought, incorrectly, by the general public to be associated with dangerousness and extreme madness and thus carries a stigma which other diagnoses do not (Martin, Pescosolido and Tuch, 2000; Szasz, 2003). Symptoms can include the following.

- *Hallucinations* These are problems to do with sensory perception which are very real for the person who experiences them. They include auditory hallucinations (including hearing voices) and somatic hallucinations where the person believes that they are experiencing phenomena like electricity running through their body.

- *Delusions* These are beliefs which are considered bizarre and are clearly not supported by the available evidence and yet are held in an unshakable manner by the person concerned. Delusions can be part of systematic thought or appear to be completely random. These are usually culturally specific, so for example in the UK, some people are deluded into grandiose thinking, believing that they are related to the royal family or are relatives of the prime minister. Similarly, other culturally specific beliefs may be present and require of the worker an appropriate level of culturally specific awareness (Littlewood and Lipsedge, 1997; Fernando, 2003).

- *Interference with thought* Thought insertion is a form of delusion involving the belief that someone else's thoughts can be placed in the person's mind. This can also be perceived as a form of *thought control* where it is believed that someone outside is controlling your thoughts, or that your private thoughts are being broadcast to the general public.

Schizophrenia affects about 1 per cent of the population. The onset is usually during adolescence or early adulthood but can occur later on in life. Before an accurate diagnosis is made the symptoms should have been noted over at least six months and must include at least one active psychotic phase. Early recognition and treatment significantly improves the overall prognosis for the user; consequently, social workers should be aware of this and raise schizophrenia as a possible diagnosis earlier rather than later. Early medication can alter the course of schizophrenia (Frangou and Bryne, 2000).

Features associated with schizophrenia

Episodes may consist of three phases in which normal functioning is interrupted as follows:

- *Pre-onset or prodromal phase* In ths phase noticeable changes occur including social isolation, difficulty in functioning, odd behaviour, blunted affect, bizarre ideas and a marked lack of energy. Friends and relatives may describe the person's behaviour during this phase as he/she is not the same person as they used to be.

- *Onset or active phase* This phase is where the behaviours and thoughts of the person are acutely psychotic and will often include delusions, hallucinations, incoherence, thought insertion or control and feelings of persecution. These need to be present for at least a week in order to meet the diagnostic criteria associated with schizophrenia and they can be the result of some form of psychosocial or other trauma.

- *Residual phase* This phase is very similar to the pre-onset phase except that the person may experience negative affect and a flattening of emotions. They could still be hearing voices or experience other psychotic features but these are less strong.

Treatment and management

The usual treatment regime is a combination of medication and psychosocial interventions. While medication does not offer a cure, it can dramatically correct serious and abnormal phenomena such as hallucinations or delusions.

The over-representation of young Afro-Caribbean males who are diagnosed as having schizophrenia is of major concern, and points to the lack of culturally sensitive practice (Littlewood and Lipsedge, 1997; Fernando, 2003). It will be interesting to note whether similar concerns arise over the coming years with regard to other cultural groupings given the increase in migration for both economic and other reasons, including the search for asylum.

What is the social work role?

Social work intervention can include:

- education with the service user and their family;

- helping to arrange appropriate low-stress accommodation;

- networking with the service user to provide community support;

- the use of behavioural techniques to modify behaviours;

- encouraging compliance with medication;

- acting as an advocate for the service user where appropriate.

What is the outlook or prognosis for people with schizophrenia?

About one-third of people who are diagnosed with schizophrenia will completely recover, but for the remainder the outlook is one that will include at least one more episode and for some this illness will turn into a major challenge for them and their families for a considerable period of time. The picture is much better than it was twenty years ago, in large part due to more effective interventions and the emergence of the newer anti-psychotic drugs that have fewer side effects than their predecessors, but it can be a debilitating long-term condition for some. Chapter 7 has an illustrative example concerning schizophrenia.

Mood disorders

Depression

Depression is a group of mental disorders that can affect any of us at some point in our lives and is often overlooked among the very young (Scottish Executive, 2001b; Barnes, 2003; Heads Up Scotland, 2007) and the elderly (Burroughs et al., 2006; Scogin and Shah, 2006). Depression is a disorder characterised by mood change which explains why this disorder is termed a mood or *affective* disorder. There are different types of depression including manic depression, post-natal depression and clinical or major depression that affect about 3–4 per cent of the population in any one year. More females are affected than males.

Depression is categorised into three levels of severity: mild, moderate or severe. The ICD-10 is a good source for further information about these levels. Where the depression is mild, people may receive treatment from their GPs and continue as normal with much of their lives. Where it is moderate, the person may begin to struggle to continue with their social, work or domestic lives and where depression is severe, it is unlikely that the person will be able to live a 'normal' life and suicide is a distinct risk.

Features associated with depression

Anyone can suffer from depression from time to time and it only becomes of clinical interest when the severity increases or the duration of the episode is longer than might be expected. Assessment is carried out using some psychiatric rating scales like the Beck Depression Inventory.

RESEARCH SUMMARY

Depression and other affective disorders were the fifth most common group of conditions reported to GPs during 2005/6. One important measure of mental well-being is the General Health Questionnaire (GHQ12). This is a widely-used standard measure of mental distress and psychological ill health. It rates areas such as concentration, sleep patterns, stress levels, feelings of self-esteem, despair, depression and confidence. A GHQ12 score of four or more would indicate the possible presence of a psychiatric disorder, whereas a score of zero would be considered to be a strong indicator of positive mental health. Figure 1.3 gives GHQ12 scores from 1995, 1998 and 2003.

Treatment and management

A range of treatments is possible depending upon the severity of the depression. Among the treatments indicated are courses of anti-depressant medications, including the use of Prozac which interacts with the neuro chemical pathways both in the brain and elsewhere in the body. The use of medication is often combined with a range of psychosocial interventions to provide effective treatment. In severe depression it is important to take the risk of suicide seriously and to consult about risk with your medical and other colleagues. The person should always be asked about thoughts of suicide (suicidal ideation) and where they exhibit plans for suicide or a preoccupation with it, this should be seen as clear intent and action taken. (See Chapter 6 for a discussion on suicide.)

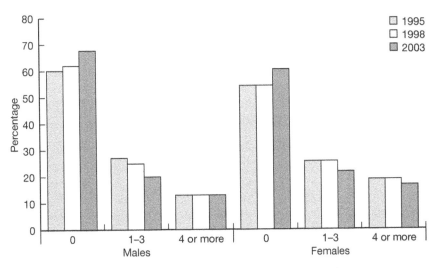

Figure 1.3: GHQ12 Scores by gender, ages 16–64 (1995/1998/2003)

Source: High level summary of statistics: Health and Community Care, Scottish Executive Statistics 2006. Available from: www.scotland.gov.uk/Topics/Statistics/Browse/Health/TrendPDF. Reproduced under the terms of Crown Copyright Policy Guidance issued by HMSO.

Bipolar affective disorder (manic depression)

This is a disorder in which the person can feel intermittently depressed and occasionally elated. In the ICD-10, mania and depression are cited as opposite ends of the same spectrum, hence the term bipolar. *Mania* is characterised by extreme elevation of mood and an increase in physical and mental energy and activity. This disorder can either exist in its own right at the depressed end of the spectrum or, more uncommonly, at the other extreme of mania (unipolar) but usually it is accompanied by at least one episode of its opposite. During mania, the user will often believe that they are well and treatment can become difficult. In such phases the personal, social, emotional and financial consequences can be very damaging as the individual may squander their money or become extravagant and disinhibited in many other ways. Consequently, hospital in-patient treatment may be required in order to provide treatment to return the person's mood to normal as well as, in some cases, providing a level of protection for them against the consequences of their own excesses.

The main medication is lithium, although there are other medications available. This is a mood stabiliser that works by controlling the extent of racing thoughts rather than acting sedatively, and although it takes a few weeks to work it does seem to prevent a swing into depression. It is particularly effective in the prevention of relapse among patients who have previously been diagnosed.

Dual diagnosis

The term dual diagnosis or co-morbidity (EMCDDA, 2004) covers a spectrum of disorders that combine with mental disorder. As discussed above, this can include mental disorder and learning disability. It also refers to mental disorder and substance misuse. This latter category has presented acute wards in hospitals with some of the most serious of challenges. In some areas, many of the patients admitted to hospital have experience of substance misuse, a habit which some try to continue while they are on the ward. The most common forms of misuse are drugs and alcohol (Buckley and Brown, 2006; Laker, 2006; Scottish Executive, 2003b, 2006b).

In Scotland, the issue of coexistent mental health problems and some form of substance misuse has for some time been recognised as a priority area requiring action. In 2003, the report of the joint working group of the Scottish Advisory Committee on Drug Misuse (SACDM) and the Scottish Advisory Committee on Alcohol Misuse (SACAM) entitled '*Mind the Gaps*' (Scottish Executive, 2003b), stated that:

> There is a large group of men and women in our society with a mixture of mental health problems and problems arising from alcohol and substance misuse. Many lead troubled lives, seeking help from individual services, both voluntary and statutory, from time to time. But the individual's experiences and service components do not generally run smoothly. The client's experience and the way that services perceive themselves and others are not coherent. (p5)

Concerns around the poor integration of service delivery in relation to this group of people have been the subject of recent research (Scottish Executive, 2006b) and policy statements (Scottish Executive, 2006c) (see www.scotland.gov.uk/Resource/Doc/127647/0030582.pdf).

Dual diagnosis and co-morbidity are rather complex issues, particularly as both are often used interchangeably. Dual diagnosis is defined as being the presence of an alcohol or drug misuse/abuse problem in addition to another, usually a psychiatric, diagnosis (WHO, 2004). Co-morbidity is used in a somewhat more complex way and can include concurrent (two or more disorders at the same time) or successive (disorders occur at different times) morbidity (Crome, 1999). The relationship between these conditions and the interactive effects are complex, for example:

- psychiatric or psychological symptoms which may be triggered by substance use/misuse, dependence, intoxication or withdrawal;

- psychological problems, perhaps not amounting to a mental disorder, which may precipitate substance use which can lead to the development of a mental disorder;

- the presence of a mental disorder itself which may lead to the use/abuse of substances;

- mental disorder which is worsened by the overlay of substance abuse;

- intoxication and/or substance abuse which results in psychological symptoms.

(Adapted from Scottish Executive, 2006b. See also Bannerjee, Clancy and Crome, 2002; Manley, 2005; Laker, 2006.)

RESEARCH SUMMARY

Dual diagnosis

The OPCS National Psychiatric Morbidity Study revealed that within the population of those with a diagnosed mental disorder, the prevalence of dual diagnosis was 29 per cent. Anti-social personality disorder had the highest rate of co-morbid substance use disorders (84 per cent met the criteria), with schizophrenia having a 47 per cent rate of co-morbidity. Those with affective disorders were noted as having a co-morbidity rate of 32 per cent (Farrell et al., 2003).

Generally speaking, people with a dual diagnosis tend to have a poorer prognosis of good recovery. There is an increased risk of suicide for people with dual diagnosis and as substance misuse is becoming more common it should always be looked for in assessments. There are also increased risks around self-harm, suicide and early death, as well as an increased likelihood of psychological problems, high rates of relapse, hospitalisation, homelessness and physical health problems, often serious (Scottish Executive, 2006b).

Treatment can involve motivational interviewing, assertive outreach, cognitive behavioural therapies, individual counselling and most importantly providing an integrated service (Barrowclough et al., 2006; Conrod and Stewart, 2006).

What is the social work role?

Social work interventions can include:

- the identification and management of risk;

- encouraging service users to take prescribed medication;

- individual counselling;

- cognitive behavioural therapy (CBT);

- referral for specialist psychotherapy;

- community networking.

Organic disorders

The organic disorders considered here are those associated with increasing age, most notably dementia. However, don't forget that older people can also experience depression and other mental disorders in much the same way as their younger counterparts. The presence of depression in older people should be actively considered in any assessment as the person's presentation can mean that an organic disorder is masked behind some other form of mental disorder.

Alzheimer's disease is a degenerative disease where the brain has been irreversibly damaged. Similar symptoms can also occur through excessive and prolonged consumption of alcohol (Korsakoff's Syndrome) or as a result of traumatic injury, a stroke or the misuse of drugs. In the case of Alzheimer's disease which is considered a chronic condition, there is a progressive degeneration of the brain which results in impaired intellect, disorientation and eventually death.

Features associated with Alzheimer's

It is important to distinguish between the 'normal' effects of ageing and the development of a progressive disorder like Alzheimer's. We all suffer the loss of brain cells as we age but with this disorder, cell loss is more rapid and profound than would normally be expected. The rate of degeneration does vary but it is usual for this to increase as the disorder progresses.

Treatment and management

The early stages can be accompanied by depression, anxiety and severe sleep disturbance as the person may have insight into the progressive nature of this disorder. Older people do better in familiar surroundings than in institutional care, but admission to residential care may be necessary where there is increased vulnerability. In Scotland, recourse to the Adults with Incapacity (Scotland) Act 2000 may be necessary where degenerative conditions like Alzheimer's disease affect the individual's capacity to make decisions and to protect themselves. There is also the Adult Support and Protection (Scotland) Act 2007 (see Payne, 2006a, 2006b) which allows public authorities to intervene in the lives of people who are vulnerable and at risk because of debilitating illnesses like Alzheimer's disease. (For information on the 2007 Act go to www.opsi.gov.uk/legislation/scotland/acts2007/20070010.htm.)

What is the social work role?

Social workers will be part of a team that will provide a system of care that encompasses the provision of support services of different kinds to the user and their carers and family, depending on their level of need (Blackstock et al., 2005). The social work role includes arranging welfare benefits, providing information and explanations of the person's situation to family and others as appropriate as well as possibly arranging and financing social support systems and, eventually, specialist nursing care if this is necessary.

The whole issue regarding the role of the social worker *per se* has been the subject of considerable scrutiny in Scotland recently, culminating in the publication of the report of the 21st Century Social Work Review team, *Changing lives* (Scottish Executive, 2006a). A number of supporting papers produced during the consultation process focus specifically on this important issue (Scottish Executive, 2005b, 2005c, 2005d) and are worthy of study.

Of particular importance within this context is the notion of the *reserved functions* of social workers. The 21st Century Social Work Review undertook to review those particular functions that should only be undertaken by social workers because of their special knowledge and training. One of these reserved functions is that concerning issues around mental health and incapacity where specialist social workers should be responsible for the exercise of functions under the Mental Health (Care and Treatment) (Scotland) Act 2003 and the Adults with Incapacity (Scotland) Act 2000 (Scottish Executive, 2005b).

Critical psychiatry

While for the last fifty years or so the medical model has dominated the explanatory landscape of mental illness, there have been pockets of disaffection that have gained their followers. Among these, several key names, themselves psychiatrists, are to be found including Thomas Szasz who, in the controversially influential book *The myth of mental illness* (1972), opposed the use of compulsion to treat people who in his view were struggling with problems of everyday life rather than some form of mental illness. Ronald Laing (1985), another dissenter, saw the family and its various power struggles as accounting for much of what we call schizophrenia, and more recently a movement called 'critical psychiatry' has emerged. Psychiatrist Duncan Double (2006) is one of a small number of professionals who look beyond conventional explanations for and treatment of people who have a mental illness.

Why is it that a movement called 'critical psychiatry' can find favour? The answer lies in part in the general need by public and professionals alike to examine alternatives to conventional treatments of a range of health problems. The increased use of supplements to assist diet and the use of acupuncture and homeopathy all stand testimony to the general dissatisfaction with the increased technical and scientific focus of medicine in general and, by inference, psychiatry more specifically. They do not absolutely reject the use of medication and other 'conventional' means, but see these as one of a *range* of treatments and approaches rather than, as it sometimes is seen, as the *only* treatment or approach.

The fundamental tenet of critical psychiatry is to challenge the evidence base upon which 'traditional' psychiatry is founded and in so doing inevitably to look at the psychosocial aspects of the service user's life. Phil Thomas, a consultant psychiatrist, puts this over very succinctly on the critical psychiatry website www.critpsynet.freeuk.com/.

> *Critical psychiatry is part academic, part practical. Theoretically it is influenced by critical philosophical and political theories, and it has three elements. It challenges the dominance of clinical neuroscience in psychiatry (but does not exclude it); it introduces a strong ethical perspective on psychiatric knowledge and practice; it politicises mental health issues. Critical psychiatry is deeply sceptical about the reductionist claims of neuroscience to explain psychosis and other forms of emotional distress. It follows that we are sceptical about the claims of the pharmaceutical industry for the role of psychotropic drugs in the 'treatment' of psychiatric conditions. Like other psychiatrists we use drugs, but we see them as having a minor role in the resolution of psychosis or depression. We attach greater importance to dealing with social factors, such as unemployment, bad housing, poverty, stigma and social isolation. Most people who use psychiatric services regard these factors as more important than drugs. We reject the medical model in psychiatry and prefer a social model, which we find more appropriate in a multicultural society characterised by deep inequalities.*

In a recent book, Double (2006) explains that the main aim of critical psychiatry is to develop a more open approach to psychiatry and that professionals like social workers need to remain sceptical about the claims that drug companies make for the efficacy of their products. This is not about ignoring the advances in medication nor to minimise the assistance it can offer, but is more about seeing this as only one component of the 'mental illness toolkit'.

To work in a truly empowering way can run counter to the imposition of a biomedical regime in which it is possible to see control and restraint as dominant features rather than as enabling and understanding. It is important to understand the cultural context in which service users experience mental illness and the role that poverty, poor housing and oppression play in relation to this. This is where the alternative explanation called the 'Social Model' needs consideration.

The social model

The social model fits well with the general holistic approach of social work and is the underlying rationale for mental health social work, although it is by no means as influential as the medical model. Nevertheless, there are numerous examples of practice where the social model underpins effective practice (Mulvany, 2000; Ramon, 2001; Tew, 2002; Barnes and Mercer, 2005).

There are several different perspectives even within this model:

- social causation;
- labelling;
- critical theory;
- social constructivism; and
- social realism.

Whereas the conventional medical approach puts illness down to genetics, viruses or some other biomedical cause, the social model looks at social and environmental factors. The implications of the medical model are that illness is a matter of bad luck and one that needs an individual response, whereas the social model highlights the role of social causes and hence invites a social response. This latter approach brings into play issues of power, oppression and social exclusion (Tew, 2002; Swain, French and Cameron, 2003; Borsay, 2004; Scottish Executive, 2005f).

Social causation

Social causation is a particular perspective that helps us to understand the interaction between social disadvantage and mental disorder. A psychiatric diagnosis is largely accepted and the interest of the sociologist is in the effect that societal inequalities and social exclusion have had on the person's mental health. Other variables such as gender, ethnicity and class can be incorporated into this explanatory model.

The concentration of people who are diagnosed as having schizophrenia in inner-city areas is an interesting example of this perspective. For although it is a 'fact' that the incidence of schizophrenia in inner-city areas is much higher than in the suburbs and that schizophrenia is predominantly a lower class disorder, this is far from being a causal relationship.

ACTIVITY **1.5**

What factor do you think could explain the concentration of people with schizophrenia in inner city areas? Write down your ideas.

Comment

There are many possibilities but among those in the literature are the following:

- The 'drift theory', in which people who are long-term sufferers of schizophrenia migrate from rural areas into cities where they can blend in more easily and where services are more likely to be concentrated. People with schizophrenia from the so-called 'upper classes' may find that the debilitating effect of this disorder results in them being unable to maintain their position in society and a downward drift into the 'lower classes' occurs.

- Alternatively it could be that being in poverty in cities is harder and more alienating for people and that this could result in increased incidences of the disorder.

Within Scotland, as in many other parts of the UK and the world, the whole issue of delivering services to *rural* communities has to be considered (Cheers and Pugh, 2008). Given the physical and social geography of Scotland, these matters are likely to occupy the minds of service planners and practitioners (Pugh, 2000, 2003; Lehmann, 2005; Innes et al., 2006) and offer particular challenges to those working in the field of mental health, particularly with regard to preventive services and the development and sustainability of local support networks.

ACTIVITY **1.6**

What particular issues present themselves to service users, carers and professionals in relation to rural locations? Note down your thoughts.

Comment

In relation to service users and their carers, concerns around the physical distance from populated areas can create anxieties when someone feels unwell or a crisis develops. These concerns can be elevated in periods of bad weather when some roads can be closed because of snow, etc. Not *knowing* that someone can and will get there can cause a lot of distress and add to the difficulties. In terms of ongoing supports and the availability of social networks, being in a rural location can make these more difficult to develop and sustain. Issues around stigma can affect the nature of help-seeking behaviour by people and lead to increased isolation. Conversely, some people may feel that their local community is very supportive of them and actually receive a great deal of help from neighbours.

From the perspective of the professional, working within rural areas requires that forward planning is essential as travelling times are increased. Visits to rural and particularly *isolated* locations require that extra attention be given to considerations of safety. Letting people know where you are, who you are visiting and when you expect to return are important things to remember. It is also important to remember that mobile communications may be interrupted or unavailable in some areas which is a factor to consider in crisis situations. Offering ongoing support to people in rural settings through the use of support groups, etc. can be difficult to arrange and sustain, particularly where attendance at these groups and events is likely to require additional effort on the part of the service user because of geography. Where lack of motivation is a feature of a disorder, these demands may be even more difficult to accommodate and so creative thinking is required.

Psychosocial causes of mental disorder

The early part of this chapter concentrated on the medical model in which work with service users is focused upon trying to identify the cause of the mental disorder in order that we can intervene to restore better mental health. We then briefly looked at the social model and now need to see how these two models can be applied to everyday practice. Most professionals accept that the most likely cause of any mental disorder is a complex interaction between the biological, the psychological and the social. Newton (1988) is one of many academics who have constructed models that not only help us to see possible causes, but also to identify what might be done with the service user to improve their functioning.

A simplified version of these models is set out in Figure 1.4 and shows how a number of factors can interact to determine whether in any given circumstance a person will develop either good or poor mental health and/or a mental illness. These factors include:

• predisposing or vulnerability factors including genetic components and any previous family or personal history of mental health problems;

• social causative factors including the issues of class, social exclusion and racism in rein-forcing mental disorder;

• psychological factors including loss, threats, highly critical relationships, levels of resilience in relation to adverse events and the extent of social support networks that may precipitate or trigger the onset of a disorder.

It is important that you realise that these models are an oversimplification of complex situations and that different authors use different terminology. Nevertheless they at least provide an indication of where people might be vulnerable and offer the possibility of intervention to help strengthen the weak areas.

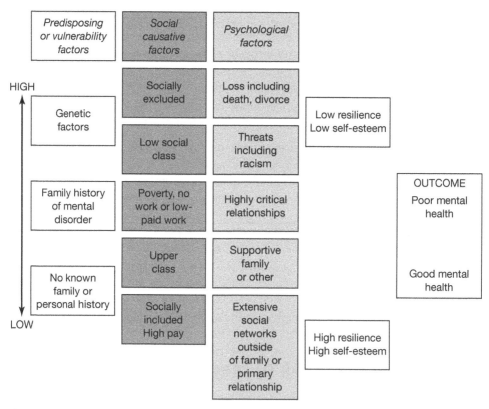

Figure 1.4: Psychosocial model

This approach allows you to weigh up the factors and, with the service user, to work out what could be achieved to promote their mental good health. It also helps to explain how people can face similar events but react differently. Thus although the service user may have a history of family mental health problems and mental illness, they may be in a well-paid, satisfying job with a network of social support. These factors could interact to provide protective rather than vulnerability factors. Of course the opposite might occur where no previous history of mental disorder is known but social exclusion and the resultant stress may increase the person's vulnerability to mental health problems and mental illness. These apparent differences can be explained by reference to the interplay between the person and their environment where the intrapersonal and the interpersonal interact with environmental factors and, alongside wider system variables, affect the phenomenological or subjective experience of each person to bring about differing outcomes in response to similar circumstances (Vygotsky, 1978; Bronfenbrenner, 1979, 1986; Lewin, 1997; Hothersall, 2006).

Social work practice in a psychosocial context

The reality of intervening in people's lives is that you are working with something that is very complex and multifaceted (O'Sullivan, 1999; Walker and Beckett, 2003; Healy, 2005). At the centre of our work is helping service users to manage their lives in more effective ways to counter the negative effects of their illness. However, any intervention carries with it a degree of uncertainty about the effect it might have.

The present drive to integrate services for people with a mental disorder opens up (in theory at least) the opportunity to provide a 'seamless' service (Scottish Executive, 2000c, 2006c). Social workers will work alongside health colleagues and it should be obvious to both just what they each bring to the situation, although it is important that we do not operate solely on the basis of assumptions about collaborative practice (see Chapter 8). The need for quality evidence on which to support the specific intervention is long overdue and the establishment of centres for evidence-based practice (Huxley, 2002, p198) suggests that social care is beginning to embrace the idea of measuring changes that have occurred as a result of their and others' interventions, from the perspectives of both professionals and service users and their carers (Adams and Drake, 2006; Nelson et al., 2006; Scheyett, McCarthy and Rausch, 2006).

The Cochrane Centre provides access to a number of systematic reviews of the effects of health care interventions and has a number of mental health groups in the collaboration, all of which can be accessed through their website www.cochrane.org. In Scotland, the National Programme for Improving Mental Health and Well-Being has linked a number of mental health groups, all of which can be accessed via www.wellscotland.info/contacts/. The evidence that we have already shows that psychosocial intervention can have a powerful effect on rehabilitation. Respite care of some sort can help to relieve the impact on carers and can sometimes delay or even prevent hospitalisation, while family-based interventions can alleviate some of the negative aspects of living with someone who has a mental disorder and reduce the stress of family life. Interventions aimed at improving the broad living environment (Bradshaw, Harris and Lovell, 2005) and creating or supporting social networks can therefore be very effective, and what appears to work less well is psychological debriefing after trauma, simple crisis intervention approaches and strict case management (Huxley, 2002; Bonynge, Lee and Thurber, 2005; Ritchie, Watson and Friedman, 2006). It is therefore important for the whole team (including the service user) to approach interventions carefully, critically and collaboratively.

Stress as an intervening variable

Of course, you probably realise that people experience similar events differently – the loss of employment to one person could be a crushing blow that results in vulnerability to depression, while to another it could be the very opportunity to go to college to become better qualified, or to just take some time out. The choice will almost certainly be influenced by previous experience, family circumstances and financial position.

Epstein (1983) suggests that it is possible to learn better ways of coping with stress while writers like Cochrane (1983) point to the role that stress plays in pushing people either towards positive mental health or in the other direction. It is not just the experience of losing your job, but the way in which this impacts upon you and how you perceive the event. This approach does open up the prospect of working with the service users to recognise what makes them overstressed and to identify better ways to help them manage this. It is clearly not possible to reduce all the adverse events that affect a person's life, but it *is* possible to get better at managing these situations (Hankin and Abela, 2005).

EXAMPLE

Social workers who work with families of young people who are on the road to recovery from an eating disorder can utilise a number of short-term techniques to assist in reducing the stress in such situations. These might include working with the family to ensure that they do not:

- *ask about what the person has eaten;*
- *make comments about the food;*
- *make comments about shape or size;*
- *make comments about their weight.*

This puts the consideration of weight and size into the professional domain and removes everyday comments from family members that may be considered stressful.

Promoting mental well-being: a political approach

Newton (1988 – see above) provides information about what is needed to provide the necessary conditions to prevent mental disorder. Two possible approaches to prevention are either to work to reduce the vulnerability factors or to help people develop more positive responses and therefore increase their resilience to withstand stressful situations better. These approaches include a socio-political dimension as many of the social factors include the effects of social exclusion, racism and poverty (Platt, 2007).

Work that falls into the category of reducing vulnerability would include social workers being placed in schools (Scottish Executive/HMIe, 2006) and projects with specific funding, such as Sure Start (Akhurst et al., 2005; Cunningham-Burley et al., 2006). In both instances the work can be focused upon the young person and their families. Some of the work compensates for social disadvantage and could have a positive impact on mental health (Scottish Executive, 2005g; Hothersall, 2006).

The National Programme for Improving Mental Health and Well-Being

The Scottish Executive introduced the National Programme for Improving Mental Health and Well-Being in 2003. The programme has four key aims:

- Raising awareness and promoting mental health and well-being;
- Eliminating stigma and discrimination around mental ill health;
- Preventing suicide and supporting those bereaved by it;
- Promoting and supporting recovery from mental health problems.

These aims are applicable in relation to the promotion of positive mental health in everyone, but there are five priority areas targeted for urgent action:

- infant mental health;
- the mental health of children and young people;
- mental health and well-being in employment and working life;
- mental health and well-being in later life;
- improving community mental health and well-being.

In line with the key aims and priorities of the National Programme, there are several key initiatives which, through a number of major mental health charities and public health bodies, aim to address and support the priority areas in different ways. These include:

- *Breathing Space* This is a free, confidential phone-line service for those people experiencing low mood and depression.
- *Choose Life* This is a major initiative which works to prevent suicide in Scotland.
- *Scottish Recovery Network* The emphasis here is on promoting and supporting recovery from mental illness.
- *See Me* This campaign works to stop the stigma of mental illness.
- *Scotland's Mental Health First Aid* see www.healthscotland.org.uk/smhfa/.

The National Programme is supported by the provisions of the 2003 Act, in particular s 23–31.

For more information go to www.wellscotland.info/mentalhealth/national-programme.html.

The mental health and well-being of children and young people has recently been a particular focus for the Scottish Government and the NHS with the development of a framework for promotion, prevention and care (Scottish Executive, 2005g). This is covered in detail in Chapter 5.

ACTIVITY 1.7

Go back to Figure 1.4 and think where would be the best focus for a suicide prevention strategy. What factor would make people more vulnerable to suicidal thoughts? Jot down your ideas.

Comment

You probably came up with most of the factors identified within the National Programme policy document. These would include people who are:

• in low-paid, unskilled work;

• unemployed;

• breaking up from a relationship;

• socially isolated;

• misusing drugs or alcohol.

Having an impact in all these areas would help and we do not actually know which one would make the biggest difference. This requires a mixture of social policy and community initiatives. Equally though, working with service users who are depressed to improve their social networks would help, and so would encouraging them to continue taking their medication.

Despite the methodological problems the government has moved forward with its intentions to affect the number of suicides with year-on-year reductions set as targets. Progress is being made but even so over 833 people aged 15+ took their own lives in Scotland during 2004 (Scottish Executive, 2007a – see Table 1.2).

Table 1.2: Suicide among people age 15 and over, by sex and year, Scotland, 1989–2004

Year	Male		Female	
	Number of deaths	Rate per 100,000	Number of deaths	Rate per 100,000
1989	487	24.9	208	9.6
1990	543	27.7	181	8.3
1991	521	26.6	182	8.4
1992	575	29.4	217	10.0
1993	668	34.1	230	10.6
1994	607	31.0	222	10.2
1995	618	31.5	209	9.6
1996	613	31.3	224	10.3
1997	648	33.1	218	10.0
1998	648	33.1	225	10.3
1999	660	33.7	208	9.5
2000	671	34.2	199	9.1
2001	644	32.7	240	10.9
2002	673	34.1	221	10.1
2003	576	29.0	216	9.8
2004	607	30.3	226	10.2

Source: Scottish Executive (2007a, p17). Reproduced under the terms of Crown Copyright Policy Guidance issued by HMSO.

In order to effect some level of change, a number of related measures have been introduced which include:

- reducing the pack sizes of aspirin and paracetamol in an attempt to make it more difficult for people to purchase large quantities of these tablets;

- improving the risk assessment on inpatient wards where acute patients are liable to be detained;

- establishing a research forum to improve the quality of the information that is available to professionals to ensure that professional practice is evidence based;

- working more closely with service user groups;

- setting up a number of pilot projects to target key at-risk groups such as young men (Scottish Executive, 2002a, 2006d).

It is too early to comment authoritatively about the effectiveness of this plan although evaluations are ongoing (Scottish Executive, 2006d). However, you may have your own views.

C H A P T E R   S U M M A R Y

- We have seen the impact that values and ethics have on mental health social work. These values are set down by the professional bodies and, in the case of social work, by the Scottish Social Services Council.

- Transforming social work in the twenty-first century requires workers to be able to recognise their own prejudices and biases and to move beyond these to develop a practice that is culturally competent, demonstrated by workers' awareness of the service user's culture, including religion and traits.

- Transforming practice means also engaging in more than the rhetoric of anti-oppressive practice and value-based practice.

- It means demonstrating that these major ideas have influenced everyday mental health work. This means seeing the person not just as the mental health problem that they exhibit and not being influenced by stereotypes. Listening to what users have to say about their experiences is an important part of this process.

- The chapter has introduced you to the two main theoretical approaches to understanding mental health and mental illness and you should have developed your knowledge of the critical and research-based explanations that contribute to the knowledge base of social work, including the application to practice.

- Detail has been provided about mental disorder, intervention and treatment. Included in this has been a description of the main types of medication that are currently in use, and all this should help you to feel more confident and knowledgeable about mental health and mental illness.

- The role of social workers in working with people who have mental disorder or poor mental health has been outlined and the provision of a schematic outline of psychosocial factors will help you to see where the best intervention ought to be made.

- In-depth case studies are provided in later chapters that will build up your specific knowledge of depression, schizophrenia and eating disorders.

FURTHER READING

Pilgrim, D and Rogers, A (1999) *A sociology of mental health and illness.* 2nd edn. Bukingham: Open University Press.

A very useful text that illustrates the key perspectives on mental health. It has good chapters on social class inequalities and mental health, gender, race and ethnicity and age, all of which make for interesting and relevant reading.

Littlewood, R and Lipsedge, M (1997) *Aliens and alienists: ethnic minorities and psychiatry.* 3rd edn. Abingdon: Routledge.

This is a very useful text which considers important issues around trans-cultural psychiatry. Written from the perspectives of both psychiatry and anthropology, it explains how bio-chemical problems such as schizophrenia or depression involving neurological and neurochemical problems inside the brain will be expressed differently by people from different cultural backgrounds.

Patrick, H (2006) *Mental health, incapacity and the law in Scotland.* Edinburgh: Tottel Publishing.

This is an excellent text which looks, in detail, at the current law in Scotland in relation to mental disorder and incapacity. It presents highly technical information in a very accessible way.

WEBSITES

Scottish statistics on mental health can be obtained from:
- **www.scotland.gov.uk/Topics/Statistics/Browse/Health**

The Sainsbury Centre for Mental Health:
- **www.scmh.org.uk/80256FBD004F6342/vWeb/wpKHAL6S2HVE**

The Scottish Association for Mental Health:
- **www.samh.org.uk/frontend/index.cfm**

For useful information concerning relevant research around mental health issues and social work practice, go to:
- **www.rip.org.uk/** (children and families)
- **www.ripfa.org.uk/** (adults)

The various mental well-being policy initiatives discussed above may be accessed through the Scottish Government website at:
- **www.scotland.gov.uk and via www.wellontheweb.com**

The Scottish Personality Disorder Network has a very accessible website at:
- **www.scottishpersonalitydisorder.org/treatment.php**

Notes

1   The name of the Scottish Civil Service was changed from the Scottish Executive to the Scottish Government by the First Minister in September 2007. We have retained the title Scottish Executive for all references to its work before that date and to all pre-September 2007 publications. We only call it the Scottish Government for those few references to it post-September 2007.

Chapter 2

The legal and policy context (I): the Mental Health (Care and Treatment) (Scotland) Act 2003

A C H I E V I N G   A   S O C I A L   W O R K   D E G R E E

This chapter will help you to begin to meet the following (Scottish) Standards in Social Work Education (SiSWE) (Scottish Executive, 2003a), available at www.scotland.gov.uk/library5/social/ffsw.pdf.

Key Role 1: Prepare for, and work with, individuals, families, carers, groups and communities to assess their needs and circumstances.

Learning Focus:

1.1 Preparing for social work contact and involvement.

1.2 Working with individuals, families, carers, groups and communities so they can make informed decisions.

1.3 Assessing needs and options in order to recommend a course of action.

Key Role 2: Plan, carry out, review and evaluate social work practice with individuals, families, carers, groups, communities and other professionals.

Learning Focus:

2.1 Identifying and responding to crisis situations.

2.2 Working with individuals, families, carers, groups and communities to achieve change, promote dignity, realise potential and improve life opportunities.

2.3 Producing, implementing and evaluating plans with individuals, families, carers, groups, communities and colleagues.

2.4 Developing networks to meet assessed needs and planned outcomes.

2.5 Working with groups to promote choice and independent living.

2.6 Tackling behaviour which presents a risk to individuals, families, carers, groups, communities and the wider public.

Key Role 3: Assess and manage risk to individuals, families, carers, groups, communities, self and colleagues.

Learning Focus:

3.1 Assessing and managing risks to individuals, families, carers, groups and communities.

3.2 Assessing and managing risk to self and colleagues.

Key Role 4: Demonstrate professional competence in social work practice.

Learning Focus:

4.1 Evaluating and using up-to-date knowledge of, and research into, social work practice.

4.2 Working within agreed standards of social work practice.

4.3 Understanding and managing complex ethical issues, dilemmas and conflicts.

4.4 Promoting best social work practice, adapting positively to change.

Key Role 5: *Manage and be accountable, with supervision and support, for their own social work practice within their organisation.*
  Learning Focus:
  5.1 Managing one's own work in an accountable way.
  5.3 Contributing to the management of resources and services.
  5.4 Managing, presenting and sharing records and reports.
  5.5 Preparing for, and taking part in, decision-making forums.
  5.6 Working effectively with professionals within integrated, multidisciplinary and other service settings.

Key Role 6: *Support individuals to represent and manage their needs, views and circumstances.*
  Learning Focus:
  6.1 Representing, in partnership with, and on behalf of individuals, families, carers, groups and communities to help them achieve and maintain greater independence.

Introduction

The end of law is, not to abolish or restrain, but to preserve and enlarge freedom.
(John Locke, 1690)

It was necessary ... to say in what way mental illness was different from physical illness, and in what circumstances the ethical duty of respect for autonomy could be overridden. This statement was from an unidentified respondent to the question 'Is a Mental Health Act necessary?' in the Millan Committee's consultation on the need for a revision of the Mental Health (Scotland) Act 1984 (Scottish Executive, 2001c).

This chapter concentrates upon the principles and practice of the main statute that relates to mental disorder, as defined in the last chapter. As the title *the Mental Health (Care and Treatment) (Scotland) Act 2003* suggests, it is an exclusively Scottish piece of legislation and it does not just relate to providing treatment, but to the provision of the entire gamut of care to people who have difficulties in managing their own needs arising out of having a mental disorder. In order to work effectively in multidisciplinary settings you need to have a broad knowledge of the processes that will directly or indirectly impact upon service users with whom you work.

Clarification of terminology

On points of terminology, having carefully separated out the terms and defined mental disorder in the last chapter, it may seem confusing to have the legislation called a *Mental Health* Act when the 2003 Act deals with problems faced by those with a wider range of disabilities than mental illness only. However, after much debate it was decided that it should be so called because most people understood the euphemistic term of reference (Scottish Executive, 2001c, p15). In the rest of this book we will follow Millan's lead in Scottish Executive (2001c) but apply quotation marks to show our deliberate use of a term which we have acknowledged is misleading. Thus we will refer to the body of legislation relating to mental disorder as 'mental health' law. Further more, we will use the quotes around 'mental health' to denote its usage in common place terms like 'mental health' services.

Our focus will generally be upon mental illness. At certain points in the text the term *patient* is used to refer to the person with a mental disorder who becomes subject to the powers of the Act. While it may be regrettable that this law uses such a medicalised term, we use it as a word of convenience. For the sake of brevity, the lengthy but proper name for the Act will be shortened to *the 2003 Act*. While on the subject of brevity, may we apologise in advance for the number of abbreviations used later in this chapter. To dabble in this area of law is to become acquainted with many lengthy legal terms which inevitably become abbreviated through use. Therefore, when you read that, *for the CTO, the MHO remained the same, but the AMP became the RMO following approval by MHTS* you will know that this is how practitioners speak!

A very short history of 'mental health' law

Some form of law relating to mental disorder has been an integral part of British legislation for several hundreds of years, albeit under now old-fashioned sounding names such as the Lunacy Acts. Locking 'mad' people away in the 'asylum' under some formal legal process was a feature in the writings of Charles Dickens, Thomas Hardy and others. The use of the law to deprive someone of their liberty because of mental illness is well established in public consciousness and *sectioning* people into hospital is a relatively common theme in police and hospital television drama. However, if Locke was correct in the words quoted above, is it not contradictory to have a law that deprives someone of their freedom because of their mental condition?

Why have a 'Mental Health' Act?

If it is right to have a law which takes away people's rights to make decisions about care and treatment when mentally ill, why not have a similar law restricting people who are physically ill? There is some very limited public health statute allowing the restraint of people who have serious communicable diseases such as typhoid, but its use is extremely rare (Public Health (Control of Disease) Act 1984). Think about the annual flu mortality figures and the cost to the nation of millions of pounds through days lost from work. Is there not far more reason to have an Influenza Act to confine sufferers to their beds than there is reason to have a 'Mental Health' Act?

ACTIVITY **2.1**

Think about why people who experience mental disorder should be subject to legislation. Try to list three reasons.

Comment

You probably listed things such as:

- people who experience mental disorder may be incapable of looking after their own best interests;

- they may not be able to make reasonable decisions;

- they may not be able to consent to treatment;

- they may pose a danger to themselves or others.

However, reading the foregoing paragraph, you may have begun to think that, despite the occasional glaring and sensationalised newspaper headlines about people who commit dangerous acts while mentally ill, people with flu represent far more public danger than do mentally disordered people, only a tiny minority of whom commit any offences what-soever.[1] You may also reflect that most of us do unwise things and act outside our best interests, so why make an exception of people affected by mental disorder?

There is a curious paradox operating here, which, setting aside *incapacity law* as discussed in Chapter 3, does not apply to any other area of health and social care. It is this: when you have an extremely serious mental disorder, the state is prepared to use the law to pro-tect you from your own impaired decision-making by restricting your freedom. The reason for this is that, broadly speaking, we agree that we all are fallible beings who have an enti-tlement to make mistakes and act unwisely, even when we are physically ill. However, by our very understanding of what it means to be mentally ill, we think that the experience of mental illness in itself can make us do unwise things or make unreasonable decisions. It therefore elevates mental illness into a special category in which we are not always responsible for our actions. The same is considered true for personality disorder, the second component of mental disorder. It is also accepted that having a learning disability of any degree of severity may hamper one's understanding to the point where it impairs decision-making. Therefore these three conditions are lumped together as conditions for the intervention of 'mental health' law under a legal principle called *parens patrae* – the state's responsibility to care for its more vulnerable citizens.

Tensions between protection of welfare and safety and individual freedom

While much of the focus of 'mental health' law is upon medical aspects of the condition called mental illness, the law recognises that there are social consequences of such an ill-ness. Therefore, when we look at the conditions that must be present for a person's individual liberty to be impinged upon under the 2003 Act, we will see that welfare is high on the agenda, and social risks (such as safety) figure as largely as do risks to health. It is all strongly related to human rights. The paradox discussed above suggests that we have potentially conflicting rights which must be resolved at the point when a person poses serious risk to self or others because of mental disorder. There are rights to freedom of belief, choice and expression which conflict with the state's responsibility to protect the person from harm when mentally unwell (the Human Rights Act 1998). We can see how they are resolved when we examine the extreme case of Roz, a woman who suffers from severe depression to the extent that she is seriously planning to kill herself.

ACTIVITY **2.2**

You have been told very little about Roz, other than that she has been diagnosed by her doctor as having depression and she feels so desperate and hopeless about life that she can stand it no longer and wants it to be over. Take a moment to reflect and write a list of reasons why she ought to be allowed to kill herself and why she ought to be prevented, if need be by forceful restraint, from doing so.

Note: *Because of past experiences or because you are feeling fragile and vulnerable yourself at the moment, it may be distressing for you to be asked to undertake this exercise. Such things are not at all unusual. If this applies to you, it is sometimes wise to talk to someone you trust about it or to seek counselling or professional support.*

Comment

It is extremely difficult to look squarely at the reality that people do kill themselves and to consider the rights and wrongs of such actions. On one side you may have noted that it may be ethically wrong for one person to decide on behalf of another that their life is worth living. To live or not to live may be the most personal of decisions and who are we to intervene?

On the other hand, depression is perhaps the most treatable form of mental illness today. Therefore, if prevented from committing suicide, Roz may well live to find life worthwhile again, and if, after recovering from her depression, she still wished to be dead, that may be another matter. However, if anyone proposed to Roz that she should be detained in hospital for treatment so that she would no longer feel the need to commit suicide, she would presumably answer that she does not want to go to hospital. Roz wants to be dead because her existence is so painful to her. Yet, if we accept her right to kill herself (suicide no longer being against the law), we will be depriving Roz of her right to life and her right to make any subsequent decisions. Therefore it seems most reasonable to protect Roz's right to life by temporarily denying her the right to determine to kill herself.

Before moving on to outline salient aspects of the 2003 Act, there remain two issues to clarify. The first is that the coercive aspects of the Act will only ever apply to a minority of the most seriously mentally ill people. The Scottish Government's policy on enhancing the mental well-being of the nation frequently points out that one in four of us will have a mental health problem in adult life (www.wellscotland.info – see Chapter 1). Only something in the region of 1 or 2 per cent of the population will have serious mental illness and the vast majority of them will receive care and treatment of their own free will.

The second issue is that all of the discussion so far relates to civil codes of law. 'Mental health' law is virtually the only piece of civil law that contains powers to deprive individuals of major civil liberties. To put it bluntly, although the 2003 Act contains sweeping powers to lock people in hospital for potentially lengthy periods of time, to force treatment upon them, to restrict their choices in the community and to limit other freedoms, the people who are subjected to it have broken no law, committed no crime. There are aspects of the law which deal with people who are both mentally disordered and commit crimes. These will be discussed in Chapter 4.

A brief history of the 2003 Act

The 2003 Act is a new piece of legislation, in fact the first major piece of law created by the young Scottish Parliament. It replaced the 1984 Act after a lengthy process of consultation and review. The main building blocks of the 2003 Act were formed out of the Millan Report – a far-reaching report by a committee instigated by parliament and convened by the Rt Hon Bruce Millan (Scottish Executive, 2001c).

The principles

Modern Scottish welfare legislation is characterised by the inclusion of overarching *principles* through which all actions under that law must be mediated. Setting binding principles in law is a way of ensuring that people's human rights are preserved and, of course, since the Human Rights Act 1998, all UK law must conform to our rights as set out in the Articles of the European Convention of Human Rights (Convention for the Protection of Human Rights and Fundamental Freedoms as amended by Protocol No. 11, Rome, 4.xi.1950).

The 2003 Act has a detailed set of *principles* set out in s 1, 2 and 3. They make it a binding duty for anyone who has formal powers under the Act to make decisions and commit actions only with regard to these principles. For example in making a decision to detain a person in hospital for treatment, all the people involved in the process must have regard for the wishes and feelings of the person subject to the detention. They can only invoke powers that are the least restrictive necessary in relation to the freedom of the subject. They must take account of the views of other significant people such as the person's carer.

The 'Short Introduction' to the 2003 Act gives a good summary of the principles:

- non-discrimination;

- equality;

- respect for diversity;

- reciprocity (where compulsory powers are imposed by law, a parallel obligation is imposed on providers of care and treatment services to provide appropriate services);

- informal care (should be considered before formal compulsion);

- participation (of service users as far as possible in the process);

- respect for carers;

- least restrictive alternative;

- benefit (any compulsory intervention should be of benefit to the *patient*).

There is also a special set of principles with specific regard to the needs and rights of children who may be subject to the Act (Scottish Executive, 2005n).

The framework for compulsion

You may have noticed us using the term *compulsion*. It is used to reflect the width of powers of compulsory intervention in people's lives that the 2003 Act may invoke. Since most people affected by mental disorder live in the community, even while very unwell, 'mental health' law is no longer just concerned with detaining people in hospital for treatment. For example, the law can compel people to accept other forms of care and support, it can require the person to live in a certain place such as a hostel or supported accommodation and it can require them to attend day services or give access to people to come into the place where the person lives to provide care and support.

The term *framework* (used in the heading above) implies that there is a structured response to the following questions: *How can a person be made subject to compulsion?* and *What sort of situation would justify taking away such freedom?* Dealing with the last of these questions first, the law sets down very strict conditions under which compulsion may be invoked. The conditions vary in detail from lesser measures of compulsion to the more long lasting and far reaching powers, but they do share general features.

Clearly, the person must be suffering from a form of mental disorder to justify loss of liberty. Given what we have already said about one in four of us having some form of mental health problem in adult life, the disorder from which the person suffers would have to be one of such a severity as to merit the loss of liberty as a protective measure. The judgement about when a person has such a disorder is given by a doctor who, in most cases has to be a highly specialised psychiatrist.

However, having a severe mental disorder does not necessarily mean that the person will need measures of compulsion. Remember that most of Scotland's 2 per cent of the population who have severe mental illness willingly receive treatment without being so compelled by law. There have to be special risks present in the situation – risks to the person's own health, safety or welfare, or risks that require another person to be protected from the actions of the mentally disordered person. Furthermore, the degree of that risk must be considerable to justify the loss of liberty. Finally, in most situations where compulsion is being considered, there is a *test of incapacity:*[2] it has to be demonstrated that, because of the mental disorder, the person lacks the ability to make reasoned treatment decisions in relation to their condition.

CASE STUDY

This last point is an important one. Consider, for example, Scott. Scott has schizophrenia and through the chaos of his illness he has risked homelessness by non-payment of his rent. His illness leads Scott to trust no one and so he is refusing services and will not even reply to notices of eviction, which he believes to be part of a plot to persecute him. This is a condition that psychiatrists would refer to as paranoia. Scott has a serious mental disorder in that it seriously affects his life. It is mid-winter and he is at risk to his safety and welfare, as would be anyone who is imminently homeless. However, the law considers that, as long as Scott can make a rational decision in respect of treatment, the law cannot restrict his choice to act as he does. Therefore, suppose Scott is fully aware that he has schizophrenia, that he understands his uncontrollable mistrust of others to be paranoia and he accepts that there is medical treatment available to him such as would alleviate his condition, making him less paranoid and more able to work with others to avoid eviction. However, Scott dislikes the side effects of the treatment so much that he prefers his current options to the feelings while taking the treatment. In this case, service providers could only stand by and try to offer such gentle persuasion as Scott would accept in order to try to help him, because the law considers it to be his right to determine his freedom not to take the drugs, even at risk of eviction.

Once these conditions for compulsion have been established, the question arises as to *how can a person be made subject to compulsion?* Here, the framework of the 2003 Act unfolds a range of measures from a very short *emergency detention* in hospital allowing for loss of liberty for up to 72 hours, through a more extended *short-term detention* lasting up to 28 days and allowing for the subject to receive certain treatments for mental disorder against his or her will, to a longer lasting *compulsory treatment order* (CTO).

While the emergency and short-term detentions have powers of compulsion limited to detention (and, in the case of short-term detention, treatment) in hospital only, the CTO has wide ranging powers such as the power:

- to detain in hospital;

- to apply a range of treatment for mental disorder against the subject's wishes, either in or outside hospital;

- to compel the person to reside at a particular place;

- to compel him or her to attend specified places for specified purposes such as to receive treatment, training or care; and

- to compel the person to allow certain others access to his or her home.

The CTO lasts for up to six months and is renewable at set periods of time, indefinitely.

To counterbalance the great powers of the CTO, it has a stringent process of scrutiny. To set it in motion, emergency detention only requires the agreement of a doctor that the conditions apply and, unless it is impracticable, the consent of a *mental health officer* (see below for discussion of the role of the MHO, but note the euphemistic use of the term 'mental health' yet again). Short-term detention requires the agreement of a specially qualified doctor (an *approved medical practitioner* – AMP) and, at all times, the consent of an MHO. A CTO requires special reports from two independent doctors, one of whom must be an AMP. On the basis of these reports, it further requires an MHO to apply to a body called the Mental Health Tribunal for Scotland (see below). The MHO makes a detailed assessment of the person in relation to the conditions for compulsion and the case is examined by a specially convened tribunal which decides whether or not to grant the application and has powers to vary the recommended measures of compulsion.

There are other wide-ranging provisions in the 2003 Act, such as warrants of entry into the privacy of a person's home, powers to create flexible variations of CTO and to briefly extend short-term detention so that a tribunal hearing for a CTO may be heard, duties upon the local authority to investigate circumstances where a person seems to be living at risk because of mental disorder and police powers to remove a person into a place of safety because they appear to be suffering from a mental disorder.

The role of the mental health officer

An MHO is a specially qualified and expert social worker who, by qualification, has legally specific powers to participate in the decision-making processes by which a person can be made subject to compulsion. MHOs stand at the gateway to virtually all routes of compulsion under the Act. They have responsibility for giving consent to most *emergency detentions* and all *short-term detentions* and they make applications for all CTOs. They also have other powers and duties. MHOs are employees of local authorities and their employers have a duty under s 32 of the Act to provide enough MHOs to fulfil their duties in the area.

As will be seen, MHOs also have duties under the Adults with Incapacity (Scotland) Act 2000 (see Chapter 3) and, in respect of mentally disordered offenders, under the Criminal Procedure (Scotland) Act 1995 (see Chapter 4).

The role of others

There are roles given to a wide range of others under the 2003 Act: nurses, police, hospital managers, the local authority and health board, doctors including GPs and others. However, alongside MHOs, the other major role is that of the *approved medical practitioner*. AMPs are specially trained psychiatrists, usually consultant psychiatrists, who have responsibility for making decisions about short-term detention and assessment for CTO. When a patient falls under the care of a particular AMP, for example when he or she becomes subject to a CTO, the AMP becomes the patient's *responsible medical officer* (RMO), with more specific duties to monitor and review the care and treatment of the patient and to apply for renewals of the CTO if the conditions for compulsion still apply when it expires.

The Act makes a distinction between the roles of formal agents who have powers and duties conferred upon them in relation to compulsion and other people who may be there in roles supportive of the 'patient'. The principles are binding on the actions of these formal agents, but not upon those of others. Most significant among these other people are the patient's *named person* and *advocate*.

The named person is someone identified by the patient as an autonomous point of reference and support. The named person may be a friend or family member or a trusted person in the patient's life. Named persons have a number of roles when the patient becomes subject to compulsion. For example, it is a duty of the MHO to seek their views, they have a right to receive any legal papers relating to detention or CTO and they may attend tribunal hearings.

Patients have a right to *advocacy* services which should enable the patient to express his or her views in the very challenging processes of detention or a tribunal hearing. Advocacy is a very different role from that of a legal representative at such a hearing. The patient's lawyer would be there to represent the patient's legal case in the context of a legal hearing. The advocate is simply the voice of the patient.

CASE STUDY

Calum MacAlistair is 18. He has just moved to university in Glasgow, having lived all his life in a small, remote island community. Used to a life which hinged around the church in a close-knit community, he has found the size and bustle of a busy city both stimulating and difficult to cope with. However, Calum has made new friends in a Christian group in the halls of residence where he now lives, immersing himself in study and student life.

Over a few weeks he has found it harder and harder to sleep. This is matched by an increasing excitability and overflowing sense of high energy, accompanied by what he sees as brilliant and creative ideas. Ordinarily shy, Calum enjoys his new state of mind, but he also has a growing sense of anxiety that his mood is out of his control.

His new friends just think that he is a bit wild and they first of all enjoy his drive and energy. However, they do get fed up when he pesters them at all hours of the night to join him in fun adventures. Finally, they become alarmed when he wakes them up at five in the morning dressed only in a bed-sheet wrapped like a toga, shouting that he is God. Since they, like Calum, are all Christian, the reference to God is offensive. Since he neither drinks nor takes drugs, these cannot be blamed for his condition.

ACTIVITY 2.3

Consider what risks there might be if Calum were not detained in hospital at this moment? Jot down your thoughts and compare with the comment below.

Comment

If you do not know a great deal about hypomania,[3] some of the more serious risks might be difficult to ascertain. In an advanced, untreated state, hypomania can cause death by exhaustion. More commonly, however, it can cause the person affected by it to do out-of-character and socially damaging things such as breaking the law, unwisely spending money on a grand scale, getting into fights and so on. You may have been able to see the beginnings of some of these risks if you recognised that Calum's friends might get fed up with him, making him more and more isolated at a time when he needs friends. If you further recognised the risks that he might get thrown out of the halls of residence and that he might not be able to keep up his studies, then you have correctly begun to recognise some of the long-term and damaging negative effects of untreated mental disorder.

CASE STUDY

The manager of the halls contacts the on-call GP who is quick to diagnose hypomania. Calum has no previous experience of mental illness and is unable to accept that he might be ill and in need of hospital admission. Recognising this, and ascertaining that Calum will not come to hospital of his own free will, the GP contacts the MHO service. On arrival, the MHO uses her skills to interview Calum even though he is in a state of great agitation. She makes an assessment of his inability to comply with treatment and his need for hospital admission. She verifies that emergency detention would be the only means of getting Calum into hospital at this moment. She obtains family details in order to address who might be his named person. She explains to him what is happening in terms of his rights and the availability of an independent advocacy service to support him at this difficult time. She does all of this with a careful eye to the principles of the 2003 Act which protect Calum's human rights.

As soon as possible after his admission, Calum is seen by the consultant psychiatrist, his RMO, who consults with the MHO to make a short-term detention. If, as would be likely, in such a situation, Calum was still unable to agree to being a voluntary patient at the end of 28 days, a CTO would have been applied for by the MHO and a tribunal (see below) convened to decide whether or not it should be granted to secure a longer period of compulsion.

Advance statements

The 2003 Act sets out provision for the *patients* themselves to have a voice in their own treatment, even should they become too unwell to make competent decisions. The advance statement is a document in which the patient can register the kind of treatment he or she wishes to receive or not receive, should he or she ever become so unwell that it would become impossible to give valid instruction at the time. The statement can be altered as often as the patient likes, up to the point when he or she loses capacity to do so. Its status is that any doctor giving treatment *must have regard for its content*. That is to say that the doctor would have to justify (if need be before a tribunal) why he/she had overridden the patient's wishes as recorded in the advance statement, if that was deemed necessary.

Unfortunately, at the time of writing, advance statements remain one of the under-used parts of the Act and work is required to realise their empowering potential.

The role of the Mental Health Tribunal for Scotland

As we have already discussed, the use of the 2003 Act for the necessary protection of a person's health, safety or welfare can be so powerfully sweeping as to jeopardise other aspects of that person's human rights. Therefore the exercise of such powers requires strong and independent protections. The location of the right to advocacy at the gateways to compulsion is one such protection. The rights that the patient has to appeal against detention and orders is another. The existence of an independent decision-making body to hear these appeals and grant or refuse CTO applications is yet another.

The Mental Health Tribunal for Scotland (MHTS) is the independent office convened under the 2003 Act for this purpose. It receives, administers and deals with all applications for CTOs, all related applications for renewal and variation of orders and all appeals against measures of compulsion under the Act.[4] The MHTS does this through a central administration and by employing members to sit on specially convened tribunals. Each tribunal is a panel of three people, convened by a lawyer with a medical member and a general member. General members are drawn from professions such as nursing and social work and from people who have experience of mental disorder either by having been service users themselves or by being a carer to a service user. The panel thus reflects a range of legal, medical and other experience by which to make decisions about people's liberty and needs for protection.

When the MHTS receives an application for a CTO from the MHO, it sets up a tribunal. Ordinarily, the tribunal will look at the papers and have a hearing to meet with the RMO, MHO, patient and any other relevant people to discuss the case for and against the application and to decide what ought to be done. The tribunal has wide powers to accept or reject the application outright or to change the powers recommended in it or the time-scale for the running of the order (www.mhts.scotland.gsi.gov.uk).

The role of the Mental Welfare Commission for Scotland

The Mental Welfare Commission (MWC) is another independent organisation with powers to safeguard the rights of patients. Different in role from the MHTS, it monitors the operation of the Act and, where required, it makes inquiries into deficiencies of care. As such, it scrutinises the work of the MHTS, as it does the work of MHOs and doctors, hospitals, health boards and local authorities, among others. The MWC gathers and analyses statistics about the operation of the Act and publishes an annual report in which it outlines its work of the year, visiting hospitals and other facilities and visiting patients subject to the powers of the Act. It also publishes its inquiries, which can make recommendations to health boards, local authorities and providers of care. The recommendations of the MWC can be far-reaching and there could be very serious consequences for any organisation which chose not to act upon them. For example, the Adult Care and Protection (Scotland) Act 2007 (Scottish Executive, 2007j), which we will discuss in the next chapter, largely arose from needs highlighted in the Mental Welfare Commission's (2003) *Investigations into the Scottish Borders Council and NHS Borders Services for people with learning disability*, the so-called Miss X, or Borders Inquiry into long-term gross neglect and deficiencies in the care of a woman with learning disabilities.

A brief overview of mental health policy

Policy is that strand of activity which sets the general direction for services to attain the objectives of those in government. To put it plainly, policy is a set of directives made by government to ensure that its plans get put into action. For example, in terms of mental health, the Scottish Parliament wants to increase the responsibility that every citizen takes for their own health and it wants to erode the nation's extremely poor record of mental health, the one-in-four statistic that is reflected in suicide and self-harm statistics far above the norm for a developed and wealthy country (see Chapter 1). Therefore the Scottish Government has devised a wide-ranging set of policies on the theme of improving the nation's mental health and well-being (www.wellontheweb.com).

Policy can also be conceived as a middle layer, mediating between the will of the governing politicians and the services which are directed at the ordinary people of the land. As such, policy is largely the province of the Scottish Government. The Scottish Government has a wide portfolio of Directorates (or departments) covering matters relating to Environment, Fisheries and Agriculture through to Health, Justice and Education. Each of these directorates produces and monitors its own policies under the auspices of its own Minister and alongside its partner agencies. The Mental Health Division, dealing with mental health policy and law, is a sub-set of the Health Directorate. Its partners include the NHS and the health boards of Scotland, the 32 Scottish local authorities (the providers of statutory social work services and hence MHO services), a range of voluntary and private service providers, groups of service users, carers and professional interest bodies such as the Association of Directors on Social Work. It is with and through these agencies that the Mental Health Division works to put its policies into action.

Policy and the law

Clearly, government would get into grave difficulties if their policies were at odds with their laws. Indeed, policy and law can be seen as twin tramlines along which services develop. Not all current mental health policy has a strong relationship with the mainstay of the 2003 Act. If we think of the population challenged by poor mental health as a pyramid, with the minority of the most vulnerable at the tip (section 1 in Figure 2.1), most (though not all) of the 2003 Act is focused upon that tip. Those at risk of receiving specialist care from psychiatric services would be in sections 1 and 2. The policy to enhance mental well-being is more targeted upon the majority population at the base of the pyramid (section 3 in Figure 2.1). In this way, if we are all encouraged to take more care of our mental health and to become more emotionally literate, it is supposed that less of us will slip down the path to greater mental ill health (Scottish Executive, 2006c).

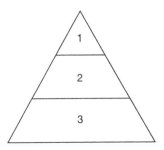

Figure 2.1: Poor mental health shown as a pyramid

While much of this may be helpful in directing resources and in changing the way that the public think about mental health and mental illness, as we acknowledged in Chapter 1, the relationship between mental health and mental illness is not a simple one and the much needed focus on Scotland's poor mental health record may not reduce the rate of serious mental illness in any significant way.

However, there is also a raft of policies directly targeted upon the workings of the 2003 Act. There are policies to direct health boards to improve their services for children and young people and their services for women with post-natal mental illnesses, policies directing local authorities to provide standardised mental health officer services and guidance on how to operate the 2003 Act itself.

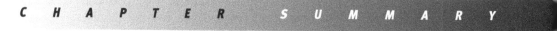

C H A P T E R   S U M M A R Y

This chapter has:

- introduced you to the need for 'mental health' legislation and its place within 'mental health' service provision;

- introduced you to the need to balance powers that the law has to intervene in people's lives for the purpose of protection and the civil rights of people to determine their own choices (the role of the principles in protecting individual human rights and the need to follow a rational and lawful process in restricting liberty);

- introduced you to the Mental Health (Care and Treatment) (Scotland) Act 2003 as the core piece of legislation in this field;

- introduced you to the salient powers of compulsion and the processes whereby these powers can be obtained (emergency and short-term detention, CTO, application and appeal to the Tribunal, etc.);

- introduced you to the principal conditions which must be present for a person to be made subject to these powers (risk to health, safety, welfare or the need to protect an other person, test of capacity to make treatment decisions, etc.).

- introduced you to the principal roles of those individuals and agencies with powers and roles under the Act (the MHO, RMO, Mental Welfare Commission, Tribunal, etc.);

- introduced some of the most current policy developments in enhancing the general mental health of the people in Scotland and the policy as it relates to implementation of the 2003 Act; and

- introduced you to the relationship between law and policy.

FURTHER READING

Unfortunately because of the relative newness of the 2003 Act, there is little written about it in books. Most of the material is contained in websites, policy directives and reports. However, the following may be of interest in supporting some of your learning from this chapter.

Visit the MWC website at **www.mwcscot.org.uk**. Look at the pages on reports and inquiries and get a flavour of the range of their work, the sort of situations they make inquiry into and the sort of recommendations they make. Also look at the sort of statistical information they present in their annual reports. Remember that Scotland is a small country of about 5 million people and match this against the numbers and rates of people made subject to various forms of compulsion under the Acts. Try to get an overview of how the Commision presents its work to convey both formality and openness and approachability.

Visit the MHTS website at **www.mhts.scotland.gsi.gov.uk** and look at the range of work it does do from the mechnics of timing and co-ordinating tribunals to tracking, monitoring and standardising how tribunals work and the decisions they make.

The Scottish Government's Mental Health Division has an interesting web page on policy developments, in which you can find the Delivery Plan and other items discussed above at **www.scotland.gov.uk/Topics/Health/health/mental-health/mhlaw**.

Probably the most technically detailed and authoritative book on this subject at the moment is that by Hilary Patrick (2006), entitled *Mental health, incapacity and the lay in Scotland* (Edinburgh: Tottel Publishing).

The Act itself is worth perusing if you are unfamiliar with how law is written and what it contains: The Mental Health (Care and Treatment) (Scotland) Act 2003.

Alongside the Act is a three-volume Code of Practice, published by the Scottish Executive. While it is preoccupied with detail of meeting the legislation in practice, it is also worth perusing.

The Scottish Executive also publishes a series of short guides to the 2003 Act for various purposes, for example:

- *The New Mental Health Act – An easy read guide*
- *The New Mental Health Act – A guide to advance statements*
- *The New Mental Health Act – A guide to compulsory treatment orders*

These may be ordered through Blackwells bookshops who are agents for the Scottish Goverment publishers. They may also be viewed via the internet (see Websites below), where a full list of the guides available can be found.

WEBSITES

The following site accesses an introduction to the 2003 Act:

- **www.scotland.gov.uk/Publications/2003/11/18547/29201**

The following page accesses the Code of Practice in electronic form and all the short guide/easy-read leaflets available:

- **www.scotland.gov.uk/Topics/Health/health/mental-health/mhlaw/guidance**

The Mental Welfare Commission's annual report gives a good flavour of its work and the most recent and previous reports may be viewed on:

- **www.mwcscot.org.uk/publications/annualreports/annualreport**

A specific suite of materials for inducting MHOs into the 2003 Act contains good practice orientation to the Act and can be found on:

- **www.scotland.gov.uk/Topics/Health/health/mental-health/mhlaw/mhotraining**

The 2003 Act itself can be viewed electronically on:

- **www.opsi.gov.uk/legislation/scotland/en2003/2003en13.htm**

Notes

1. While Scotland has a population of around 5 million, 1.25 million (1 in 4) are estimated to have mild to moderate mental health problems, 50–100,000 (between 1 in 100 and 1 in 50) have severe mental illness and only 500 (one in 10,000) are 'restricted patients', i.e. patients detained under mental health law through criminal procedures and subject to restriction because they represent a serious risk to the public (Scottish Executive, 2006l).

2. Tests in law are threshold conditions that must be satisfied. The *test of incapacity* is a set of conditions that mean that the person cannot be compelled under the Act unless he or she suffers from incapacity of a justifiably serious

nature or degree. *Incapacity* is an inability to make competent decisions or choices (in this case, only in relation to treatment for the mental disorder). The concept of incapacity is more fully discussed in the next chapter.

3. Hypomania is a reference to the elated mood extreme of bipolar affective disorder (see Chapter 1) at the opposite end of the spectrum of mood from depression.

4. Note the use of language here: CTOs are *applied* for to the MHTS, who convene a tribunal to examine the facts (a bit like a children's hearing) and, if persuaded by the case, to *grant the order*. Since emergency and short-term detentions are made by a more simple process of certification, there is no application or hearing but, once in place, short-term detention does carry a right of appeal against it. Because of the short 72-hour time-frame, emergency detention cannot have any appeal. The patient has rights both to contest the application for CTO and to appeal the order if the application has been granted by the tribunal.

Chapter 3

The legal and policy context (II): support and protection of vulnerable adults

A C H I E V I N G   A   S O C I A L   W O R K   D E G R E E

This chapter will help you to begin to meet the following (Scottish) Standards in Social Work Education (SiSWE) (Scottish Executive, 2003a), available at www.scotland.gov.uk/library5/social/ffsw.pdf.

Key Role 1: Prepare for, and work with, individuals, families, carers, groups and communities to assess their needs and circumstances.

Learning Focus:

1.1 Preparing for social work contact and involvement.

1.2 Working with individuals, families, carers, groups and communities so they can make informed decisions.

1.3 Assessing needs and options in order to recommend a course of action.

Key Role 2: Plan, carry out, review and evaluate social work practice with individuals, families, carers, groups, communities and other professionals.

Learning Focus:

2.1 Identifying and responding to crisis situations.

2.2 Working with individuals, families, carers, groups and communities to achieve change, promote dignity, realise potential and improve life opportunities.

2.3 Producing, implementing and evaluating plans with individuals, families, carers, groups, communities and colleagues.

2.4 Developing networks to meet assessed needs and planned outcomes.

2.5 Working with groups to promote choice and independent living.

2.6 Tackling behaviour which presents a risk to individuals, families, carers, groups, communities and the wider public.

Key Role 3: Assess and manage risk to individuals, families, carers, groups, communities, self and colleagues.

Learning Focus:

3.1 Assessing and managing risks to individuals, families, carers, groups and communities.

3.2 Assessing and managing risk to self and colleagues.

Key Role 4: Demonstrate professional competence in social work practice.

Learning Focus:

4.1 Evaluating and using up-to-date knowledge of and research into, social work practice.

4.2 Working within agreed standards of social work practice.

4.3 Understanding and managing complex ethical issues, dilemmas and conflicts.

4.4 Promoting best social work practice, adapting positively to change.

> **Key Role 5: Manage and be accountable, with supervision and support, for their own social work practice within their organisation.**
>   Learning Focus:
>   5.4 Managing, presenting and sharing records and reports.
>   5.5 Preparing for, and taking part in, decision-making forums.
>   5.6 Working effectively with professionals within integrated, multi-disciplinary and other service settings.
> **Key Role 6: Support individuals to represent and manage their needs, views and circumstances.**
>   Learning Focus:
>   6.1 Representing, in partnership with, and on behalf of, individuals, families, carers, groups and communities to help them achieve and maintain greater independence.

Introduction

Dear Sir

I am in a Madhouse & quite forget your Name or who you are. You must excuse me for I have nothing to communicate or tell of & why I am shut up I don't know. I have nothing to say so I conclude

Yours respectfully,

John Clare

(Kermode and Kermode, 1995)

The above quotation from John Clare, the Norfolk peasant poet, from a letter written from the Norfolk General Lunatic Asylum dated 8 March 1860, painfully describes something of the subject matter of this chapter: what would popularly be described as *losing one's mind* and, for our purposes, the regard that the law ought to have in such cases.

This is the second of three chapters on 'mental health' law. It explores the law that protects individuals who are vulnerable because they are affected by mental disorder to such a degree as to be unable to make competent decisions governing their lives. It also touches upon the very new law relating to protection of adults who are vulnerable to abuse and exploitation. Before introducing the pieces of legislation, it may be worth reflecting that, along with the civil powers of the 2003 Act, the Scottish Government has introduced a package of legislation which brings to vulnerable adults the concept of *adult protection* in a holistic way, much as *child protection* revolutionised care of our children and young people in the 1990s. In this regard, adult protection covers a wide range of reasons why an adult might be so vulnerable as to need protection. For example, as well as reasons of mental disorder, an adult may require protection because of poor health or infirmity of old age. As we enter into this new world, some issues of how far the state ought to intervene into private lives must be debated. However, our focus here will be, as ever, on adult protection in relation solely to mental disorder.

What is mental incapacity?

Before answering the above question, we need to ask: *What is mental **capacity**?* This question relates closely to the discussion we had in the previous chapter about the need for a

'Mental Health' Act. As a legal concept, *capacity* refers to our ability to make competent decisions determining our life choices. It is based on the assumption that the state does not seek to intervene unnecessarily in the lives of its citizens and will therefore not interfere with the choices anyone makes, provided that they are lawful choices. In other words, *by and large*, provided you do not chose to break any laws, the state will not assume any authority to take control of the decisions you make, no matter how unwise they may seem to others. Note the italicised 'by and large' in the above sentence. This is because, as you will see, this assumption of capacity in its citizens is not absolute on behalf of the state. Note also that we have carefully set aside *illegal* decisions that anyone may choose to make. This is because if, for example, you are planning to rob a bank tonight, the state will very definitely seek to interfere with your decision. By setting criminal activity aside, the assumption of capacity is firmly placed in civil law, much as is the core of 'mental health' law in the previous chapter. The only thing that the law will seek to do about capacity in terms of criminal law is to establish that the perpetrator of any crime did not have a mental disorder which might interfere with his or her capacity to understand the consequences of his or her actions. This subject will be discussed more fully in the next chapter.

ACTIVITY **3.1**

The discussion about capacity so far suggests that we all make a vast array of decisions in life about which the state generally assumes we have competence to determine. You may never before have thought about the fact that you lead your life in these terms. This is largely because the freedoms that we enjoy are so wide that we take them for granted and they become invisible. To illustrate the contrast, were we living in 1930s Stalinist Russia, where the state intervened greatly in people's lives, we would have a much more limited view of our freedom to choose and it would be painfully visible to us. Therefore take a moment to reflect upon the types of decisions you make about how to lead your life. List as varied a range of these decisions as you can, from the everyday, mundane ones about clothes, food, work and so on, to the less frequently occurring ones and even those sorts of decisions you may only make once or twice in a lifetime.

Comment

The suggestion that you could use a moment to do any justice to listing the decisions you make in life is ridiculous. The list is, literally, potentially endless – from choosing what socks to wear in the morning to deciding whether or not to make a will; from deciding to go to work to deciding to sell your home; from deciding to brush your teeth to making major treatment decisions when confronted by serious illness; from deciding on a holiday to deciding how or whether to vote in an election.

Clearly, there are material things which might restrict your decision-making. If, for example, you do not own a pair of socks you cannot choose which pair to wear. However, there is one more overriding question which restricts the assumption of capacity in any of us and it is located in the following question:

What protection ought the state extend to people who lack capacity so as to minimise exploitation or risk through the choices and decisions they make?

This suggests that we do not all make our choices on a level playing field. Clearly, the law can only go so far in levelling off the field. It could not, for example, compensate for a lack of technical knowledge in the unwise decision that a person might make to buy a less fuel-economic car. Capacity is therefore a range of abilities from the 'good enough' to the 'expert', and the question of *incapacity* is about protecting people who fall seriously below the 'good enough' level. Bear in mind though that 'good enough' is not only relative, but socially constructed and determined (Searle, 1995).

Introducing the Adults with Incapacity (Scotland) Act 2000

In devising a protective incapacity law, account must be taken of why a person appears to lack capacity. For example, being drunk could not be a valid reason for protecting a person from risk in the decisions they made. For one reason, if being drunk were accepted as a valid form of incapacity, telling the Sheriff that you are sorry, but you were drunk at the time, would be a valid defence against a drink-driving charge. For another reason, being drunk assumes that the person started out with capacity to make the decision to get drunk. For such reasons, *incapacity* is considered in the eyes of the law to rest upon only two factors:

- The existence of a mental disorder (mental illness, personality disorder or learning disability) of a nature or degree that warrants the removal of the ability to make a decision (s 87(1), Adults with Incapacity (Scotland) Act 2000); or

- a physical disability of a nature or degree which makes the communication of any decision impossible (s 1(6), Adults with Incapacity (Scotland) Act 2000) (Scottish Executive, 2000a).

To explore the first of these reasons, clearly not everyone with a mental disorder lacks capacity to make decisions. The step of taking decision-making powers away from one person and giving them to another is such a fundamentally serious step in terms of human rights, that the degree of mental disorder must be serious enough to justify it.

CASE STUDY

*Take, for example, the case of Hugh. Hugh is 40 and has moderate learning disabilities. This does not necessarily mean that he lacks capacity in any sphere of his life. However, Hugh lacks the cognitive ability to count up to 100 and therefore, **despite any previous assessment of his capacity**, when his uncle died leaving him £100,000, he was unable to manage the sudden inheritance. But even then, Hugh would probably only truly lack capacity if he could not understand his limitations and was therefore unable to accept financial advice.*

Comment

There are some issues to note from the above case study, in order to develop your understanding of incapacity. Quickly re-read the case and note the phrase 'despite any previous assessment of his capacity' emphasized in bold. This implies that Hugh might only lack capacity in certain circumstances or upon the arrival of a certain event. Remember this point because we will return to it soon.

Regarding incapacity by virtue of physical disability, the clearest example would be that a person could not be considered able to make decisions if in a persistent vegetative state or a prolonged coma. However, there are other progressive conditions such as motor neurone disease and Parkinson's disease, which can so impede a person's ability to communicate decisions as to render them incapable. We will not dwell on this area because we are more preoccupied with mental illness in this book.

The Adults with Incapacity (Scotland) Act 2000 (the 2000 Act) (Scottish Executive, 2000a) is the legislation which deals with incapacity in Scotland. As the title of the Act suggests, it is targeted upon adults only. This is because children are generally assumed to fall under the protection of their parents who make decisions on their behalf. The law is complicated in this regard because there are different age thresholds at which one is given capacity to make decisions in one's own right. For example, one cannot buy alcohol until 18 but, at the time of writing, one can chose to leave full-time education or get married at 16. Sometimes the law makes allowance for partial capacity, as in the case of the tapered allowance that a doctor must make of the views on treatment of a patient younger than 16. For the purposes of clarity, the 2000 Act sets the definition of *adult* as anyone over the age of 16. Consequently, any person subject to the law is referred to in the Act (and in this text) as *the adult*.

What protection does the 2000 Act offer to adults with incapacity?

As already stated, taking away decision-making power is a huge step in terms of human rights. On the one hand, it removes fundamental civil liberty to determine one's own life. On the other hand, it offers fundamental protections to people who lack ability to make safe decisions for themselves. As with the 2003 Act, it has a set of overarching principles to protect human rights (s 1).

One of these principles dictates that any intervention under the Act must be the least restrictive of the adult's freedom. There is a heavy hint in the example of Hugh above that incapacity should not be seen as absolute. What this means is that someone like Hugh should be considered to have capacity until, because of mental disorder or physical inability to communicate, he is met with a situation which so severely challenges his capacity as to warrant the protection of the law. (Recall that we asked you to note the phrase *despite any previous assessment of his capacity*, in our comment on the case study.) At that point, only the minimum necessary powers may be taken to overcome this instance of incapacity and only for so long as the powers are needed.

CASE STUDY

In Hugh's case, he was so taken by his new and large fortune that he wanted to spend it all on a holiday for his friends and he did initially require someone to take control of his estate. But then it was explained to him that he might need help, which he readily agreed to accept. Therefore continuing to use legal compulsion to manage Hugh's affairs was no longer the least restrictive option and it was not lawful continue to do so.

Comment

Why might Hugh firstly appear to have incapacity in respect of his inheritance of £100,000, and then to have capacity if he is willing to follow professional advice on how to spend it? The answer is that we all encounter situations in which we are out of our depth in terms of technical knowledge and need professional advice. Like Hugh, as long as we show good enough understanding of the need for such advice, as long as we can assess the quality of advice we are given and as long as we can make reasoned judgements about how to follow that advice, no one can say we lack capacity.

All of the above discussion does raise the question:

What protection ought to be offered to adults with incapacity?

Inherent in the answer is the notion that, if one is going to protect the adult by removing the power to make certain decisions, one must replace the lost power with something. The replacing authority may firstly be understood via the useful legal concept of *proxy*. Most people are familiar with the term *proxy* in relation to voting. If you have the right to vote in an election and cannot physically manage it, for example, because you will be on holiday or will be going into hospital for an operation, you may exercise your power to give instruction to another to vote on your behalf. This is called *voting by proxy*. *Proxy* means the transfer of authority to act on behalf of one person to another. In voting by proxy, you make the decision to give your power to vote to another person. If you are wise, you also give your proxy instructions as to how to vote.

The first occurring set of powers in the 2000 Act is not unlike proxy voting in that *powers of attorney* are proxy powers that you confer upon another person by your own choice. Anyone may draft powers of attorney (called *granting powers of attorney*). In the powers, the *granter* (the person granting the powers) must name not only the person(s) he or she chooses to act as proxy, but also the powers he or she wishes to confer upon the proxy. A so-identified proxy is known as the *attorney*. For example, you may choose your brother, sister, parent, friend or whoever you wish as your attorney. You may list powers under two categories: *continuing powers of attorney* and *welfare powers of attorney*. Continuing powers relate to any matters concerning your finances and property that you chose to specify: buying and selling of property, speculation on the stock market, disposing of pension or income, dealing in bank and savings accounts, etc. Welfare powers deal with virtually everything else – deciding where you should live, what you should wear, your diet, how to meet your care needs, etc. – as far as you specify. These powers then lie dormant in the legally constituted document which you have prepared and they only become active should you ever acquire incapacity as defined in the Act.

CASE STUDY

James was a man aged 30, who was aware that both his mother and grandfather had acquired a form of hereditary dementia in their early sixties. James had seen them both lose capacity to make simple decisions about how to manage their growing care needs as the dementia progressed and, being advised by his mother's psychiatrist that he was at high risk

CASE STUDY *continued*

of encountering the same condition, he thought it wise to draw up a power of attorney granting financial and welfare powers to his wife. In time, James was affected by the disease and the powers he had granted when he had capacity to do so became activated as he lost his own decision-making powers. This enabled his wife, the person who knew him best, to work with care providers and medical services to make the sort of decisions about his care and treatment that James would have made for himself if he could have done so.

Comment

The above case should not lead you to think that it is only worth drafting powers of attorney if, like James, you have reason to believe that you may acquire incapacity in later life. None of us can foresee the unimaginable and numerous potential causes of incapacity (accidentally acquired head injury, most dementias, forms of mental illness, etc.) are not at all predictable. Therefore, it might be prudent for all of us to grant such powers now.

This leads us to the next question:

ACTIVITY **3.2**

Take a moment to reflect upon what you think ought to happen in cases where incapacity is lost before the adult has the foresight to make a power of attorney? Make a brief note of your thoughts.

Comment

Did you think that it is simply a matter that the individual who has not had the foresight to grant powers of attorney should face the consequences that their finances, property and welfare will not be protected should they lose capacity? This way of looking at it would be much like the model used in the insurance trade. Apart from those instances where the law requires you to have insurance (such as motor insurance) it is your own tough luck if your house burns down and you have not bought insurance.

On the other hand, did you think that the state has to take responsibility for the protection of adults with incapacity because they are especially vulnerable? If you thought this, you are a wise student of human nature. Most people will not be aware of their ability to grant such powers. Were you aware of it before it was pointed out in this text? Of those who are aware, many will never get round to granting powers even if they think they ought to do so. To quantify this, one only has to ask the parallel question: *Why do so many people die before making a will?*

Following from this one only has to think of the costs in human misery, legal arguments over misspent estates, etc. to see that it would be a bad idea to continue to do nothing for people who fail to provide for themselves with powers of attorney.

A series of questions flow from this consideration:

- How should the state manage its responsibility?

- Should incapacity law try to define some sort of threshold beyond which the state will intervene?

- Who should have the power to manage the affairs of the adult with incapacity?

- Should there be some kind of check on how that person uses their power in case they choose to abuse it?

You may have rightly perceived that, in these cases, it is too late for the adult to grant power away to another person, because he or she has already lost the capacity necessary to authorise a proxy. You may have further noted that, in other cases such as learning disability, which is most likely a life-long condition, the person never had the necessary capacity to draft powers of attorney in the first place. In considering the insurance-type model suggested above, it would seem unfair upon people born with incapacity not to have the opportunity to get the sort of protection that others can obtain by making a power of attorney. Besides which, life and the law are so complicated that there are many reasons why any of us would not think of or might put off the decision to make a power of attorney.

Therefore, we imagine that you rightly considered that some sort of measured action must be taken by others to protect the adult. Unless these actions are regulated in law, they run the risk of being abused themselves. Many complicated issues arise from this consideration.

If we do need a law to protect adults with incapacity, there probably ought to be some sort of threshold beyond which it can be activated but, as we will discuss, deciding where it lies is a complicated process. Likewise, the law ought to define who should handle these powers and how they will be monitored to ensure their proper use. All of this is discussed below.

The powers of the 2000 Act

The answer to these problems is that the 2000 Act has mechanisms to replace certain of the adult's lesser decision-making powers such as managing a bank account or agreeing to medical treatment with limited substitute powers managed by an external party under the scrutiny of regulatory bodies. It also has mechanisms for the Sheriff to grant orders with wider and more flexible powers, removing some or all decision-making from the adult and giving the authority to another. To start with the lesser powers, the 2000 Act creates relatively simple processes whereby:

- an individual may obtain access to funds which would otherwise be locked away in the adult's bank or savings account. This power is called *intromission with funds* (s 25, 2000 Act);

- a specially registered care or nursing home may manage finances and moveable property on behalf of an adult who is resident there (s 42, 2000 Act); and

- a doctor may issue a certificate authorising medical treatment for the adult when the adult lacks capacity to agree to it (s 47, 2000 Act).

Now read the three variants of the case study below.

CASE STUDY

Willamina MacKay (Mina to her friends) is 98 years old. She has led a very active life and currently she lives with her great-granddaughter who cares for her. However, over the last two years Mina has progressively suffered from dementia and, while she used to pride herself on managing her own affairs, she gets confused with her pension, which is paid directly into her bank account for which she is the sole signatory. To ensure that Mina continues to get the essential things she needs as well as the luxuries she enjoys, her great-granddaughter can apply to the Office of the Public Guardian (see below) to intromit with funds, legally allowing her to draw money from Mina's account.

CASE STUDY

Mina's physical condition has sadly deteriorated and, even with maximum support from a complex package of care, her great-granddaughter is unable to cope with the lifting and hands-on nursing. Reluctantly Mina recognises this and agrees to go into a nearby care home. The home is registered by the Care Commission to manage finances and movable property of its residents. Since Mina tends to lose her jewellery it makes sense for them to keep it safe for her and to take over the management of her pension.

CASE STUDY

Because of deterioration in her dementia, Mina gets confused and upset about taking medication that she requires for her heart condition and respiratory problems. Rather than upsetting her by forcing her to take it, the staff at the care home agree with Mina's great-granddaughter that it would be best to mix the medication into her food. Mina's GP agrees but before anyone can do this, he must complete a certificate under Part 5 of the 2000 Act. This sets limitations on the sort of treatment which can be given to Mina without her consent.

Comment

These limited powers have checks, balances and external scrutiny built in to them (see the Office of the Public Guardian discussed below). They also have the safety net of the protection of human rights via a set of principles binding upon anyone seeking to use these powers.

Applications to the Sheriff Court

Intervention and guardianship orders

Where larger, multiple or more sweeping powers are needed the 2000 Act offers a two-tier solution. Where it is imperative for the adult's health or safety or welfare that one single thing must be done, any interested party may apply to the Sheriff Court for an *intervention order* (s 53) The law does not specify what sort of powers an intervention order may contain beyond stating that it will relate to the finances or property or welfare of the adult. For example, if a person is incapacitated by mental illness to the extent that he or she has been unable to look after their home and its roof is about to fall in, an intervention order may be sought to repair it and to recover the costs from the person's estate. If a farmer were to be admitted to hospital under the Mental Health Act and authority to care for his cattle had to transfer temporarily to another person, an intervention order might be sought. If a woman with dementia were able to live in her own home but for the risk of the gas cooker, and she refused to have it converted to electric, an intervention order might provide the solution.

For more complex situations where more powers are sought, any interested person may apply to court for a *guardianship order* (s 57, 2000 Act). There are two types of guardianship order: *financial* and *welfare orders*. Financial orders cover the range of powers in relation to finances and property and welfare orders cover any powers sought in relation to the spectrum of welfare, from medical treatment and health matters to clothing, diet, residence and other life choices. As with intervention orders, the 2000 Act does not offer a list of powers that may be granted by the Sheriff. It is up to the applicant to ask for the necessary powers and to make a reasoned case in respect of the adult's incapacity and the principles of the Act as to why these powers are necessary. It is within the scope of the Sheriff's authority when hearing an application to make any of the following decisions:

- to grant any (or all) of the powers asked for;
- to grant additional powers even if they were not asked for;
- to dispense with the guardianship application by granting a single intervention order; or
- not to grant any powers at all, thereby refusing the application.

Rather like CTO applications to the tribunal in the last chapter, applications rest on two medical reports, one of which must be made by an approved medical practitioner. Where an application for an intervention or welfare guardianship order is thought necessary by the local authority and there is no other willing applicant, the application must be made by an MHO. In practice, not surprisingly, given the cost and daunting emotional issues for friends and relatives of making applications, there are more applications by MHOs than private individuals.

Once they are granted, who exercises the powers contained in orders?

The person applying for the order need not necessarily be the person who will exercise the powers, assuming the order is granted by the Sheriff. The application itself must propose the *intervener* or *guardian* and part of the Sheriff's role is to check that the person is a suitable choice to wield these powers on behalf of the adult. It may either be a private individual (usually a relative of the adult) or the local authority (in other words the local council social work service) which may be authorised with the powers of the order. For private welfare guardians, a report on suitability must be furnished by the MHO in addition to the application and medical reports. If the order does not authorise a private guardian, the role falls to the Chief Social Work Officer (CSWO) (the highest ranking official in the social work service of the local authority). The CSWO then may delegate the role to anyone in the local authority. Usually such guardians acting on behalf of the local authority are either MHO practitioners or care managers, depending on the local policies of their employing authority.

When the Sheriff grants an order, it is given a time limit (ordinarily of three years but potentially life-long). The order must be reviewed and renewed at the Sheriff Court before it expires, or it must be terminated at any point when it is no longer needed (in keeping with the principle of *least necessary intervention*) (s 1(3), 2000 Act).

External scrutiny of orders

Much like the 2003 Act, the 2000 Act is an oddity in welfare legislation in that it can enforce its protective measures even when the vulnerable person does not want to be protected. Therefore, as well as affording the adult rights to contest any application made to the Sheriff Court and to appeal any orders granting powers to a guardian or intervener, the Act gives monitoring and scrutinising roles to two agencies. The first is the Mental Welfare Commission, already introduced in the previous chapter. The Commission's brief is in respect of all aspects of the Act in relation to the welfare of adults with incapacity. It therefore routinely visits people subject to welfare guardianship and scrutinises the work of agencies such as the local authority, as well as monitoring provision for people subject to the Act.

The Act specifically constituted an independent agency for monitoring and regulating the management of finances and property. The Office of the Public Guardian (OPG) receives all powers of attorney, all applications to intromit with funds and notification from the Sheriff Court of all financial guardianship orders. It monitors the people exercising these powers.

CASE STUDY

Huntington's disease is a genetic disorder which carries a high likelihood that it will be passed from parents to offspring. It is a terminal disease which manifests in involuntary movements or tics, which ultimately become so marked that the person cannot swallow and struggles to breathe. It is also characterised by depression and sometimes psychotic experiences.

Georgina, who calls herself George, is 27 years old and has been living with the illness for three years now. She helped nurse her mother through the terminal phase of the illness so she knows that dying from it can be a long and difficult process. Her chronically depressed mood and involuntary bodily movements mean that she can no longer work. She lives alone in a small rented flat and has so far refused any level of care. She prefers to go out little, being very self-conscious and having been tormented by local children for her ill-kept appearance and erratic movements. George has an alcohol problem, resolving to drink herself to death before the illness kills her. She also rejects any offers of help or medication. Consequently she lives in considerable chaos and squalor.

However, George's GP was so concerned about her poor self-care and her drinking that she referred the case to the practice social worker, who convened a case conference where it was agreed to pursue an MHO assessment. Following from this, the MHO made

---

an application for guardianship through the Sheriff Court, accompanied by medical reports from the GP and an approved medical practitioner. Despite George's legal representation in court that it was her right to drink herself to death, the Sheriff was persuaded by the argument that she was so depressed that she could not make such a choice. The guardianship order was granted, authorising specific powers for care staff to go into George's home and give her help and support even if she does not wish it. The order also authorises the community psychiatric nurse (CPN) to supervise anti-depressant medication and other treatment under the direction of George's psychiatrist and it requires George to attend a local day facility which is run for support of people with Huntington's disease.

George has no close relatives and, other than drinking partners, she is quite isolated. She lacks anyone who might reasonably be appointed as guardian. Therefore the court was minded to accept the MHO's recommendation that the Chief Social Work Officer (CSWO) be appointed as guardian. In reality, the policies of the local authority delegate this role to the care manager coordinating the care of the person subject to the order.

Imagine for a moment that you are George's care manager and you are given the task of co-ordinating services for her. How would the existence of the guardianship order affect your role?

In considering this, it may be helpful to think about the powers that the order contains and how they might be managed. Make a note of your answer.

Comment

In answering this question, did you note that the order grants you the powers of guardian (albeit on behalf of your CSWO), in this instance:

- to afford access to anybody employed or contracted to give care to George;

- to allow the CPN to supervise the taking of medication; and

- to require George to attend the day support facility for people with Huntington's disease.

As the effective guardian on behalf of the CSWO, you could use means that you would otherwise wish to stop short of to achieve these ends. There would not be grounds to use force, unless in exceptional circumstances, to perform any of these tasks but, for example, you could give keys to George's flat to any carers to allow them access. You might want to use strong persuasion to get her to take transport to the day support facility and, if need be, the CPN could secretly hide the anti-depressants in food or drink if that was the only way to ensure George taking them. At the centre, the door could be locked against George leaving, although it must be considered that the more forceful the measure, the more likely it is to strengthen George's resistance. Persuasion is always best and staff would need careful help in how to do this.

Effectively, one of the things that these powers do is to draw clearer limits on what is acceptable practice with a person who may be awkward and resistant but is not subject to such an order. Before Scotland had such focused use of powers through the 2000 Act, carers were sometimes forced to informally hide medication in food or to lock doors against a person leaving without the backing of the law. With the 2000 Act all of this becomes dangerously illegal practice and an entire culture of mostly well-intentioned practice must be turned around.

Adult Support and Protection (Scotland) Act 2007

This new piece of legislation adds another dimension to the array of protective law for vulnerable adults. Under it there are several amendments to the 2000 Act, allowing for greater flexibility in certificating for treatment and in meeting the needs of some adults who show no signs of objecting to the provision of services following an assessment of needs. It also makes some technical amendments to the 2003 Act. However, the mainstay of the 2007 Act is the provision of protection from harm of vulnerable adults who are unable to protect themselves. As with the 2000 and 2003 Acts, it protects the rights of potential subjects with an overarching set of principles (Patrick, 2006, 2007).

Anyone who reads through the principles of the 2000, 2003 and 2007 Acts will see a necessary repetition in their core principles – all of them speak of intervention that is the least restrictive to the freedom of the subject, intervention that is targeted upon maximum benefit to the subject and the need to take account of the wishes and feelings of the subject.

The legislation sets up *Adult Protection Committees* which will review local arrangements for protecting vulnerable adults. Powers of the Act include the requirement of an assessment of the need for protection when an adult appears to be at risk of harm. Harm includes physical, psychological or financial harm or exploitation and may include deliberate self-harm and neglect. The basis for intervention will rest upon the adult's inability to take protective measures and, as such, it will be based upon a test of capacity. As with the 2000 and 2003 Acts, it limits the causal reasons why a person's lack of capacity may necessitate their protection. However, the definition of causes of vulnerability is far broader than the 2000 Act's *mental disorder or inability to communicate because of physical disability*. They are:

- disability;
- mental disorder;
- illness; or
- infirmity.

In situations of extreme vulnerability the 2007 Act offers controversial powers to take the adult into protective care, to exclude the perpetrator of harm from access to the adult and to offer continuing supervision and monitoring of any situation in which an adult may be at risk. These orders will be made by application to the Sheriff Court and, while none of them may be made if the adult opposes them, the Sheriff will have powers to overrule the adult's opposition if he or she feels that the adult has been placed under *undue pressure*.

It should be noted that some critics have objected that, by giving the Sheriff power to overrule the adult's objection, the Act may discourage people from coming forward to seek its protection.

CASE STUDY

To see how this works, take the example of Jimmy, a man in his late sixties. He has schizophrenia and is a heavy smoker, suffering from a heart condition. Jimmy has a comfortable-enough income from Disabled Living Allowance but his son, who has a heroin addiction, takes most of his money, leaving Jimmy only enough for his cigarettes. Jimmy is facing eviction for non-payment of his rent and he is malnourished from an inadequate diet. He has been offered protection under the 2007 Act in that his son may be banned from visiting him and the situation could be monitored. However, Jimmy is afraid of his son, who can be aggressive and bullying and he has therefore refused help. If an order is placed before the Sheriff, he can make a ruling that Jimmy is under undue pressure from his son, thereby overruling Jimmy's objection to the intervention.

The burden of these powers and duties will fall upon the local authority and, while the not-yet published codes of practice and guidance may indicate specific roles for MHOs and social workers, the Act itself places the burden of intervention on *officers of the local authority*, which could be non-social work qualified employees such as care managers.

Negotiating the area of overlap between the 2000, 2003 and 2007 Acts.

If as you read this in conjunction with the previous chapter you are experiencing a growing confusion about when a person might become a patient under compulsion of the 2003 Act or might be an adult in need of protection under the 2000 Act, then you are developing a good understanding of this complicated subject. It is easiest to define the core territory of each Act. However, having done so, the remaining areas of overlap are still a subject for debate among the most skilled of professionals. Before explaining the core areas of each Act it is important to acknowledge the value of overlapping legislation – that it is better to have slight duplication of the areas of protection extended by different laws than to have gaps in the provision. The 2007 Act fills an important gap.

The core territory of the 2003 Act is the care and treatment of anyone with a mental disorder who is so adversely affected by it that they cannot make critical treatment decisions and are therefore a risk to their own health, safety or welfare or another person may require protection from their actions. The purpose of the principle interventions under the 2003 Act is to secure care and treatment for the patient even in circumstances where the patient objects to receiving such help and protection. The treatments enforceable under the compulsion of the 2003 Act are limited to specific treatments for mental disorder. In other words, it could be used to force treatment for depression but not for appendicitis, angina or a broken leg.

The core territory of the 2000 Act is the wide-ranging protection of any adult who experiences incapacity because of mental disorder or inability to communicate because of physical disability. The 2000 Act's powers to protect are by removal of the adult's authority to make decisions and determine choices by the transfer of those powers to another person (such as a welfare or financial attorney or guardian). The powers are not determined by a fixed list contained in the Act but are intended to be of as wide a scope as will be of help to the adult with incapacity. Powers of treatment under the Act are not just fixed upon treatments for mental disorder but may extend to dentistry and physical health treatments. While the 2003 Act has no powers to intervene in the management of finances and property, this is core territory of the 2000 Act.

The 2007 Act is intended to fill some specific gaps in the powers of the other Acts. While the 2000 Act is about transplanting the adult's authority to make choices and decisions onto another person, the 2007 Act is about preventing others from harming or exploiting the adult. It is intended to strengthen the powers of any vulnerable adult in order to protect him or her from harm and it is not designed to replace decision-making powers with any proxy powers or to force a person into protective care or to receive protective treatment.

C H A P T E R   S U M M A R Y

In this chapter you have been:

- introduced to the concept of adult protection for people made vulnerable by a range of factors;

- introduced to the concepts of capacity and incapacity in relation to mental disorder and the law;

- introduced to the balance of rights and power to intervene in the lives of vulnerable adults and the role of the principles in law as a protection of human rights;

- introduced to the Adults with Incapacity (Scotland) Act 2000 and the Adult Support and Protection (Scotland) Act 2007 (Scottish Executive, 2007j) as the main provisions in this area;

- introduced to the salient features and powers available under these laws (powers of attorney, powers to intromit with funds, powers to manage residents' finances, powers to certificate for treatment, intervention and guardianship orders, and powers to intervene in the lives of vulnerable adults under the 2007 Act);

- introduced to the roles of those with major duties under the law (MHO, RMO, Mental Welfare Commission, Office of the Public Guardian, the courts, etc.); and

- introduced to the need for and complications caused by overlapping legislation of the 2003, 2000 and 2007 Acts in a framework of adult protection.

FURTHER READING

As with the previous chapter, there has as yet been little published at the level of this book that might help you by way of further reading. However, the Scottish Executive has published a set of introductory packs for the 2000 Act, of which Packs 1 and 2 make good interactive reading and are available on the website **www.scotland.gov.uk/justice/incapacity** (Maas-Lowit, 2002a, 2002b). See also Patrick (2006).

Look up the principles of the 2000 Act. If you cannot access a copy in your library, it can be found on the internet at: **www.opsi.gov.uk/legislation/scotland/acts2000/20000004.htm**.

The principles are contained in s 1. Read them through, paying attention to the sort of language used by the law. Try to imagine what they mean with reference to protecting the rights of those people so vulnerable because of mental disorder as to need protection under the Act.

Chapter 4

The legal and policy context (III): the law relating to mentally disordered offenders

A C H I E V I N G A S O C I A L W O R K D E G R E E

This chapter will help you to begin to meet the following (Scottish) Standards in Social Work Education (SiSWE) (Scottish Executive, 2003a), available at www.scotland.gov.uk/library5/social/ffsw.pdf.

Key Role 1: Prepare for, and work with, individuals, families, carers, groups and communities to assess their needs and circumstances.

Learning Focus:

1.1 Preparing for social work contact and involvement.

1.2 Working with individuals, families, carers, groups and communities so they can make informed decisions.

1.3 Assessing needs and options in order to recommend a course of action.

Key Role 2: Plan, carry out, review and evaluate social work practice with individuals, families, carers, groups, communities and other professionals.

Learning Focus:

2.1 Identifying and responding to crisis situations.

2.2 Working with individuals, families, carers, groups and communities to achieve change, promote dignity, realise potential and improve life opportunities.

2.3 Producing, implementing and evaluating plans with individuals, families, carers, groups, communities and colleagues.

2.6 Tackling behaviour which presents a risk to individuals, families, carers, groups, communities and the wider public.

Key Role 3: Assess and manage risk to individuals, families, carers, groups, communities, self and colleagues.

Learning Focus:

3.1 Assessing and managing risks to individuals, families, carers, groups and communities.

3.2 Assessing and managing risk to self and colleagues.

Key Role 4: Demonstrate professional competence in social work practice.

Learning Focus:

4.1 Evaluating and using up-to-date knowledge of, and research into, social work practice.

4.2 Working within agreed standards of social work practice.

4.3 Understanding and managing complex ethical issues, dilemmas and conflicts.

4.4 Promoting best social work practice, adapting positively to change.

Key Role 5: Manage and be accountable, with supervision and support, for their own social work practice within their organisation.

Learning Focus:

5.1 Managing one's own work in an accountable way.

5.2 Taking responsibility for one's own continuing professional development.

5.3 Contributing to the management of resources and services.

5.4 Managing, presenting and sharing records and reports.

5.5 Preparing for, and taking part in, decision-making forums.

5.6 Working effectively with professionals within integrated, multi-disciplinary and other service settings.

Key Role 6: Support individuals to represent and manage their needs, views and circumstances.
Learning Focus:

6.1 Representing, in partnership with, and on behalf of individuals, families, carers, groups and communities to help them achieve and maintain greater independence.

Introduction

My life has been one chain of contradictions,

Madhouses, prisons, whore-shops ...

(John Clare, *Child Harold*, 1841)

In the discussion of 'mental health' law in Chapter 2, we saw how much of the attention of the 2003 Act is focused upon civil law solutions to the outstanding needs of those most vulnerable because of mental disorder. We only briefly mentioned that the law did have regard for a far smaller, but no less vulnerable, group of people: those who come to 'mental health' services via the processes of criminal justice services because they have committed offences while mentally disordered. This chapter discusses the legislation, legal system and care and treatment services available to support and manage this group. In the previous two chapters we have had occasion to use legal terminology to identify people. That terminology has not always been compatible with the language preferred by social workers in reference to service users. For example, the 2003 Act makes perpetual use of the term *patient* to describe the subject of actions under the Act when that person may only be a patient in respect of the medical treatment he or she receives. While many service users may take issue with the phrase *mental disorder* to sum up their experiences, the criminal justice components of 'mental health' law make reference to the term *mentally disordered offender* to mean a mentally disordered person who has or appears to have committed a criminal offence. While it may have a slightly harsh and depersonalising ring to it, we will abbreviate it to MDO and use the term here for the sake of legal correctness.

Orientation to the criminal justice system

A basic understanding of the processes of criminal justice is required before starting to explore the resources for MDOs. When the police have reason to believe that a person has broken the law, they have powers of arrest. The *accused* (the person who stands accused of committing the offence) may be questioned *in situ* or taken to a police station and questioned, following which, if charged, the person may be held in police custody (in the cells) or released to be recalled for questioning or to a court hearing. The police send a report to the Procurator Fiscal's Office[1] and it is here that a decision is made whether to continue the process to a hearing in court. There are various courts to which the case may be remitted, depending on the nature and severity of the charge. The two criminal courts which are central to the processes for MDOs are the Sheriff Court and the High Court (for more serious cases and for jury trials), although, when we discuss lesser or *low-tariff* offences below, the magistrates' court[2] is also a feature. Once referred to the Sheriff Court, there may be several hearings in sequence – to establish the offence(s) with which the person is charged, to establish whether the accused intends to plead guilty or not guilty, to hear the case if the accused pleads *not guilty* (the trial) and to make a sentence. The outcome of the final court hearing will either be a discharge because the accused was found *not guilty*, or it will be one of a range of options at the disposal of the Sheriff (admonishment, probation, fine, compensation orders, supervised attendance orders, community service, deferred sentence, custodial sentences, restriction of liberty or so-called *tagging* and drug testing orders).

Offending behaviour and mental disorder

To boil the rationale of the justice system down to its essence, the intention is to maintain public order, to catch criminals and to deter them from committing further crimes. In this process there are elements of:

- *punishment* – doing unpleasant things to people who have behaved wrongly, in order that they may learn not to commit wrongs in the future;

- *retribution* – the public element that justice is seen to be done;

- *reparation* – the public dimension of punishment which restores the wrong that a person has done by making them pay in some way; and

- *rehabilitation* – the restoration of the offender to social life in such a way that it is less likely that he or she will commit a subsequent offence.

Setting aside a critical view of how well any justice system achieves these goals, all of this assumes that the offender has a degree of awareness that they have committed a crime and an understanding that it is a wrong from which they can learn. This poses an interesting question.

ACTIVITY 4.1

How do people fit into this notion of punishment, retribution, reparation and rehabilitation when their offending behaviour is caused by or amplified by mental disorder? Jot down a note of your answer.

Comment

Knowing what you now know from your reading of this book so far, did you find it difficult to fit the notion of *punishment* to a group of people who may not understand that they have done a wrong that requires punishing? It may still be true that the victim and society have a right to expect that the crime must have negative consequences for the offender, but did you also note that the idea of learning to move on from criminal activity is complicated by the existence of mental disorder? Therefore, did you also note that rehabilitation must be tied to *treatment of the disorder*? If one commits an offence because of mental illness, one cannot be assumed to be free of the risk of reoffending until the illness is treated.

These are complicated issues. To enable you to begin the process of thinking about how people ought to be treated when they lack capacity to be fully responsible for their actions in relation to a crime they have committed, take a moment to reflect upon the above exercise one more time. In doing so, note that a careful reading of the question shows two possibilities – firstly, that the mental disorder *causes* some sort of criminal behaviour, and secondly, that it has *played a part in amplifying* a pre-existing tendency to criminal behaviour. To illustrate a situation, let us look at a couple of short case studies before we comment on the exercise. Read the two variants in the case study and use them to help you in jotting down some notes about how the criminal component of a person's action relates to the mental disorder. You will need these notes for the following Activity 4.2.

CASE STUDY

To understand how illness might generate criminal actions, consider the following. I steal a car because I have a paranoid illness that leads me to believe that I must meet the Prime Minister as soon as possible because I am the only person who knows that the country is being infiltrated by dangerous aliens disguised as human beings. In this case, do you think I should be blamed for my actions?

Consider, on the other hand, a case where emotional upset amounting to a serious mental health problem is a contributing factor in criminal behaviour. I am very depressed because I feel the government has wronged me in some way, and I decide to end my life by trying to assassinate the Prime Minister. For example, if I was bereaved and depressed because my son joined the army and got killed in Iraq (and I hold the government responsible), it cannot be said that my illness is entirely generating the crime, but it does influence my actions. In this case, do you think that the influence of my depression ought to be taken into account in sentencing me in court?

ACTIVITY 4.2

In either case, do you think that I should be punished fully for the offence in the same way as I ought to be if I was an ideologically committed political extremist trying to assassinate the Prime Minister for the ends of my political organisation?

Comment

These are not easy issues to resolve. You may have noted that, regardless of the role my mental disorder plays in my actions, on the one hand I am behaving in a way which seriously affects national security. Therefore I must be stopped and deterred from repeating my actions. Furthermore, the public must be assured that I will not be able to repeat my deed. On the other hand, setting aside other people's view that I am mentally ill, from inside my perception of the world, I may be doing the right thing. You might therefore have concluded that I should not be punished, because the one aspect missing in my actions is any deliberate awareness of wrong-doing on my behalf. You may also have noted that, because I have a mental illness, it may be unlikely that I will ever be deterred from my actions until my illness is treated. Finally, if you noted that those administering the law are attempting to sort out *criminogenic* behaviour from that caused by illness, then you are getting to terms with this complicated sphere of thought.

Sorting out blame from need for treatment in mentally disordered offending behaviour

We have now painted a picture that suggests that the influence of mental disorder upon a person's criminal actions is seldom absolute. It is usually a question of the court having to decide to what degree mental disorder was an influencing factor and determining what to do about it. This involves sorting out *culpability* (the aspects of the offending behaviour for which the person can be held to account) from absolution from blame because the person was, to some degree, *insane*. Insanity here may sound like an old-fashioned term, but it is the one used by the law. It is a very complicated matter which usually involves a thorough assessment of causal factors by a forensic psychiatrist, MHO and others in the clinical team, and it relates to the continuing risk that the offender poses. For example, for a percentage of the population, taking even a moderate recreational drug like cannabis may precipitate a severe and sometimes lasting psychotic episode.

ACTIVITY 4.3

In order to think further about this concept of culpability in relation to mental disorder, take a moment to reflect upon the next question: Where does the culpability end and the absolution from blame begin if, having precipitated a cannabis induced psychosis by knowingly smoking the drug, I become paranoid and commit a serious assault upon an innocent passer-by, believing him to be in some way truly evil? Take five minutes away from your reading to reflect upon this and make a brief note of your answer.

Comment

To answer this question you may feel that you need more information, such as whether or not I had had a psychotic reaction to the drug upon taking it in the past and therefore that I knew the risk I was taking in smoking it. However, either way, did you agree that there is an element that I was doing something illegal by smoking the drug and that, so intoxicated, I did have a degree of responsibility? This argument is a bit like the one that prevents a drink-driver from using the defence that he or she was drunk at the time and therefore not responsible for his or her actions – the person knowingly got drunk, one drink at a time, and so did make the decision to be in the state where he or she could not manage his or her actions as well as a sober person would.

The solution is that the process of administering justice must take account of the mental disorder and treat the person according to the degree to which it has influenced the criminal actions and to which it influences the process of court hearings. To take the most extreme example, a person who is so mentally ill following an offence that he or she is unable to recognise the court proceedings may be considered too mentally ill to stand trial. The trial would be postponed while the accused undergoes treatment and becomes well enough to stand trial.

A more commonly occurring situation is where the MDO is recognised to be ill but is able to stand trial. In more serious cases or cases involving complexity, this may require a period of assessment in order for medical reports to be placed before the court to inform the Sheriff's sentencing on issues such as those discussed above.

Introducing the Criminal Procedure (Scotland) Act 1995, as amended by the 2003 Act

The above discussion implies an interface of two very different systems – the justice and the health care systems. Therefore the 2003 Act (which is preoccupied with delivery of 'mental health' and social care) makes a series of substantial amendments to the law which sets out the processes of court hearings towards justice (the Criminal Procedures (Scotland) Act 1995, or the 1995 Act, as we will call it) (Scottish Office, 1995). In these amendments there are *assessment orders,* to allow the MDO to be placed in hospital for assessment of the disorder and its relation to the offence. At this stage, the purpose of the assessment is to report back to the court. There are also *treatment orders* to allow for a period of treatment in hospital before sentencing, allowing the court to see how the person responds to treatment and to manage the mental disorder throughout the processes of justice in court.

Once the court has all the requisite knowledge to take account of the mental disorder in relation to the offence, it may sentence the person. Sentencing of MDOs may take many forms. Just because a person has a mental disorder does not necessarily mean that specific disposals designed for MDOs must be used (for example, where the criminogenic factors far outweigh the influence of illness in commission of the offence). Therefore the range of disposals available to non-MDOs (as listed above) may be called for. However, in *lower-tariff* offences probation may be given, with a requirement that the offender receives treatment for the mental disorder. In this case, the offender would be in breach of probation were he or she to fail to comply with any psychiatric treatment.

Ordinarily, in criminal justice, there is a relationship between the seriousness of the offence and the severity of the disposal. A drink-driver who kills five school children is as unlikely to receive a small fine as a person found guilty of breach of the peace is to be sent to prison. This relation of offence to severity of disposal breaks down somewhat in relation to mentally disordered offenders. This is because, in most cases, the purpose of the disposal is to force the offender to receive treatment for the disorder that caused the offending behaviour. Therefore the MDO may have his or her freedom deprived for as long as it takes to treat the mental disorder, regardless of whether or not he or she would have been given a custodial sentence if not mentally disordered and regardless of how long that sentence might have been. In this way, unlikely though it may be, in theory, the person convicted of a minor offence such as breach of the peace could be placed in hospital for as lengthy a period as someone who had committed murder if the mental disorder was one that was difficult to treat. However, the risk that the offender poses also goes into this equation, as we will discuss below, bringing issues of public protection to the fore in the degree of risk that can be taken in rehabilitating an MDO. And risk of committing murder requires more careful management than does risk that someone will reoffend by breaching the peace.

The mainstay court disposal in this regard, the *compulsion order*, is a requirement to receive measures of care and medical treatment in or out of hospital, much like its civil law counterpart, the compulsory treatment order (see Chapter 2).

MHOs and their medical counterparts, approved medical practitioners, play parts both in the provision of reports to the court and in giving and monitoring care and treatment of MDOs. The more serious cases, involving offences, such as murder or serious sexual offences, may result in a *compulsion order with a restriction order.* Called a *CORO*, it is given where a custodial sentence would ordinarily have been indicated. This means that the care and treatment of the patient is given in a framework of greater security and that decisions about conditional discharge into the community can only be made by a tribunal,[3] with close monitoring by the Scottish Ministers (the Ministers of the Scottish Government, headed by the First Minister). There are about 500 such *restricted patients* in Scotland, and the First Minister is dependent upon a team of civil servants and a psychiatric advisor to monitor decisions about them on his behalf.

The forensic framework

The term *forensic* is used to refer to that branch of psychiatry and psychiatric nursing given to the care and treatment of MDOs. Given the almost prejudicial, sensationalised press that the least well-informed of the media give to overemphasise the link between mental illness and violence, it is important to have a balanced view of the risks that mentally ill people pose. In actual fact a very small number of people affected by mental illness pose any threat to themselves or others. Of those who pose any threat at all, it is most likely to be to themselves, through self-harm or suicide. However, it has to be recognised that some of Scotland's 500 restricted patients would be classifiable as extremely dangerous and therefore the issue of *public protection* comes into play in their care and treatment. The levels of security in the community and in any open psychiatric ward are not adequate to protect the public. Therefore there is a system of *secure units* operating in three tiers. Every health board has access to a *lower security* forensic ward which would operate at a level of security where patients and visitors are closely monitored, doors constantly locked and widows cannot be opened to the outside. These would contain most of the in-patient MDOs subject to compulsion orders or on assessment or treatment orders in the process of court hearings. For MDOs who have committed more serious offences or whose behaviour requires more close management, recent policy is creating three *medium secure units* in Scotland. (Two are open, in Edinburgh and Glasgow, and one serving the

North of Scotland is planned for Perth.) Despite the fact that they are built for offenders, these units are hospitals, not prisons. They are designed to have no outside windows, open-space access being inward-looking into a large courtyard with garden features. These would also receive people who are in the rehabilitation process from the State Hospital into the community. *The State Hospital,* located near the village of Carstairs in South Lanarkshire, is Scotland's only *high security unit.* It is here that people who need the highest level of security, comparable to the most secure prison facilities, are treated. It has a secure high perimeter fence, automatically locking remote-controlled double doors and electronic tracking of visitors. Use of mobile phones is banned for prisoners and visitors and other stringent security features prevail. However, it also has very good exercise, therapeutic and recreational resources.

Assessing and managing risk

Setting aside the media-driven misconceptions about dangerousness and mental illness as discussed below, there is a very clear and serious issue of public protection around the small proportion of mentally disordered offenders who do pose serious threats to public safety. Even in this discussion we do need to be very careful in how we present the issues. Very few people affected by mental disorder present any risk to anyone other than to themselves. In reality, the statistics suggest that 20% of all homicides happen within the family and of these about 80% are committed by someone known to the victim. In a similar way, a person is more likely to be sexually abused by a family member or a trusted family friend than a stranger and if you are aged between 16 and 30 you are more likely to be the subject of a random physical attack from someone under the influence of alcohol than you are from someone with a mental disorder (see the statistics on homicide in Scotland in Further Reading at the end of this chapter and Scottish Executive, 2007f).

None of this suggests that the common perpetrators of violent and sexual crimes have any mental disorder. However, a small minority do and while by no means all MDOs are predisposed to violence, by definition most people who have committed serious acts of violence while mentally disordered become MDOs through the process of prosecution of their offences.

We have outlined (above) a system which allocates MDOs into high, medium and low security. For that to happen, a system of risk assessment and management has to be in place.

Dangerousness: who decides?

Care in the community seems to have had consistently bad press since the move to close down many hospitals and to relocate services in the community. The popular press reporting of the killing in 1992 of Jonathon Zito by Christopher Clunis at a London Underground station caught the public imagination and created a form of moral panic. While this happened 15 years ago, it was a significant moment and the linking by the media of dangerousness and 'mental health' has meant that the few incidents that have been reported have left an impression in the public mind that is difficult to erase. The effect of this has been unnecessary fear and also to put 'mental health' professionals in the front line where any mistakes are very public. While Christopher Clunis and most other high-profile media cases have occurred in England, the average reader might not make the distinction that Scotland has its own separate 'mental health' framework.

The reality is that the thousands of decisions that are made correctly seldom get coverage. For those of you who are football fans, the 'mental health' professional is rather like the goalkeeper who makes hundreds of saves and is hardly noticed, but if one error is made no one lets him/her forget. This is not to condone poor practice as this needs eradicating where it exists. Nor is it to deny the need for investigations when things do go wrong, but in work that is necessarily complex and involves risk management, things will not always work out as you predicted.

It is important that we study the cases where things have gone wrong and make sure that we learn from them. Many inquiries show a degree of what is called *system failure*, characterised by a breakdown in communication and understanding between the various agencies that are involved. A report from the Scottish Executive listed the needs for improved inter-agency working, better communication between agencies, better understanding of how other agencies work and improved information sharing as the top four items most commonly occurring in major inquiry reports (Galilee, 2005). These were certainly high in the findings of the Mental Welfare Commission report into Mr L and Mr M (MWC, 2006), when a man with addiction problems, personality disorder and a paranoid illness killed a friend.

This risked a lack of trust not only by the public in services, but also in government ministers who will always be wary of the impact of adverse publicity because of the ballot box. While this tendency has driven the 'mental health' agenda in England and Wales more than in Scotland, it would be foolish to pretend it does not exist North of the Border. Being a smaller country, Scotland enjoys smaller-scale systems and, relative to England, has not had the high-profile media interest when things have gone wrong in its 'mental health' delivery. The impact on public awareness of Mr L and Mr M in Scotland has been less than the impact of Clunis in England. However, as the 2003 Act and related policy begins to increase the flow of restricted patients from high to medium security, and as restricted patients are increasingly managed in the community, it would be fair to say that the Scottish Ministers too feel a sense of nervousness. In England, the degree of panic reaction which created difficulties and years of delay in revising 'mental health' law has and is being conducted largely in a research vacuum. The reality is that, while assessment of MDO risk is based upon statistically validated instruments which often require special training to use, risk assessment is only ever *predictive*. In other words, it attempts to predict what a person *might do* in the future, based upon past behaviour and various other factors such as use of drugs, measurement of personality and so on. However good these tools are, in reality we often simply cannot know if the public is at an increased level of risk from any given mentally disordered person (Coid, 1996).

The ability to predict who will carry out such acts is limited and far from a science in the sense of the physical sciences which, for example, can predict how an object will behave when subjected to the force of gravity. With this in mind Coid (1996, p967) calls for:

- better training for 'mental health' professionals in assessment and treatment;
- more effective training in risk assessment and management; and
- patients who behave dangerously and default from treatment not to be allowed to become ill in the community.

To this end, a national body, the Risk Management Authority (RMA), has been established by s 3 of the Criminal Justice (Scotland) Act 2003 (Scottish Executive, 2003g). The RMA is an independent non-departmental public body, accountable to the Scottish Ministers through the offices of the Scottish Government Justice Directorate. It works to assist agencies within the criminal justice system to endorse all risk assessments of those who pose a high level of risk to the public, such as serious sex offenders. The RMA also proposes more widespread use of shared inter-agency risk assessments. As we will discuss later under 'Policy and Guidance', this framework of multi-agency public protection arrangements (MAPPA) has just been revised to include risk assessment and management plans for seriously violent mentally disordered offenders.

It is important to distinguish between what is verifiable evidence and what is speculation. There are many risk assessment tools in use to assist in disentangling these issues, however they have to be approached with caution. They are *tools* and as such, they are only as good as the person using them. They ought to be considered as aids to support good practice, not answers in themselves. As an example, let us look at HCR20 (Webster et al., 1997), so called because it rests on an assessment of:

- historical factors (such as childhood abuse or history of alcohol abuse related to violence);

- clinical factors (such as predisposition to psychotic episodes); and

- risk management factors (such as the need to control access to children).

(For more on HCR20, see Further Reading at the end of the chapter.)

Positive assessment of risk

All the discussion so far throws risk in a very negative light. However, if we take a broader view, every gambler plays with risk in the hopes of benefiting from it by winning. Therefore risk ought to be seen as *the possibility of beneficial and harmful outcomes and the likelihood of their occurrence in a stated time-scale* (Titterton, 2004).

By this assessment, we ought not forget that there is no such thing as a risk-free environment and that all of us benefit from risk-taking because that is how we develop in life.

ACTIVITY 4.4

Consider your own situation as a student or as a newly qualified worker. List the negative risks that you took in applying to study or for your current job. Now list the positive benefits which attracted you to do so.

Comment

I imagine that you took on board the risk that you might fail the course or not be up to the job; the risk that study is a costly business and work eats into your free time; perhaps there were physical challenges in travelling to your study or work or even in relocating your home. Whatever the negatives, you must have assessed that the positive gains outweighed them in terms of your personal growth and opportunities.

It is perhaps most difficult to apply this view of risk-taking to that most dangerous group of people – restricted patients. However, good practice suggests that even here we ought not to attempt to totally restrict every opportunity to take risks. There is of course a big caveat to this statement: any positive risk-taking with restricted patients must be undertaken in a carefully controlled environment, and by limited degrees. This is how the person progresses towards being managed in lower levels of security and eventually being rehabilitated in the community or as near to it as public safety will allow.

Involving service users in risk assessment and management

Research commissioned by the Joseph Rowntree Foundation examined the involvement of users in their own risk assessment and management. The work was carried out in England and interviews were in-depth with users, carers and professionals. The findings (Joseph Rowntree Foundation, 2004a) include:

- Many service users were aware that they could pose a risk to other people when experiencing psychosis and wanted to reduce the chances of this happening.

- Levels of agreement between service users and professionals about risk and how to respond to it ranged from full agreement to very little or none, and serious gaps were sometimes found in information held about service users that potentially put themselves and others at risk.

This shows that there is a lack of consistency in the overall approach to working with risk and risk management and much depends upon the individual professional. The researchers suggest that there needs to be a format for assessing risk and the subsequent management plan incorporates service users' views (Langan and Lindow, 2004).

Low-tariff mentally disordered offenders

So far, we have focused on the law and systems to manage those who commit high-tariff offences and require major risk management for the protection of the public. At the other end of the spectrum there exists a larger group of people who seem to preoccupy justice services far more than they do 'mental health' services. These are described as low-tariff repeat offenders with mental health issues. We use the phrase *mental health issues* here because many of them will either never have been diagnosed with any mental disorder or will not have one but will still be troubled by poor mental health resulting from poor life chances, emotional trauma and lifestyles involving substance misuse. This description could fit the picture of the vast majority of offenders in the criminal justice system and we do have to be careful that we do not depart from the focus of this book. Therefore consider a sliding scale as in Figure 4.1, as we described in Chapter 1.

+ Good mental health   Poor mental health –

Figure 4.1 Range of mental illness

On this scale, the mental health of the offender becomes more a significant factor as it moves towards the *poor* extremity. As in the discussion in Chapter 1, we also need to recall the relationship between poor mental health and the existence of any mental illness. Not only is this the case, but *personality disorder* appears to figure largely as a problem for this group.

As a student you are far more likely to encounter members of this group on practice learning experiences in criminal justice settings than you are to encounter seriously mentally disordered offenders on COROs. The problem in engaging with this group from a mental health perspective is this: where health care is a limited commodity, it is preoccupied with giving its services to those more seriously ill (and in the sphere of MDOs, those of highest risk). Therefore this far larger group of people who repeatedly commit minor crimes such as public order offences are unlikely to ever get to see a forensic psychiatrist or MHO for an expert assessment. They may also go largely untreated and while research is not very robust, it appears that some of the overcrowding among Scotland's high prison population is caused by the routine assumption that mental disorder does not play a role in their offending behaviour.

This all suggests a poor service to a very needy group whose offending behaviour does impact upon the public.

Policy and guidance

Policy governing the forensic system is preoccupied with two things: *public safety* and *patient flow*. 'Patient flow' is a term that suggests that even the most dangerous patient, requiring the highest level of security, has human rights which entitle him or her to a plan that extends some hope of eventual rehabilitation to a lower level of security. It also suggests that most MDOs will eventually move to live in the community with appropriate supports and may eventually be discharged and rehabilitated at no risk to the public. As discussed above, the ever present threat of prejudicial, ill-informed and sensationalised tabloid headlines such as *MADNESS – Carstairs maniacs on the road to freedom: only place for these savages is Carstairs* (*Scottish Daily Record*, 26 March 2007) poses a high level of political risk to the First Minister should things go wrong and public safety be threatened. Therefore the entire system has to be closely monitored. Events like the case of Mr L and Mr M trigger inquiries by the Mental Welfare Commission (MWC, 2006). The findings of such inquiries produce recommendations which agencies like the health board and local authority must follow. For example, in the case of Mr L and Mr M, a recommendation was that every restricted patient on conditional discharge in the community must be supervised by, among others, an MHO.

Such large-scale requirements have to be addressed throughout the system and result in numerous smaller-scale policy revisions such as the review of how much training MHOs receive in working with MDOs. Since some of the people reading this book now will go on to undertake MHO training later in their careers, it could be said that the decision to include a chapter specifically addressing MDOs has been influenced by the MWC inquiry as well.

If the nature of forensic services brings justice into close proximity with services for people with mental disorder, clearly some of the policy orientation must bend towards closer working between the two systems. At the same time as the Millan Committee Report was being considered, the McLean Committee produced a parallel report on the management of serious violent and sexual offenders to present before the Scottish Parliament (Scottish Executive, 2000b). McLean contained recommendations about use of structured risk assessment and management tools and clearer frameworks in which to share those risks across agencies. Following McLean, the Risk Management Authority (as discussed earlier) was established to standardise risk assessment of dangerous offenders. From this came the multi-agency public protection arrangements or MAPPA (Scottish Executive, 2007h) and structured guidance on what should be in place in each area to share risk assessment and management in order to secure public protection. So far, MAPPA have been clearly established for violent offenders and serious sexual offenders. The current round of policy formulation is bringing MAPPA into closer relationship with 'mental health', to balance the rights of mentally disordered offenders with public safety. The Care Programme Approach (Scottish Office, 1997b) is a structured policy to secure appropriate services for people with severe mental disorder and to make sure they do not fall through the net of care upon discharge from hospital (see Chapter 7). There is therefore a specific CPA for MDOs to ensure, co-ordinate and review appropriate levels of service provision (Scottish Executive, 2007i).

To return to consideration of that group of low-tariff repeat offenders, it seems that there are problems caused by the policy that has encouraged social work to increasingly move into three separate partnership arrangements. The three partnership arrangements are:

1. Adult care/care management (including health care and 'mental health' social work) in partnership with health services under an arrangement called *Joint Futures*.

2. Criminal justice social work which has been 100 per cent funded by the Justice Department of the Scottish Government for several years now and is moving into partnership with police, courts, etc. called *Justice Authorities*.

3. Children and family social work, which is increasingly partnered with education in local authorities.

The benefits of this split are that social work can engage in closer partnerships with those other professions which most concern their target area. For example, mental health social workers now work more closely with psychiatrists and nursing colleagues (see Chapter 8). However, the problems occur when a group such as low-tariff repeat offenders with mental health issues only have their needs met in relation to justice and not health. Policymakers are slowly becoming aware of this issue and are beginning to address the gap.

Who are mentally disordered offenders?

So far we have talked around law and policy and given a rather faceless, impersonal impression of this group of people. They are after all a group of people around whom it is easy to spin stereotype or mythology. The fact is that, if one in four of us will have a mental health problem in our lives, any one of us may become subject to mental illness. However, it will mostly be things like depression and anxiety. Any of us who commits an offence while depressed could become a mentally disordered offender. For example, consider a man in his forties who is unemployed, divorced and becomes more and more depressed to the point where he thinks of killing himself. He disconnects the gas flow from his central heating, allows it to flow for an hour and ignites it, causing an explosion which wrecks his flat but does not kill him. He is now a mentally disordered offender guilty of a very serious offence (most likely arson).

Because of the strong relationship between drink, drugs and mental illness, there is a core relationship between a significant number of MDOs and substance abuse. (Certain drugs have a strong causal, triggering or amplifying effect upon mental illness in certain people.) One of the attributes of personality disorder (see Chapter 1) is a difficulty in learning certain social behaviours and this too makes it a common factor in MDO. Mentally disordered offending like most offending is more frequent amongst people from deprived backgrounds who have been failed by the education system and suffer from social exclusion.

In Chapter 1, we briefly discussed the concept of co-morbidity and *dual diagnosis* (meaning a person who has two concurrent diagnoses) with reference to people with mental illness and learning disability. Dual diagnoses are frequently issues for MDOs who may have co-morbidity of dual diagnosis of personality disorder and mental illness or substance misuse and mental illness or even multiple diagnoses of all three. It would actually not be uncommon for a person to have a *quadruple diagnosis* (although the term would not really be used) of mild learning disability, personality disorder, mental illness and substance misuse.

It is stereotyping to talk of 'the typical mentally disordered offender'. We have suggested above that there is a degree of risk that anyone may find themselves so labelled. However, in attempting to give more commonly occurring attributes, we do begin to build up a picture. A reading of the Mental Welfare Commission's inquiry into Mr L and Mr M would confirm some of this picture of psychotic illness, personality disorder, drink, drugs, social exclusion and deprivation, but it must be exercised with caution (MWC, 2006). The most common feature of MDOs is their own extreme vulnerability and the destructiveness that mental disorder has imposed upon their lives.

Social work with mentally disordered offenders

Because much of the system for managing MDOs is hedged in by security and court procedure and because it is heavily regulated by the need to maintain public safety, it may be less apparent what exactly social workers do in this sphere of work. The answer is disarmingly simple. While they have to manage their roles within the legal, policy and procedural systems (for example, a social worker ought never lend a restricted patient his or her mobile phone or give out personal details) the roles and purpose remain the same as those described elsewhere in this book.

The specialised task of MHOs is regulated by legal duties and Codes of Practice (Scottish Executive, 2005i), but the tasks of care management and social work remain focused on the assessment of need, relationship building and support, and the management of services and resources to meet that need.

CASE STUDY

Mark is 25 years old. He grew up in a chaotic home where both parents drank heavily and his father was frequently absent. His mother died of a drug overdose when he was 16 and he moved in with his sister until she threw him out at 17. He has been failed by the education system, has rarely worked, has often been homeless and has frequently relied upon illegal drugs. Off and on from the age of 12 he suffered from depression but rarely was it identified and he seemed unable to manage any consistent regime of treatment for it. More readily identified was an emergent pattern of disregard for authority, an inability to pay attention and a lack of remorse for wrong-doing which both resulted in expulsion from various schools and a diagnosis of anti-social personality disorder. These attributes have led him into frequent violent disputes with other people, particularly people in authority, and into a string of petty offences such as breaches of the peace.

Aged 20, Mark so seriously injured an acquaintance in a fight in a pub that it is unlikely the person will ever recover his sight. Mark was heavily using amphetamines and crack cocaine at the time and his erratic behaviour in police custody led to a psychiatric referral and diagnosis of drug-induced paranoid psychosis. The trial process entailed a period of enforced assessment in hospital under a sequence of 'mental health'/criminal procedure orders. The final outcome was a compulsion order with restriction and a brief period in the State Hospital, followed by lower security detention more local to his home.

Mark is now about to be released into the community while subject to conditional discharge from his compulsion order with restriction order. This means that, while still subject to the CORO, his liberty will be closely restricted by a package of imposed care and treatment and no change can be made to this without the ruling of a Shrieval Tribunal[3] or the agreement of the First Minister. It will be carefully managed and monitored by his MHO, his RMO and a community forensic psychiatric nurse, and if he breaks the conditions of his conditional discharge in any way he will be immediately recalled into hospital.

ACTIVITY 4.5

If you were involved in Mark's care in the community, for example if you were working in the hostel in which he has to stay, how would you expect the service you deliver to differ from the sort of service that a person under civil compulsion of a CTO might receive? Make a brief note of your answers.

Comment

If you have noticed that issues of *public safety* loom large, you must have read this chapter very closely. It therefore follows that, while the care and treatment elements of Mark's care would differ little from those of someone with a similar package of care under a CTO, they must be delivered with greater attention to security. For example, if Mark missed a routine appointment, or if there was any indication of a change for the worse in his mental condition, it would be of primary importance to notify the care team *immediately*.

Did you also note that part of the continuing work is to enable Mark to make connections between his mental illness and his offending behaviour. How this is done should be delineated in a structured care plan and it is likely that you would play a part in this in your everyday interactions with him. This might involve helping him to develop awareness of his tendency to illness (see Chapter 7 for more details) and discussing his attitude to his offence to help him develop empathy for his victim. This is called *victim awareness*. Victim awareness is a particularly difficult issue for people with certain personality disorders because, by definition, they would struggle to recognise other people's needs and feelings.

It also follows that, whatever acts Mark has committed in the past, he deserves to be treated with respect and dignity.

Social work and mentally disordered offenders

Because of the weight we have given to the formality of working with MDOs, a reading of this chapter may wrongly lead you to conclude that the main roles for those working in this area are given to formal agents such as the RMO, the MHO and the Scottish Ministers. However, the day-to-day care of MDOs falls to nursing staff in hospital and the same ranks of carers and social workers in the community who provide services to others seriously affected by mental disorder. While there are complications of public safety, risk management and the structures of law around MDOs, much of the role is little different from that described in Chapter 7, which is about working with people who have long-term involvement as services. However, the comment above suggests that workers also need to be aware that the focus on keeping everyone safe from the risk of reoffending requires a particular emphasis. Therefore, were you working with Mark, you would need to be sensitive to certain things in your interactions with him. Were there any evidence that he was using or even contemplating using any drugs, it would be a matter that you would *immediately* have to report to his RMO. To keep an eye on this issue, you might be encouraged to have an open dialogue with him about drug taking and his attitude to it. For example, were you watching television together and drug use was featured in a programme you were watching, you might use it as an opportunity to gently sound him out.

Linked to this is the issue of violence and Mark's attitude to it. This can be judged not just by discussion but by watching his behaviour. You might also want to help Mark to grow and develop by discussing with him the things which trigger his arousal to violence. This could be done with reference to the offence itself, by asking questions like *what do you remember of events just before you assaulted Mr H* [the victim]*?*

The most obvious triggers were that Mark had taken a drug which made him clinically paranoid. However, there may be other triggers of which he could become aware. Mark could then learn to respond to them in ways other than with violence. Suppose, for example, that Mark had some distinguishing physical feature for which he had been bullied at school. Let us imagine that Mark is not very tall. If he disclosed that he assaulted Mr H because he thought Mr H was laughing at his short stature, you might explore this sensitively with him. If you then found out that Mark always gets into fights because he thinks people are laughing at his height behind his back, you might enable him to assess the situation differently and respond to it differently, thereby reducing the likelihood that he will reoffend.

The key to working with MDOs is that it involves close teamwork. You would therefore have to be aware of what work had been done with Mark before you ever met him. He would have been closely assessed and he would likely have been engaged in work with psychologists, forensic psychiatrists, MHOs, social workers and forensic nurses before he left secure hospital. There will be closely devised care plans. You would have to be aware of all of this before you set up some sort of working relationship with him. You would have to discuss your intentions and their results with the other members of the multidisciplinary team.

FURTHER ACTIVITY

Because of levels of security and issues of confidentiality and public safety, it is unlikely that you would get to visit any facilities specifically for the care and management of mentally disordered offenders. That does not by any means imply that all MDOs are extremely dangerous, that they all use specialised and separate services and that none use mainstream facilities like leisure centres, libraries, etc. However, it might be important to get a flavour of the dedicated and secure services for MDOs because the difference between hospital and prison may be confusing at this high-security level: visit the State Hospital website at: www.tsh.scot.nhs.uk.

Visit the pages on 'Patient Information' and 'Relatives' Information'. As you read about the way that money, mail and daily activities are handled, try to read between the lines about what is implied about managing security.

CHAPTER SUMMARY

In this chapter we have discussed 'mental health' law as it relates to criminal justice. You have been introduced to:

- the difference between civil and criminal powers to compel people to receive care and treatment;

- the Criminal Procedure (Scotland) Act 1995, and the major amendments made to it by the 2003 Act, inserting into it flexible powers for courts to make 'mental health' disposals;

- the need to balance rights with public protection in relation to mentally disordered offenders;

- the range of policy structures that govern the workings of the law and assist those who work within the justice, 'mental health' and forensic systems (the Memorandum of Procedure, MAPPA, CPA, etc.);

- mentally disordered offenders as a body of vulnerable and sometimes dangerous people who require care, treatment, protection and secure monitoring;

- restricted patients as a specific sub-group of offenders who pose a particular level of risk and therefore require particular frameworks of security and risk management;

- some basic concepts around risk assessment, management and the positive benefits of risk-taking; and

- the impact of inquiries into failings in the system and most notably that of Mr L and Mr M (MWC, 2006).

The case of Mr L and Mr M gives a very good flavour of both MWC inquiries and their outcome recommendations. It is also a good introduction to the various systems for managing MDOs. It paints a careful portrait of a mentally disordered offender: (see **www.mwcscot.org.uk/web/FILES/Publications/ Mental_Welfare_Inquiry.pdf**).

While the new CPA guidance for restricted patients had not yet been published at the time of writing, its broad outline can be found in the Memorandum of Procedure (Scottish Executive, 2006m).

A good overview of MAPPA guidance can be found in the Scottish Executive, Circular No. JD/15/2006.

An overview of the Risk Management Authority can be found in its annual report.

While the MAPPA Guidance and the Memorandum of Procedure make heavy reading, a gloss through them will give the reader a flavour of the sort of issues they address, the seriousness of the risk to public safety and the structures that are in place to carefully manage seriously violent and sexual offenders.

A good overview of the risk assessment tool HCR20 can be found at: **www.fnrh.freeserve.co.uk/ hcr20.html**.

Statistics on homicide in Scotland

Calculating rates of unlawful killing depends upon police statistics rather than those of courts after successful prosecution because the perpetrator is not found or brought to successful prosecution in every case. The 2003 statistics from the Scottish Executive show that 38 victims in every million of the population were male (over six times the rate for females). Male victims aged 16 to 30 represented 72 homicides per million population (the highest rate).

There were 105 killings where an accused person was identified in 2003:

> *The accused ... was known to the victim in almost four-fifths of cases; 20 per cent of victims were presumed to have been killed by a relative or partner, and 59 per cent were presumed to have been killed by an acquaintance. Of the 21 victims in 2003 who were recorded as having been killed by a relative, 6 were killed by their partner.* (www.scotland.gov.uk/Publications/2004/11/20292/47178)

Notes

1   In Scotland, the police process of making the arrest is separated from the decision-making process about whether or not the accused ought to be prosecuted for the offence. This decision is made by the Procurator Fiscal under the Crown Office, which is both independent of the police and the court. The decision to prosecute is based on satisfying a number of tests such as whether there is sufficient evidence to bring a successful prosecution and whether there is a public interest in prosecuting.

2   The magistrate's court is the lowest level of court in Scotland, presided over not by a Sheriff but by lay magistrates who dispose of petty offences such as breach of the peace.

3   Tribunals which hear cases involving restricted patients must be chaired by a Sheriff or by the President of the Mental Health Tribunal for Scotland. They are called Shrieval Tribunals.

Chapter 5

Working with vulnerable people: mental health and disorder in children and young people

A C H I E V I N G   A   S O C I A L   W O R K   D E G R E E

This chapter will help you to begin to meet the following (Scottish) Standards in Social Work Education (SiSWE) (Scottish Executive, 2003a), available at www.scotland.gov.uk/library5/social/ffsw.pdf.

Key Role 1: Prepare for, and work with, individuals, families, carers, groups and communities to assess their needs and circumstances.

Learning Focus:

1.1 Preparing for social work contact and involvement.

1.2 Working with individuals, families, carers, groups and communities so they can make informed decisions.

1.3 Assessing needs and options in order to recommend a course of action.

Key Role 2: Plan, carry out, review and evaluate social work practice with individuals, families, carers, groups, communities and other professionals.

Learning Focus:

2.1 Identifying and responding to crisis situations.

2.2 Working with individuals, families, carers, groups and communities to achieve change, promote dignity, realise potential and improve life opportunities.

2.3 Producing, implementing and evaluating plans with individuals, families, carers, groups, communities and colleagues.

24 Developing networks to meet assessed needs and planned outcomes.

2.5 Working with groups to promote choice and independent living.

2.6 Tackling behaviour which presents a risk to individuals, families, carers, groups, communities and the wider public.

Key Role 3: Assess and manage risk to individuals, families, carers, groups, communities, self and colleagues.

Learning Focus:

3.1 Assessing and managing risks to individuals, families, carers, groups and communities.

3.2 Assessing and managing risk to self and colleagues.

Key Role 4: Demonstrate professional competence in social work practice.

Learning Focus:

4.1 Evaluating and using up-to-date knowledge of, and research into, social work practice.

4.2 Working within agreed standards of social work practice.

4.3 Understanding and managing complex ethical issues, dilemmas and conflicts.

4.4 Promoting best social work practice, adapting positively to change.

Key Role 5: Manage and be accountable, with supervision and support, for their own social work practice within their organisation.
Learning Focus:
  5.1 Managing one's own work in an accountable way.
  5.2 Taking responsibility for one's own continuing professional development.
  5.3 Contributing to the management of resources and services.
  5.4 Managing, presenting and sharing records and reports.
  5.5 Preparing for, and taking part in, decision-making forums.
  5.6 Working effectively with professionals within integrated, multidisciplinary and other service settings.
Key Role 6: Support individuals to represent and manage their needs, views and circumstances.
  Learning Focus:
  6.1 Representing, in partnership with, and on behalf of, individuals, families, carers, groups and communities to help them achieve and maintain greater independence.

Introduction

In this chapter we will consider the kind of issues and knowledge that social workers need in order to carry out effective work with children and young people who have poor mental health or a mental illness. This will help you to understand the nature of these and how to respond effectively to them. Later on the focus is on working with young people who are dealing with the problems of eating disorders, self-harm, dissociative disorder and depression.

Before this, we shall look briefly at the current framework for children's services in Scotland and locate mental health services within this in order that you have an integrated picture (see also YoungMinds, 2003).

Children's services in Scotland

The organisation and delivery of children's services in Scotland is governed primarily by the Children (Scotland) Act 1995 (available at www.opsi.gov.uk/acts/acts1995/Uk pga_19950036_en_1.htm) and associated regulations and guidance. In line with the recommendations of *For Scotland's children* concerning the level of integration of children's services (Scottish Executive, 2001b, available at www.scotland.gov.uk/library3/education/fcsr-00.asp) and those of the child protection audit and review (Scottish Executive, 2002b, available at http://www.scotland.gov.uk/Publications/2002/ 11/15820/ 14009) the Scottish Executive launched a major reform of child protection (see www.scotland.gov.uk/Topics/People/Young-People/children-families/17834/10238) and a subsequent review of all children's services under the heading of 'Getting It Right for Every Child' (GIRFEC) (available at www.scotland.gov.uk/Topics/People/Young-People/childrensservices/girfec/Background). GIRFEC is intended to offer a broad framework for the development, design and delivery of services which aims to ensure that these are (more) child-centred, well integrated across all agencies and have a clear focus upon the child's needs while maximising positive outcomes. One of the key underpinning principles of GIRFEC is to reduce many of the barriers which exist in relation to joint working and joint service planning and delivery. In areas of practice like mental health, joint working, planning and reviewing is essential.

One means by which this may be assisted is by the implementation of new legislation which would amend aspects of the Children (Scotland) Act 1995 as well as introducing a range of new measures (see Children's Services (Scotland) Bill and accompanying information at www.scotland.gov.uk/Publications/2006/12/18140606/0) to facilitate more effective working practices. As with much primary legislation, the intention is to enable rather than to pre-scribe, with local authorities and, significantly, voluntary organisations having the scope to be flexible in terms of how its provisions will be implemented. (At the time of writing, the Children's Services (Scotland) Bill 2007 has not progressed through the Scottish Parliament.)

Within Scotland, services for children, young people and their families tend to be delivered by specialist child care workers based within a variety of team structures and organisa-tional settings in much the same way that specialist mental health social workers deliver services to children within teams located within the broader context of child and adoles-cent mental health services (CAMHS). It is important to remember that mental health, good, bad or indifferent, is not the preserve of any one organisation or profession – every-one has their part to play. This, it is felt, offers a sense of the central importance of effective collaboration within this area of practice. These matters are covered in more detail in Chapter 8.

If you are a social worker located within a CAMHS team or its equivalent and have a spe-cialist remit, it is important that you work closely with the child's social worker as it is likely that s/he will have one, given the way services are currently structured. If you are the child's social worker, perhaps based in a children and families team or a school setting for example (Scottish Office, 1998a; Scottish Executive, 2002c), it is likewise important that you work closely with any social worker (or other professional) with a specialist mental health remit. It is also vitally important that all professionals work closely with parents and/or carers so long as this is consistent with the best interests, and in some instances the wishes, of the child.

Hothersall (2006) provides a comprehensive account of social work with children, young people and their families in Scotland, with detailed commentary on the current legal and policy structures, including the Children's Hearing System.

What do social workers need to know to work effectively with children and young people?

Social work with children and young people who are experiencing poor mental health or who have a mental illness has until recently received relatively little attention (Meltzer et al., 2000, 2004; Green et al., 2005). However, the Scottish Government has recently endorsed the importance of the need for effective community and specialist services for this group (Scottish Executive, 2005g). Social workers have the skills necessary to work effectively with children and young people and to be key workers in multidisciplinary settings. However, it is important that all social workers are clear about their respective roles and responsibilities as well as being sure of their own personal and professional capabilities in relation to under-taking work with children and young people, particularly where there are issues around mental health and/or illness.

There are many approaches that social workers and others use, some more effective than others (Payne, 2005). All have behind them a set of assumptions that raise issues for you, the service user and their carers. For example, when working with a young person who displays behaviour associated with depression, is the young person the primary client or is it the worried parent? Working with the young person to help them to articulate their feelings and their needs may be at odds with what the family wants and believes should happen. A child may be bottling up feelings because they inwardly feel that to open up is to risk the alienation of the family, yet it may be in their interests to express these. Dilemmas such as these often lie at the heart of effective practice and when working with mental health and illness, core skills in relation to working with children and young people as well as those associated with mental health related approaches are essential (see Scottish Executive, 2006g).

As a social worker, you need to understand what the various mental disorders are and how they *typically* manifest in order that you can work alongside other professionals, as well as undertake direct work yourself where this is appropriate. This is a complex area and you need to resist making simplistic assessments of complex situations and playing the role of amateur psychiatrist. Where your strengths lie is in using an empowering approach when you can work with people to help them discover explanations for their situations that they themselves understand and suggest ways of intervening that actually work for them, using relevant knowledge, theory, values and other skills, particularly your communication and relationship skills (Koprowska, 2005). The real 'experts' are the service users and their families themselves who have experienced first-hand the impact of mental disorder.

You could be working with children, young people and their families as part of a team approach or in your own right (see above) and the kinds of problems you might be helping to deal with can be broadly categorised as follows (see also Carr, 2006):

Infancy and early childhood:

- communication problems;
- sleeping difficulties;
- toileting problems;
- learning problems;
- unusually strong or long-lasting tantrums;
- children who are suffering anxieties after major trauma or major life events such as divorce or separation of parents;
- children who are insecurely attached.

(See Barnes, 2003; YoungMinds, 2004; Angold and Egger, 2007; Heads Up Scotland, 2007.)

Middle childhood:

- conduct problems;
- attention and overactivity;
- fear and anxiety problems;

- repetition problems;

- somatic problems including bedwetting and/or soiling;

- relationship problems;

- attachment related difficulties (see Cassidy and Shaver, 1999; Sroufe et al., 2005; Crittenden, 2006; Prior and Glaser, 2006);

- behavioural problems at home and/or school;

- school refusal problems.

Adolescence:

- eating disorders;

- behavioural problems;

- anxiety states;

- self-harm;

- depression;

- attachment and/or relational difficulties;

- substance misuse (Scottish Executive, 2003b, 2003c, 2006b, 2006e, 2006f, 2007b; Wanigaratne et al., 2005);

(See also Biglan et al., 2005; Campbell, 2006; Wolfe and Mash, 2006; Eisen, 2007; Rutherford, Quinn and Mathur, 2007; Vostanis, 2007.)

Of course, before social workers become involved someone must perceive these problems as either dysfunctional, disruptive or otherwise problematic. Therefore it is essential to determine if the behaviour is within 'normal' or acceptable limits and to come to some initial understanding of the possible reasons for it. Being in a position to do this requires that you have an understanding of the usual developmental progression of children and young people (Bee and Boyd, 2004; Crawford and Walker, 2007) and some knowledge of the kind of mental health problems and mental disorders that children and young people may face. There are some disorders that are more closely associated with children and young people, even though they may also occur in adults.

One area which has only relatively recently received appropriate attention is that concerning the mental health and well-being of *infants*. There is a commitment from the Scottish Government to enhance the level of awareness of these matters through the National Programme. However, as practitioners you need to be aware of the significance of the interface between infancy, development and the possibility of poor infant mental health (Barnes, 2003; Heads Up Scotland, 2007), particularly in relation to significant early (attachment) relationships. This area has perhaps been subjected to a kind of 'taboo' for many, many years, largely because of our unwillingness and/or our inability to publicly acknowledge that our infants may be suffering from poor mental health. Some might see this as a terrible indictment of ourselves, our parenting practices and society as a whole. However that may be, we have now acknowledged that there are a number of very young children who are in need of help and support and practice in this area is development.

Definitions of mental health in the context of child and adolescent development

Chapter 1 covered the main elements that make up a diagnosis of mental disorder and helped us to appreciate some of the issues involved. It is worth revisiting this in the context of children and young people, as there is a view held by some that what we might see as a mental disorder might actually be signs of growing up and adapting that all of us have experience of. In other words, if these 'problems' are part of normal growth and development, the chances are that the young people will 'grow out of them' and therefore we should intervene only as a last resort when their presence is determined as being due to some underlying pathology, psychological or otherwise. The other view is that we should intervene earlier where there are issues around functioning and/or adaptation and try to deal with these before they manifest as something more serious. As a social worker, you need to be clear about where you stand in this respect, as much of your work is at the crossover point between these sometimes conflicting views. This is perhaps worthy of some thought given the tendency for people to deny that there may be a problem in relation to someone's mental well-being. Issues of stigma around mental illness have a very powerful effect and sometimes it is easier to attribute problematic functioning to global and sometimes ill-defined concepts such as 'the terrible twos' or 'adolescence', thereby avoiding the issues and effectively normalising what may in fact be abnormal functioning because of underlying psychopathology (see Butcher et al., 2004; Carr, 2006).

In relation to early and middle childhood, it is important to be alert to the *function* certain behaviours appear to have. All behaviours are context-specific and are therefore designed to be functional, although some may well be symptomatic of an underlying pathology, either within the individual *or* within the environment (Crittenden, 1992). It is important not to overlook the importance of effective parenting in the early years as poor parenting practice can be the cause of many difficulties for children and later as adolescents (Hoghughi and Long, 2004; McKinney, Donnelly and Renk, 2007). Equally, the impact of parenting upon the development of attachment relationships should always be explored in any assessment (O'Connor and Byrne, 2007; Prior and Glaser, 2006) and we should always be alert to the impact of adverse early experience upon brain development *per se* (Karr-Morse and Wiley, 2000; Glaser, 2001; Bellis, 2005).

Adolescence is a period of development in life characterised by accelerated learning, physical changes to the body and the brain and the assimilation of new ideas. These factors all contribute to a period where becoming a social being and accepting, rejecting and modifying one's position in relation to social mores all converge. Writing about adolescence and the life course, Lerner (2002), referring to Lerner and Spanier (1980), suggests that:

> Adolescence is a period of transition, one when the biological, psychological, and social characteristics typical of children change in an integrated manner to become the biological, psychological, and social characteristics typical of adults. When most of an individual's characteristics are in this state of change, that person is an adolescent. (p5)

For many, adolescence can be an intense time with significant pressures put on young people to perform at school and college and to reach certain developmental and social milestones. For others, it can be experienced as a period of exclusion and disinterest from others leading to intense feelings of isolation and loneliness. Petersen (1988), in Lerner (2002, p5), describes the phenomenon of adolescence well when he says that: *[A]dolescence may be described as a phase of life beginning in biology and ending in society.*

This comment perhaps offers an illustration of the way in which adolescence is both a biologically determined experience and a socially mediated one. Although everyone experiences similar biological events at this time of life, 'adolescence' as we conceive of it in the West is a socially defined and, to some extent, a socially mediated event, as is the broader concept of childhood (James and Prout, 2003). The pressures upon adolescents in terms of type may well be no less significant across different cultures, although their form will vary. These pressures can produce stress, which as we have seen earlier, is one of the key intervening variables in the probable cause of mental health problems and the onset of disorder. (Chapter 1 provides more detail.)

These views need to be put alongside the popular view, often represented in the media, that young people are becoming more and more troublesome, which can be contrasted with the romantic view of 'childhood innocence'.

For a general overview of both child and adolescent development, see Lerner, (2000), Smith, Cowie and Blades (2003), Carpendale and Lewis (2006) and Newman and Newman (2007).

RESEARCH SUMMARY

In 2004, the Office for National Statistics (ONS) carried out a second nationally representative survey of the mental health of children and young people across the UK (Green et al., 2005). The findings indicated that one in ten children and young people aged 5–16 had a clinically diagnosed mental disorder. Boys were also more likely than girls to have a mental disorder and the overall prevalence of mental disorders was greater in children who were:

- *in lone parent and reconstituted families;*
- *in families where parents had a low level of educational achievement;*
- *in families with neither parent working;*
- *in families with a low gross weekly income;*
- *in families where the main occupational grouping of the parent(s) was non-professional;*
- *in families who lived in social housing or privately rented properties; and*
- *in families who lived in areas classed as 'hard pressed'.*

(See Green et al., 2005; available at: www.statistics.gov.uk/downloads/theme_health/ GB2004.pdf (full report), and at: www.statistics.gov.uk/downloads/theme_health/ summaryreport.pdf (summary report).)

ACTIVITY *5.1*

From your experience write down what you think are some of the 'life events' that adolescents may have to deal with when growing up.

We can all draw upon our personal experiences and those of our friends to reflect upon what we went through during this stage in our development. Some of the themes might relate to conflict within the family, pressures to conform, unmet needs, etc.

The list quickly grows and with it the potential for tension between competing demands.

Mental health problems and mental disorders in children and young people

One of the challenges for us is to understand the nature and extent of mental health problems and mental disorders that children and young people can experience. The ONS Survey in 2004 (Green et al., 2005) focused upon three common groups of mental disorder: *emotional disorders* which include anxiety, depression and obsessions; *conduct disorders* which are characterised by awkward, aggressive and otherwise troublesome and anti-social behaviours; and *hyperactivity disorders* which involve inattention and overactivity. In relation to the *extent* of such problems, Table 5.1 offers details.

Table 5.1: Prevalence of mental disorders by age and sex, 2004 (all children UK)

	5– to 10–year-olds			11– to 16–year-olds			All children		
	Boys	**Girls**	**All**	**Boys**	**Girls**	**All**	**Boys**	**Girls**	**All**
	Percentage of children with each other								
Type of disorder									
Emotional disorders	2.2	2.5	2.4	4.0	6.1	5.0	3.1	4.3	3.7
Conduct disorders	6.9	2.8	4.9	8.1	5.1	6.6	7.5	3.9	5.8
Hyperkinetic disorder	2.7	0.4	1.6	2.4	0.4	1.4	2.6	0.4	1.5
Less common disorders	2.2	0.4	1.3	1.6	1.1	1.4	1.9	0.8	1.3
Any disorder	10.2	5.1	7.7	12.6	10.3	11.5	11.4	7.8	9.6
Base (weighted	2010	1916	3926	2101	1950	4051	4111	3866	7977

Source: Green et al. (2005, Summary Report, p8). Reproduced under the terms of Crown Copyright Policy Guidance issued by HMSO.

Good mental health is more than the absence of mental illness. The Mental Health Foundation (1999) suggests that mentally healthy children and young people will be those who can:

- develop psychologically, emotionally, creatively, intellectually and physically;

- sustain mutually-satisfying relationships with others;

- use and enjoy solitude;

- become aware of others and empathise with them;

- play and learn;

- develop a sense of right and wrong (see Killen and Smetana, 2005);

- deal with problems and setbacks from time to time.

In relation to this latter point, the concept of *resilience* is important. The Research Summary below looks at this in a little more detail.

Within the Scottish context, the Scottish Government is committed to ensuring that across *all* policy domains, all children are *safe, nurtured, healthy, achieving, active, respected and responsible and included*. These principles apply in relation to child and adolescent mental health services (Scottish Executive, 2005g).

These indicators are important as they set a context within which you will develop your practice as a social worker, but of course they also require interpretation and reference to any previous history of mental health problems. Equally valid is to get the young person's view of their mental health.

RESEARCH SUMMARY

The notion of resilience is a theme very current in social work with children, young people and their families. In essence, resilience refers to the capacity to 'bounce back' and overcome adversity (Fonagy et al., 1994). Much research has been undertaken highlighting those factors which appear to be associated as risk factors for poorer life-chances and difficulties in later life. A number of these are noted in the Research Summary above and impact upon individuals, families and communities. The idea of promoting resilience, which may offset the negative effects of these factors and therefore be protective, has gained considerable currency. Research has identified a number of protective factors which seem to promote resilience (Rutter, 1985, 1995; Gilligan, 1999, 2000). For a set of useful and very practical guides to resilience, see Daniel and Wassell (2002) and for an excellent review of the literature concerning this topic, see Newman and Blackburn (2002).

Resilience factors: child

Stable and even temperament	*Good social skills*
A secure attachment	*Good communication skills*
A supportive family	*Flexible coping strategies*
A sense of autonomy	*Capacity to use humour*
A sense of positive self-worth	*Appropriately affectionate*

Resilience factors: family

Close, supportive relationships	*Consistency of care*
Close ties with alternative caregivers	*Consistency of routine*
Appropriate boundaries in place	*Lack of family discord*
Sufficient material resources	*Encouragement*
Emotional availability of caregivers	*Positive role models*

RESEARCH SUMMARY *continued*

Resilience factors: community

A range of friends

Positive school experiences

Access to leisure facilities

Involvement in organised activities

Good quality of life (QoL)

Safe living space

Wide support network

Good housing

Clear value base

Safe public space

ACTIVITY 5.2

Think back to your childhood and adolescence and, using the above list from the Mental Health Foundation, see how well you were able to meet these socio-developmental goals. How many of them proved at some time in your development to be problematic? What constitutes 'normal' difficulties and what constitutes development that is not normal? What is it that determines this? Is it possible that you could have met the entire list but still have mental health problems?

Of course different people will have different experiences and some of those will be determined by your gender, ethnicity and family circumstances as well as structural reasons like poverty.

Some young people who have experienced mental health problems and disorder believe that these lists do not cover all that is necessary for positive mental health. Don't lose sight of the reality that it is adults who have determined what is satisfactory or not satisfactory about child and adolescent mental health. Walker points out that there is often little evidence of young people having been consulted about their mental health problems. Consequently it is possible that what adults may want from children may well be at odds with what they wish for themselves (Walker, 2003a).

Common mental disorders

Although mental disorder can affect people of all ages there are some that are more usually associated with certain age groups. Some of the more common mental disorders and mental health problems for children and young people are referred to below in line with some of the specific categorisations referred to in the ONS survey (Green et al., 2004). The information presented here will give you some idea of the types of issues presented by such disorders and this should inform your understanding, although as this is not a medical textbook you should refer to other sources for more detailed information, for example: Abela and Hankin (2008), Le Grange and Lock (2007), Martin and Volkmar (2007), Mash and Barkley (2007), Rutherford, Quinn and Mathur (2007), Wolfe and Mash (2006), Barkley and Murphy (2006), Geller and DelBello (2006), Rutter and Taylor (2005), Thompson, Cooper and Hooper (2005), Dogra et al. (2002).

Depressive disorders

These include major depression, bipolar affective disorder (manic depression) and adjustment disorders that all adversely affect the mood, energy and general social functioning of the young person. Most young people from time to time suffer from mood swings, depression and periods of hyperactivity, but the presence of these disorders is distinguishable by reference to the duration and intensity of the symptoms and, obviously, the extent to which it interferes with everyday life.

There is a growing belief that a small minority of young people show signs of depressive disorders much earlier than has previously been thought and that this may occur during childhood. Depression often affects males and females differently but with both it is often difficult to uncover whether they are unhappy or depressed or both. The line between unhappiness, which is usually short term, and the longer-term nature of depression is quite difficult to draw. Learning how to do this is down to experience and recognising some of the key signs (see Heads Up Scotland, 2007).

The point at which concerns are raised relates to the extent of the behaviours and their intensity. For instance, going into your bedroom for short periods and playing loud music is all part of being a young person, but going into your room, locking the door and refusing to have meals or to talk with the family is a point of concern if this lasts more than a few hours. This is a matter of degree and intensity and needs to be compared with previous behaviours.

Depressive disorders are often associated with an increased risk of suicidal behaviour (see Chapter 6) (Hawton and van Heeringen, 2000) as the young person enters the post-15 years phase. One of the problems that clinicians face in making a diagnosis is that the ICD-10 (WHO, 1992) and the Diagnostic and Statistical Manual for Mental Disorders IV (DSM-IV) (APA, 1994) use criteria that are *adult*-orientated rather than specific to young people or children. It is not that these criteria are incorrect but rather that they may be too narrow to cover the young person's behaviour (Pollack, 1999, p320; Briggs, 2002).

Once a decision has been made to intervene, medication and other 'talking treatments' may be indicated which are often combined. Both counselling and cognitive behaviour therapy can be effective and one aspect of intervention that is perhaps underemphasised is the importance of taking a detailed family and social history within the context of an ongoing assessment.

Medication may well be used, although this must be carefully monitored as much less is known about the effects of medication on children and young people compared to adults. Indeed some medications, like some of the selective serotonin reuptake inhibitors (SSRIs) which are used extensively with adults, are not licensed for use on people under the age of 18 years as a result of considerable concern about possible side effects. As we shall see below, under the terms of the Mental Health (Care and Treatment) (Scotland) Act 2003, there are particular safeguards in place regarding the treatment of children and young people which *must* be observed (Patrick, 2006). See also Miklovitz (2002), Geller and DelBello (2006), Abella and Hankin (2008).

Hyperactivity and other disorders involving inattention

Hyperkinetic disorder is the term used by British and European physicians to describe a range of disorders which affect about 1.5 per cent of the child and adolescent population in the UK (Green et al., 2005). Signs include early onset, overactivity with poorly controlled or modulated behaviour with significant inattention and impaired functioning in situations where concentration is expected, including classrooms and small group activities. From a diagnostic perspective, both impaired attention and overactivity are necessary and should be seen in more than one setting. Such disorders can co-occur with conduct-related disorders (see ICD-10 – F90.0–F90.9; Barkley, 2006; Barkley and Murphy, 2006).

Interventions can include medication, often Ritalin, or intensive behaviour modification or in some cases both. Ritalin is a psychostimulant and is from the same family as 'speed'. Although you would expect stimulants to make hyperactive young people more active, it does in fact have the opposite effect for most young people.

Stimulant medication works for a short time and can have the effect of helping the young person to concentrate and to work better at school as well as at home. Considerable gains in school performance and social ability have been reported (Frankenburger and Cannon, 1999). This medication works better when parent(s) are encouraged to provide practical and emotional support for their child. However, there has been much criticism of the use of Ritalin (Singh, 2004; Leason, 2003; Malacrida, 2002; Turner, 2002) particularly in relation to younger children, where it is suggested that poor parenting practices may be the root cause of the 'disorder'. There is now some debate around re-framing this issue (Myatt, Rostill and Wheeldon, 2004; Wallwork, 2007). Unfortunately in the US and increasingly in the UK it is reported that young people sell this medication to their classmates as it also acts as an appetite suppressant. Young people may also 'save up' their medication and take a lot at once to get the 'buzz' (Shillington et al., 2006). Where stimulants have not worked doctors will often prescribe non-stimulant medication such as imipramine, fluoxetine or clonidine. (For detailed information regarding medication, see the British National Formulary (various dates/2007b) and the BNF for Children (2007a), and available at: www.bnf.org/bnf/ (registration required).)

Social workers, in collaboration with other professionals, can provide behaviour management, counselling and some forms of psychotherapy. Many children and young people will inevitably experience low self-esteem at some point and may well be challenging to engage with in any meaningful way. Often parental attention is craved for, even when it is negative, and parents may need your help to learn how to reward positive behaviours and to ignore the negative behaviour. Children with hyperkinetic disorder benefit from being rewarded as much as anyone else, even though their extreme behaviour can be especially difficult and demanding. This approach may be as effective as prescribing medication.

It is important that you work not only with the young person and their family but also with the school so that everyone is aware of what the intervention is and what their role is in the treatment plan. In this respect, the development of Integrated Care Pathways (ICPs – see Chapters 1 and 7) (Scottish Executive, 2003e, 2005k) may represent a useful means of developing and sustaining effective practice as is the use of the Integrated Assessment Framework (IAF) in relation to children and young people (Scottish Executive, 2005h). Working collaboratively with colleagues from other disciplines, including child and family social work teams, health personnel (health visitors), etc. is seen as an integral and crucial part of good practice (Scottish Executive, 2003d; Pollard et al., 2005; Hothersall, 2006; Quinney, 2006). However, listening to what young people tell us is crucially important, and the formula 'relevant people + relevant places + relevant times = relevant services' (go to: www.youthlink.co.uk/practicedevelopment/walkthetalk) is one to consider in terms of your practice (Scottish Executive, 2005g).

Dissociative disorders

This condition affects a person's sense of who they are and the extent to which they engage with reality. The result can be a feeling of being 'disconnected' from their social world. Everyone can feel this way from time to time; for example, long-distance runners sometimes experience a 'high' as they float through a marathon, which could be considered similar. A similar experience can also occur as a result of the (side) effects of drugs or alcohol.

As you can imagine, a diagnosis of dissociative disorder is controversial (ICD-10 – F44). However, despite this it is likely that this disorder is much more common than previously thought. The diagnosis is often reached only after a series of several earlier misdiagnoses that can include borderline personality disorder and schizophrenia. The most complex of all of the dissociative disorders is known as dissociative identity disorder (DID) or multiple personality disorder (ICD-10 – F44.81) in which the person experiences different personalities, often with an overlay of depression, severe mood swings, memory loss, anxiety and panic attacks.

The cause of this range of disorders is unclear but is thought to include severe abuse in childhood and the lack of meaningful adult relationships that provide love and comfort. It is almost like the child or young person has had to be too self-reliant before they are capable of being so and has forgotten how to switch back to being a child. These disorders are diagnosed using some reliable tools such as the Dissociative Experiences Scale (DES) and the Structured Clinical Interview (SCID-D); a professional who is trained in this assessment tool must administer these. As with all mental disorders, the broad cultural context needs to be uppermost in our minds when making such a diagnosis.

Social workers may work with people who have this disorder by providing information about self-help groups and by working with the person using a range of recovery oriented approaches.

Deliberate self-harm

Intentional or deliberate self-harm, or self-mutilation (ICD-10 – Chapter xx; x60–x84), results in approximately 7,000 people receiving hospital treatment each year; an increasing number of these are children and young people (Scottish Executive, 2006i). This can consist of excessive scratching, hitting, head-banging, biting, pinching or any other form of harming their body. However, most common is the cutting or burning of oneself. It is important not to readily misinterpret these actions as suicidal gestures as they may actually imply no intent of suicide (Briggs, 2002; Smalley, Scourfield and Greenland, 2005), although in extreme cases these actions may result in accidental death (Scottish Executive, 2002a, Scottish Executive, 2006i). There is perhaps a need to consider whether relationships exist between deliberate self-harm and accidental suicide.

There is a variety of reasons as to why people would do this including self-punishment, to gain feelings of control, clearing their mind, expressing their psychological turmoil physically, seeking attention/manipulating others, and the adrenaline rush that the body naturally releases during these actions. Self-harm, when practised frequently, can escalate and become psychologically as well as physically addictive. The need to experience more severe harm in order to alleviate emotional pain and to attain an adrenaline rush is similar to the way that a heroin addict would use increasing amounts of heroin in order to feel the 'high' they initially felt. Due to this a reliance on self-harm may develop which is difficult to stop. It is important for them to form a new coping strategy to replace this addictive habit. (See Walsh, 2005; Jobes, 2006.)

Eating disorders

Eating disorders (ICD-10 – F50) involve serious disturbances of the 'normal' eating pattern and an obsessive concentration on body size and diet. There are two distinct types, *anorexia nervosa* and *bulimia nervosa*. The severity of these disorders can vary significantly and treatment and interventions may be minimal and community-based at one extreme to maximal at the other involving compulsory admission to specialist resources. Eating disorders are real, treatable mental disorders that can cause considerable distress to those who are experiencing their effects and those of their carers (Scottish Executive, 1997, 2005k). See also Le Grange and Lock (2007) and Lock and Le Grange (2004).

Other disorders: the 'Z' Group

Within the ICD-10 (WHO, 1992) are listed a group of conditions that are often found in association with other disorders. Chapter xxi includes 'Factors Influencing Health Status and Contact with Health Services' and refers to 'Problems related to negative life events in childhood' (Z61), 'Problems related to certain psychosocial circumstances' (Z64) and, of interest, Z91 which considers 'Personal history of risk-factors, not elsewhere classified'. From a social work perspective, these factors are worthy of closer scrutiny as many of these can be seen to predispose people towards mental disorder.

Psychosis

So far we have looked at some of the more common disorders which can affect children, young people and their families in differing ways to differing degrees. Psychotic illness (see Chapter 1) is less common in children and young people, but deserving of mention because of its dramatic presentation and (often) devastating consequences.

The prevalence of psychotic illness in children and adolescents is unknown although it may run to approximately 20 per cent of the under-18 population (Tiffin, 2006). In most instances, young people with a psychotic illness will experience hallucinations, delusions and other severe abnormalities of behaviour such as marked over-excitement, over-activity, psychomotor retardation and, occasionally, catatonic behaviour. Any form of psychosis may bring with it an increased risk of self-harm if not effectively managed, to both the individual and others. The treatment and management of such disorders will involve both medical and psychosocial interventions and may well involve the use of compulsory measures under the Mental Health (Care and Treatment) (Scotland) Act 2003, with special provisions regarding children being put in place (Shaw and Rapoport, 2006; Bentall et al., 2007; Hammersley et al., 2007).

Social work interventions

Interventions range from working with families to individual work. You need to reflect on some of the value and ethical issues when working with young people. In Chapter 1 the issue of who is the primary client was raised and showed some potential conflicts of interest. In particular the dilemma of conformity with parental demands may be at the expense of the young person's emergent sense of self. Equally, working in an empowering way with the young person may be liberating for them but at the cost of their relationship with their parents and families (Coppock, 2005).

Intervention can take many forms but family support is often the most common and most effective among a range of different levels of intervention (see Figure 5.1 and Hothersall, 2006, ch 3). This can consist of working with the family as a whole and/or working with individuals in the family. The thrust of government policy epitomised in *For Scotland's children* (Scottish Executive, 2001b) and the 'Getting It Right for Every Child' programme (Scottish Executive, 2004b, 2005h) is that integrated early intervention is crucial. This is echoed in recent policy statements concerning the delivery of CAMH services (Scottish Executive, 2006c) and supported by research findings (Cratsley et al., 2007).

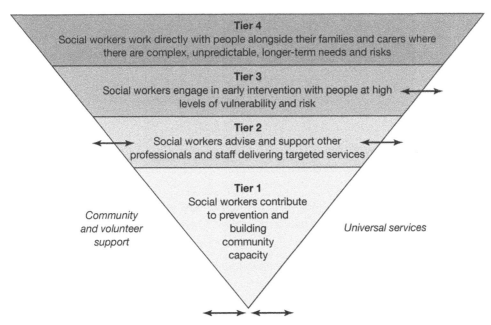

Figure 5.1: The social worker's role: a tiered approach

Source: Scottish Executive (2006a, p31) Available at: www.scotland.gov.uk/Resource/Doc/91949/0021950.pdf. Reproduced under the terms of Crown Copyright Policy Guidance issued by HMSO.

As we mentioned in Chapter 1, the whole issue of intervention was the subject of some debate during the 21st Century Review of Social Work (Scottish Executive, 2006a) and that relating to interventions with children and young people received considerable scrutiny (Scottish Executive, 2005e).

The choice of intervention is considerable and it is important that services reflect service user and family needs rather than being entirely resource driven. In this regard, it is important that children and young people are *aware* of issues around mental health and well-being and education has a lot to offer here (Woolfson, Mooney and Bryce, 2007).

Table 5.2 sets out some of the main psychosocial interventions that social workers and others might use, depending upon individual circumstances. For clarity, the Scottish Executive (2007e) note that:

> [T]he term 'Psychological Therapies' can be understood as referring to a range of interventions, based on psychological concepts and theory, which are designed to help people modify their thinking and/or behaviour in order to relieve distress or dysfunction. (p12)

Table 5.2: Main psychosocial interventions used by social workers and others

Type of intervention	Key aspects
Cognitive behaviour therapy (CBT)	Cognitive techniques challenging negative thoughts and behavioural techniques used to relieve maladaptive thoughts, beliefs and behaviours
Systemic and family therapy	Works on relationships within the family and patterns of interaction between the members
Interpersonal therapy (IPT)	Focuses on the interpersonal relationships of the service user; helps to improve communication patterns and how people relate to one another
Psycho-educational methods	This takes various forms and includes work with service users and families to help them to understand the nature of their disorder and how to promote their mental health
Counselling	Can take many different forms – usually one-to-one and gives the individual the opportunity to develop their understandings of their reactions to events

Adapted from DoH (2001).

There are occasions when a combination of interventions works; for example, CBT and IPT are effective when working with people who are depressed and help to reduce the symptoms of depression (see above).

It is important that '[a]ll Mental Health staff should be equipped with a fundamental level of psychological literacy which enables them to provide good "psychological care" based on a basic psychological conceptualisation of the patient's difficulties, and effective communication and interpersonal skills' (Scottish Executive 2007e, p9). These requirements are clearly applicable to social workers.

Services for children and young people

Child and adolescent mental health services, however configured, are currently organised into four tiers of service. These are important for professionals who are involved in this area of work to understand as is the connection between the various organisations who provide services for them.

Tier 1

This is the level at which interventions are made by GPs, health visitors, school nurses teachers and social workers. The distinguishing feature of this tier is that it is generally provided by non-specialists who can work with children and young people in ways that are non-stigmatising but still open up the possibility of early recognition of mental distress. This tier of service is usually provided at a local level wherever the professional works and is therefore a *universal* provision.

Tier 2

This level of service is provided by a uni-professional group, which includes clinical child psychologists, educational psychologists, child psychiatrists, community child nurses and social workers. This tier offers specialist training for first-tier workers and consultation for professionals and their families as well as outreach services where specialist services are not indicated and they also offer assessment for tiers 3 and 4. This level of service is provided at a smaller number of locations within the community.

Tier 3

This is a specialist level of service for people who have more severe, complex or persistent mental health problems. This is typically a multidisciplinary team often working in a community child mental health clinic or outpatient service. This will include specialist social workers, child and adolescent psychiatrists, clinical psychologists, psychotherapists, occupational therapists and art and music therapists. Assessment and treatment is the core function.

Tier 4

This offers access to highly specialised services including day and residential units including in-hospital services (Scottish Executive, 2005l). These include services for people who are severely mentally ill or who are at risk of serious self-harm or suicide. These are the most specialised of services and likely to be provided at a supra-region level as not all districts can resource this level of expertise.

It is also worth remembering that there are some children who, for a number of reasons, are potentially more susceptible (in a general sense) to poor mental health and mental illness. These groups may include those children who are part of families who are seeking asylum or have migrated (Kohli, 2007) and who can also suffer from the effects of racism (see Achenbach and Rescola, 2006). Children who are looked after by the local authority ('in care') are also at a higher risk in terms of their mental health (Hothersall, 2006), not necessarily because they are 'in care' *per se* but because of the cumulative effect of their experiences which brought them into this situation in the first place. Some children and young people are disproportionately served by mental health services and this is being addressed at a policy level by the Scottish Government in the context of the National Programme for Improving Mental Health and Well-Being (Scottish Executive, 2003d, and see also www.wellscotland.info/mentalhealth/) as well as through specific policy initiatives like 'Equal Minds' (Scottish Executive, 2005f) which aims to address mental health inequalities in Scotland.

Civil compulsory powers and other measures in respect of children and young people

The legal framework governing civil compulsory measures, which may include admission to hospital and compulsory treatment either in hospital or in the community, is complex. The Code of Practice to the Mental Health (Care and Treatment) (Scotland) Act 2003 (the 2003 Act) (Scottish Executive, 2005i) devotes considerable space to the issues that apply to children and young people. The 2003 Act defines a child as *...a person who has not attained the age of 18 years* (s 249) and therefore recognises, implicitly at least, that theoretically there should be no lower age limit to the provisions of the 2003 Act. It is, however, acknowledged that hospital admission should be seen as a last resort for very serious situations.

Earlier chapters have looked at the current legal framework regarding hospital admission and you may want to review these now. Here we shall outline the main provisions of the 2003 Act as they relate to children and young people. For an in depth account of the law here, see Patrick (2006). However, it is important to note that in all actions involving children and young people, the principles of s 1 of the 2003 Act apply, although s 2 of the 2003 Act modifies these somewhat and introduces the fundamental 'welfare principle'. You might also find it helpful to look at the Children (Scotland) Act 1995.

The 2003 Act is *explicit* in its recognition that its provisions apply to children and young people as well as adults. The earlier Mental Health (Scotland) Act 1984 made no *specific* reference to the applicability of its provisions to children and young people; the 2003 Act does so and in this respect is far more transparent in recognising the needs of this group.

The general principles and procedures governing compulsory admission to hospital apply equally to children and young people, including timescales for detention, reviews and appeals, as they do to adults. The details of these are to be found in Chapter 2. Here we look at the *special provisions* that apply.

> ### RESEARCH SUMMARY
>
> *You may wish to look at the report of the Child Health Support Group:* Inpatient working group-psychiatric inpatient services *(Scottish Executive, 2005l) which looks at the provision of inpatient services for children and young people* (Available at www.scotland.gov.uk/Resource/Doc/35596/0012563.pdf).

General issues

In most cases, the issue of whether a child or young person requires hospitalisation (whether under compulsion or voluntarily) or some form of compulsory measure regarding treatment will be one which forms part of their ongoing care planning and management. In some situations, however, emergency measures may be required or other steps taken quickly to ensure that their illness does not worsen because of non-compliance with medication, for example. Where such situations do arise, recourse to the 2003 Act may be required and the child's responsible medical officer (RMO), who should be a *child specialist* (see s 249 for a definition of this), and a mental health officer (MHO) will be actively involved as well as you, the social worker, and the child's family (assuming this is appropriate and in their interests).

In any situation where any form of compulsion is being considered, the first and foremost consideration has to be the welfare of the child. Section 2 of the 2003 Act and paras 25 and 26 of Vol 1 of the Code of Practice refer to this and make clear that everything should be done to minimise any deleterious effects such actions could have by ensuring that the necessary functions under the 2003 Act are discharged in such a way as to best secure the welfare of the child. The wishes and feelings of the child and his or her family must be taken into account at every stage in the process, as must the contents of any advance statement made by the child (s 275), although we should not confuse what a child or young person *wants* with what they may *need*, especially in cases of acute illness. Bear in mind that the capacity to make an advance statement relies upon the same principles of capacity as do issues of general consent. Sometimes wants and needs can be very different things and it is here that the professionals have a key role to play. In cases where the contents of the advance statement are not complied with, the Mental Health Tribunal may be involved and in any case the matter referred to the Mental Welfare Commission.

Consent to treatment

A major factor to be considered is that of *consent*. It is generally regarded that a person aged 12 or over has the maturity to form a view regarding matters affecting them and this includes decisions concerning medical treatment. The Age of Legal Capacity (Scotland) Act 1991, s 2(4) states that:

> *a person under the age of 16 years shall have legal capacity to consent on his own behalf to any surgical, medical or dental procedure or treatment where, in the opinion of a qualified medical practitioner attending him, he is capable of understanding the nature and possible consequences of the procedure or treatment.*

The capacity to consent to treatment brings with it the comparable capacity to *refuse* consent. Where a child or young person is deemed to be competent, refusal must be accepted *unless compulsion can be justified.* Difficulties can of course arise where it is unclear whether any refusal to treatment is based upon a real understanding of the situation or is made irrationally. The doctor and other professionals may feel that a refusal is irrational, but if the child is competent, then this has to be accepted. In some cases where a child is *unable* to give consent, then his or her parents (or whoever holds parental rights and responsibilities) can consent or *refuse* consent on the child's behalf, and this must be in writing.

Where treatment is agreed to but there are indications of resistance and/or a subsequent retraction of consent, then the treatment must stop and consideration given to the relevance of compulsion, with all its safeguards.

In relation to treatments for children and young people, there are special provisions and safeguards in place under the terms of the 2003 Act, whether compulsion is used or not. Chapters 1 and 10 of the Code of Practice to the 2003 Act give guidance on these matters and the following section of the 2003 Act is germane.

Section 244 makes reference to the Mental Health (Safeguards for Certain Informal Patients) (Scotland) Regulations 2005 and specifies safeguards in relation to informal child patients regarding electro convulsive therapy (ECT), transcranial magnetic stimulation (TMS) and vagus nerve stimulation (VNS). In practice, these treatments are likely to be rarely used. These provisions are to be read alongside those which apply to all patients under Part 16 of the 2003 Act.

It is worth noting that if a young person is deemed capable of giving consent but *refuses*, even in an emergency situation, a doctor cannot give any treatment. This has the potential of raising a number of ethical dilemmas.

Informal measures

In most situations where hospitalisation or other forms of treatment are required, recourse to the provisions of the 2003 Act will *not* be necessary. Within the context and spirit of effective partnership, informal measures are more likely to be effective. In this regard your role as the social worker can be critical in offering information, advice and *reassurance* to the child and their family about what is proposed and why. As mentioned above, there are special safeguards in place in relation to informal child patients. This is because where there is no recourse to the 2003 Act its safeguards would not apply so it was deemed important to ensure that added protection was available even where compulsion was not used. This of course endorses the value of partnership working between all those concerned and recognises the significant potential for enhancing and in some cases maintaining a therapeutic relationship even in difficult situations where hard decisions may need to be taken.

Civil compulsory powers

In some situations a child or young person may be subject to the compulsory powers of the 2003 Act. These are likely to be those where there is acute illness and serious harm is likely to befall the child or young person or someone else if action is not taken.

Any child or young person can be made the subject of an *emergency* (P 5, s 36 for up to 72 hours) or *short-term* (P 6, s 44 for up to 28 days) *detention certificate* or a *compulsory treatment order* (P 7, chapter 1, s 57–71) in the same way that an adult can (see Chapter 2).

In these situations it is important that all concerned ensure that the child or young person is fully aware of their rights under the 2003 Act and that the measures taken are part of a bigger picture in terms of their ongoing treatment and management. Section 23 places specific *duties* on health boards to ensure that any child or young person who receives treatment is provided with ... *such services and accommodation as are sufficient for the particular needs of that child or young person.* Sections 25–29 are very important here as these refer to the provision of care and support services. Section 26 has a particular relevance in relation to the ongoing care, support and treatment of children and young people and makes reference to other provisions contained within the Children (Scotland) Act 1995.

The use of compulsion in any given situation would only be as a last resort and any impact upon the child of any form of detention *per se* should be seriously considered before such steps are taken.

C H A P T E R   S U M M A R Y

This chapter has considered the way in which children's services are organised in Scotland and looked at the types of difficulties children and young people may experience which these services need to respond to. You have also been introduced to some interpretations of mental disorder within the context of child and adolescent development and looked at the range of measures available to help children and young people when they are unwell.

FURTHER READING

Vostanis, P (2007) *Mental health interventions and services for vulnerable children and young people.* London: Jessica Kingsley.

Walker, S (2003) *Social work and child and adolescent mental health.* Lyme Regis: Russell House.

In these books you will find many of the ideas in this chapter covered in more depth.

WEBSITE

There are many different organisations which offer help, advice and support to service users, their families and professionals. Some offer general advice while others are quite specialist. Below are details of the websites of some of the main organisations operating within both Scotland and the UK. These sites will also offer links to many others.

www.wellscotland.info/index.html
This links to the Scottish Executive's National Programme for Improving Mental Health and Well-Being and many other sites.

http://www.samh.org.uk/
The Scottish Association for Mental Health is Scotland's leading mental health charity. This is a good site with lots of information and links.

www.youngminds.org.uk/
A national (UK) charity dedicated to improving the mental health of children and young people. The website has a lot of interesting material.

http://www.acamh.org.uk/
The Association for Child and Adolescent Mental Health is a multidisciplinary organisation with a focus upon child and adolescent mental health. It produces the *Journal of Child Psychology and Psychiatry* as well as *Child and Adolescent Mental Health*, a journal aimed at social workers, community psychiatric nurses and other practitioners. The Association is active in training and development and is UK-wide with a Scottish branch.

Chapter 6

Working with vulnerable people: adults who are short-term service users

A C H I E V I N G   A   S O C I A L   W O R K   D E G R E E

This chapter will help you to begin to meet the following (Scottish) Standards in Social Work Education (SiSWE) (Scottish Executive, 2003a), available at www.scotland.gov.uk/library5/social/ffsw.pdf.

Key Role 1: Prepare for, and work with, individuals, families, carers, groups and communities to assess their needs and circumstances.

Learning Focus:

1.1 Preparing for social work contact and involvement.

1.2 Working with individuals, families, carers, groups and communities so they can make informed decisions.

1.3 Assessing needs and options in order to recommend a course of action.

Key Role 2: Plan, carry out, review and evaluate social work practice with individuals, families, carers, groups, communities and other professionals.

Learning Focus:

21 Identifying and responding to crisis situations.

2.2 Working with individuals, families, carers, groups and communities to achieve change, promote dignity, realise potential and improve life opportunities.

2.3 Producing, implementing and evaluating plans with individuals, families, carers, groups, communities and colleagues.

2.4 Developing networks to meet assessed needs and planned outcomes.

2.5 Working with groups to promote choice and independent living.

2.6 Tackling behaviour which presents a risk to individuals, families, carers, groups, communities and the wider public.

Key Role 3: Assess and manage risk to individuals, families, carers, groups, communities, self and colleagues.

Learning Focus:

3.1 Assessing and managing risks to individuals, families, carers, groups and communities.

3.2 Assessing and managing risk to self and colleagues.

Key Role 4: Demonstrate professional competence in social work practice.

Learning Focus:

4.1 Evaluating and using up-to-date knowledge of, and research into, social work practice.

4.2 Working within agreed standards of social work practice.

4.3 Understanding and managing complex ethical issues, dilemmas and conflicts.

4.4 Promoting best social work practice, adapting positively to change.

Key Role 5: Manage and be accountable, with supervision and support, for their own social work practice within their organisation.
Learning Focus:
5.1 Managing one's own work in an accountable way.
5.2 Taking responsibility for one's own continuing professional development.
5.3 Contributing to the management of resources and services.
5.4 Managing, presenting and sharing records and reports.
5.5 Preparing for, and taking part in, decision-making forums.
5.6 Working effectively with professionals within integrated, multidisciplinary and other service settings.

Key Role 6: Support individuals to represent and manage their needs, views and circumstances.
Learning Focus:
6.1 Representing, in partnership with, and on behalf of, individuals, families, carers, groups and communities to help them achieve and maintain greater independence.

Introduction

This chapter introduces some of the key concepts and skills that are needed for the social work role in times of meeting short-term acute need. It builds on the learning that has occurred in earlier chapters. The role of the primary care teams and the need for liaison with other professionals in this area is reinforced (see Chapter 8). Although there are different approaches when working with service users who have chronic as opposed to acute conditions, there are also overlaps between the two and today's short-term service user could develop a more protracted set of difficulties which involve long-term engagement. Indeed, for some people, positive and focused early intervention may prevent the need for longer-term involvement. To help you to unravel all of this an illustrative example is used throughout based on an older person who experiences depression.

A central issue here is that of effective assessment. The assessment of people who may pose a risk to their own health, safety or welfare is a complex and difficult task whether in the community or in hospital (Scottish Executive, (2007f). Hospital is no longer considered to be a place for people to live or even stay for any length of time beyond that which is essential. In the community one of the goals will be to achieve a balance between providing good quality intervention and the avoidance of unnecessary risks. While hospital admission is by no means the only solution to serious mental disorder, we will use admission to hospital as an example to help you to understand when it may be necessary.

A case example is used to show how social workers may need to work with a service user who is at high risk of attempting suicide. The situation highlights key areas such as the recovery process and working with people to capitalise upon their strengths rather than disempowering them and casting them in a passive role by focusing on their weaknesses.

In order to do this, we place emphasis in this chapter on working in partnership with the service user and their personal networks, using a shared approach to the assessment for services and being creative in the use of resources. This will illustrate how social workers can work with service providers to ensure that 24-hour crisis support services can be made available from a range of sources.

A note about the emotional content of the text

This chapter deals closely with suicide in relation to depression. As such it touches upon some taboo subjects which have a strong emotional impact. Given the prevalence of mental distress among all of us, we thought it wise to give a gentle suggestion to readers that, if they feel emotionally upset and they see echoes of the following text in themselves or people close to them, they ought to seek support, advice or counselling.

Policy context

The statistics

Scotland has traditionally had a higher suicide rate than the rest of the UK; however, over recent years rates are starting to come down (www.chooselife.net). Suicide is still one of the major causes of death in Scotland and accounts for approximately 15 per cent of all deaths annually although the exact numbers are unclear due in part to the reluctance sometimes of coroners to record a verdict of suicide. This is partly due to the varying criteria and also out of respect for the families. Thus it is quite likely that this figure of 15 per cent is an under-representation of the actual number of suicides. This means that 765 people in Scotland killed themselves in 2006, out of a total population of about 5 million. In this figure you will find that three out of four suicides are men and the main concern is for young men in the 15–24 age range and elderly people over the age of 74 (Scottish Executive, 2003d, 2006c, 2006d, 2007a).

National strategies

Suicide reduction

Choose Life, the national suicide prevention strategy for Scotland, was launched in 2002 with the clear if ambitious ten-year strategy of significantly reducing the death rate from suicide. Suicide rates across Europe overall have shown an upward trend since the 1980s. The European rate for men increased from 20.3 deaths per 100,000 men in 1980 to 23.1 in 2006, while the rates for females decreased from 11.3 deaths per 100,000 (1980) to 6.4 in 2006 (www.scotpho.org.uk/web/site/home/Healthwell-beinganddisease/suicides/suicide_data/suicide_international.asp).

The Scottish Public Health Observatory (ScotPHO) is the government agency which monitors health trends so that policy-makers may adjust their plans. It monitors suicide trends for Scotland (go to www.scotpho.org.uk). The good news is that rates are falling slowly. It is also important to learn about the circumstances in which people kill themselves and this is also the subject of monitoring via the ScotPHO.

Choose Life sets out a framework to ensure that action is taken nationally and locally to build skills, develop training and encourage people to seek help early, to improve knowledge and awareness of what works to prevent suicide, and to encourage partnership working and improved co-ordination between services (go to www.chooselife.net/home/Home.asp and see Chapter 1).

There is also a free 24-hour helpline called 'Breathing-Space'. Because of the links between suicide and depression, *Choose Life* relates closely to another strand of government policy given to helping people affected by depression, called 'Doing Well by People with Depression' (www.chooselife.net/Resources/Toolkit/DoingWellbyPeoplewithDepression.asp). These arm's-length government initiatives are intended to be user-friendly and accessible as opposed to the more traditional model of a rather stand-offish and remote civil service.

The Mental Health Delivery Plan

The Scottish Government's Mental Health Delivery Plan (Scottish Executive, 2006c) lists the prevention of suicide and deliberate self-harm as one of its key objectives to be achieved by 2010. This is still in keeping with the 2007 government's priorities for Scotland to be:

- wealthier and fairer;
- healthier;
- safer and stronger;
- smarter; and
- greener (Scottish Government news release, 9 September 2007).

The Delivery Plan targets high-risk groups and highlights that those with mental illness are ten times more likely to kill themselves than are the general population. It further identifies those with severe and enduring depression as the highest risk category. It endorses the 'choose life' strategy, which predates the delivery plan by four years, and it acknowledges that evidence of a falling rate of suicide in Scotland suggests that the strategy is working. Furthermore, the delivery plan sets a target for 50 per cent of front-line staff to be trained in the use of suicide assessment tools and in suicide prevention techniques such as 'Mental Health First Aid' (www.healthscotland.org.uk/smhfa/) by 2010.

Just as Choose Life relates to Doing Well by People with Depression, so too does the suicide and deliberate self-harm component of the Delivery Plan relate to its targets for reducing the high prescription rate for anti-depressants and consequently the introduction of more training for front-line staff on the use of 'talking therapies' for use with people with depression and similar conditions (Scottish Executive, 2007e).

Practice context

Depression and suicide

How common is mental disorder among older people? Depression in old age is far more common than many people think. More women are affected than men: males with a diagnosis of depression account for 63.5 per 1,000 population while females account for 118.2 per 1,000 (Scottish Executive, 2007a). Other severe forms of mental disorder are also prevalent including the organic form known as dementia. When you consider that in Scotland we are experiencing an increase in the ageing population the actual number of older people with mental disorder is gradually rising. There are about ten million people of pensionable age in the UK which is over 20 per cent of the population at large. The number of people over 85 has shown a dramatic increase to the point where in 2001 they made up 2 per cent of the population or over one million people.

How is depression linked to suicide? If you are a close reader of this text you will realise that this needs some careful examination before assuming that one necessarily leads to the other. You will have noticed that three out of every four suicides are males but the rates of depression in women over 65 is almost double that of men.

ACTIVITY *6.1*

Take a moment to reflect upon why suicide might be more prevalent in men than women. Make a brief note of your answer.

Comment

Much as with other manifestations of mental distress, suicide is an expression of inner feelings and has a cultural and sociological component to it (Durkheim, 1897/2006; Kirk, 2005; Barry and Yuill, 2007; Helliwell, 2007). For example, it is not true that the male rate is higher than the female rate in certain cultures. Therefore the reason for the far higher male rate in the Western world may relate to cultural ideas of what it means to be male and female. In your response, did you consider that men are traditionally allowed to be less emotionally expressive than women? They are generally assumed to be less 'in touch' with their feelings and they are stereotypically cast as more aggressive. This is certainly borne out in the statistics which suggest that males are more likely to express their emotion by committing crimes of violence. They may therefore be more prone to become emotionally isolated and likely to bottle feelings up. They may also be more likely to use violent means of killing themselves and such means are more likely to succeed (Oakley, 1976).

Myths about suicide

You may have heard a number of generalisations made about suicide and if you have ever worked in the field of mental health, you will almost certainly have heard some people's actions being discussed disparagingly as manipulative or attention-seeking. Before we go on to examine what this means, it is important to bear in mind that everybody who attempts or succeeds in killing themselves does so for their own unique reasons, related to their own personal history and circumstances. Therefore the only generalisations worth paying any attention to are those which are statistically valid such as that men are more likely to kill themselves than women. Even here we have to exercise extreme caution as there is a risk that you may discount the suicide risk for a woman. However, if three out of every four suicides are male, it means that one out of four is female. In other words, women do kill themselves.

The importance of suicide notes

It is true that most people who kill themselves leave a note behind. However, never assume that because a person attempts suicide without writing a note they were not serious. Many people who feel desperate may make an opportunistic attempt upon their life on the spur of the moment.

Does talking to someone about suicide make them think more about it and therefore make them more likely to do it?

This is a very common myth. The answer is very definitely no! *If one actually thinks about it, the notion that talking about suicide increases the risk is preposterous. Feeling down and desperate about one's life is sadly a very common feature of modern living. There will be a number of people reading this book now who are somewhere on the scale of this sort of desperation and it may well be that all of us find ourselves somewhere on that scale at some point in our lives. It is reasonable to hypothesise, therefore, that most of us contemplate suicide (however superficially) at some time or other. However, we, the authors of this book, are absolutely confident that by writing about suicide we are not increasing the risk that it will make any person reading it more likely to do it. Quite the reverse. Talking about anything in the right way may help the person to deal with their feelings. If you doubt this basic premise, we could legitimately ask you why you are studying social work. Do you, for example, think that a person who has an alcohol problem and is trying to give up drink will be more likely to drink by talking about it? Why should suicide be any different? At the very least, if you discuss it with the person you are in a better position to assess the risks and develop a preventative strategy.*

Do people use suicidal behaviour as a means of seeking attention and manipulating others?

Sadly, the answer is probably yes. However, two things arise from this. One is that threatening to harm yourself (or worse, making insincere attempts to do so) is a very poor way of getting your emotional and relationship needs met. One should therefore not be punitive of such behaviour (as is commonly the practice). One should help the person to meet their needs in a more constructive manner. Secondly, such behaviour is very risky and can, in itself, result in serious injury or death.

(See Schneidman, 1996; Jamison, 2001; Westwood, 2007.)

CASE STUDY

Sheila has a history of emotional problems stemming from sexual abuse by a trusted family friend in her teens. She has a steady but emotionally difficult relationship with Tommy and on a number of occasions she has taken an overdose of paracetamol tablets, knowingly timed so that Tommy will find her before they have any effect. Despite medical warnings that death by paracetamol is an irreversible process after a certain number of hours and that it is a slow and painful process taking weeks to happen, Sheila is trapped into a habit of using this high-risk strategy to communicate her emotional desperation to Tommy. It could be said that she is trying to manipulate him into giving her more emotional support. It could also be said, as nurses in the casualty ward say, that Sheila is manipulative and has no real intention of killing herself. However, one day, after an argument with Tommy, she takes an overdose, knowing that he will return home for a shower before his football practice. Unfortunately, Tommy was delayed at work. By the time he got home, Sheila was already irreversibly poisoned by the drug and she died as a result.

Suicide and old age

First the reality is that the highest suicide rate is found among elderly people and in particular those over 75. This is still the case even though the actual total number of people who successfully kill themselves has begun to fall in recent years.

General practitioners are at the front line when it comes to recognising depression in people. In the case of older people, depression can be overlooked if the GP wrongly thinks that older people are unlikely to be depressed and instead perhaps concentrates on physical problems. Identifying ways of differentiating depression from the effects of old age, which could include sleep disturbance, lowering of activity levels, lower libido and/or greater level of fatigue presents a challenge for all practitioners. There are a number of specialist rating scales that help the professional recognise the symptoms of depression including the Geriatric Depression Scale (GDS) (Ulas and Connor, 1999). Like most disorders, early recognition usually offers the best chance for a good recovery.

Traditionally services are organised in tiers or levels with access to the higher tiers being through the referral system. Primary care is the first tier with services being provided by the GP and other professionals. The general principle is that people's mental health needs should be met at the lowest tier possible and this will involve other agencies such as social services and the voluntary sector. Consider the case study below.

CASE STUDY

Duncan McBride lives with his wife in a remote community on the West coast of Scotland. He is 68 years old and she is 69 and they have lived in the same croft for the last twenty years or so. They have two children, both adults, who live in cities considerable travelling time away. It is difficult to pinpoint exactly when Mr McBride became depressed. He is a proud man and fairly inexpressive of his emotions, even to his wife. Therefore, by the time Mrs McBride knew that something was seriously wrong and by the time she was able to persuade him to see the doctor, the condition was already deeply entrenched. He had been prescribed anti-depressants by his GP, but being both unused to taking medication and sceptical of its worth, he may not have been taking the pills with regularity. Mrs McBride returned home after visiting her son for a couple of days to find her husband in a very distressed state. At first she was unsure if he had been drinking heavily but he eventually told her that he had taken a large amount of his medication all at once and washed it down with whisky. He said that he was absolutely fed up with life – it was all too much and he had had enough. She called her doctor who made arrangements for Mr McBride to be admitted informally to the local psychiatric unit. As with the vast majority of people who come into hospital, Mr McBride went voluntarily and there was no need to consider the use of compulsion.

After a week in hospital Mr McBride returns home agreeing to take the anti-depressant medication and to work with the community mental health team to develop the care plan into a more comprehensive one. As the social worker you will take on the role of care co-ordinator/key worker. This includes visiting him at home.

CASE STUDY *continued*

After two interviews with the couple it is becoming clear that their relationship is not especially strong and that Mr McBride feels ignored and isolated. Whereas at one time he was a full-time farm worker, used to being out in the hills from early morning till late, he is now retired and on a fixed and modest retirement income. His best friend died last year which has left him with a sense of despair.

Social factors

What factors contribute to depression? The psychosocial model, suggested in Chapter 1, helps to identify possible factors and as you read the case study involving Mr McBride you may notice the particular importance of loss to him.

CASE STUDY *continued*

His close friend and really only male friend in the last twenty years had been his near neighbour who died seven months ago. The two of them shared an interest in going to the nearby village pub in the neighbour's car and enjoyed the atmosphere and watching live football matches. Mr McBride has been once or twice since but felt very isolated and thought that everyone was looking at him. The only time that he gets out is to go shopping in the nearby town which he finds uninteresting.

Mr and Mrs McBride have been married for a long time, appear to have got bored with each other's company and when together they frequently niggle at each other. He is critical of how his wife spends her time and their money while she complains that he is taking root in front of the television. Whereas his wife has a circle of female friends whom she meets twice a week in the church hall Mr McBride doesn't have anyone to talk to or to confide in.

As a further complicating factor Mr McBride's car is playing up and will need major repairs or replacing soon. They both say that they cannot afford a new car or to spend a lot on the repair of their present one. Yet without the car they will be unable to go shopping or to make the odd trip to the town. Their children are adults who live quite a distance from them and only get to visit once a month at best and without a car the couple will not be able to go and see them.

The importance of loss as a significant factor in the onset of depression will probably be the first that you picked up. In this case it is a double hit as not only did Mr McBride lose his activity but also the only person with whom he appeared to have a close, confiding relationship.

The assessment of the situation the couple find themselves in is starting to take shape. You should now begin to see what factors are emerging as being of particular relevance.

Social work and suicide

Not all suicides are associated with mental disorder, although its presence increases the risk. It has been estimated that of the people who do commit suicide 90 per cent experience mental disorder of some type and of these about 30 per cent have expressed a clear intention to kill themselves while up to 25 per cent are psychiatric outpatients. This presents a real challenge to mental health practitioners. Colin Pritchard (1995) describes various ways of estimating suicide risk and uses the Lettieri scale for older men which pinpoints the following key factors:

- recent serious loss;

- depression;

- element of anger or aggression in their behaviour;

- refusal to accept help;

- previous suicidal or self-harming history;

- failure in a major role of their lives (Adapted from Pritchard, 1995.)

These represent what might be termed negative factors. This Lettieri scale is one of a number of measuring tools that assist in the prediction of suicide among the population. There are also several self-assessment scales that are in use. They vary in their clinical usefulness and the main use is to aid decision-making but not to replace it (see also Bürk, Kurz and Möller, 1985; Cochrane-Brink, Lofchy and Sakinofsky, 2000; Shea, 2002).

It is necessary to distinguish between risk of suicide in the short term and risk in the longer term. It has been estimated that about 2 per cent of those who had one attempt, will succeed within a year of the first attempt with a particular risk occurring in the first three months (see Butler and Pritchard, 1983). The difficulty that social workers and other clinicians have is assessing just who are the people who fall into this category. An additional approach is to work with the service user to help identify with them the positive factors or the *reasons for living*. This approach assumes that the service user will be able, with help, to identify reasons for their life and be able to put these alongside the more negative attributes. This helps you to work with the service user to identify their strengths or assets rather than only weaknesses or deficits. However, this approach must be used with caution in working with a person who is moderately to severely depressed. By definition, depression creates cognitive problems for the depressed person, such that he or she will be predisposed to look upon the negative side of any aspect of life. Therefore the person may not be able to identify any positives and you, the worker, might risk falling into the trap of suggesting reasons why life is worth living, reasons with which the person cannot identify at that time *because they are depressed*. However, this should not be confused with concerns about increasing the risk of suicide simply because you talk about it (see above) and professional judgement in situations like this is very important.

On the other hand, using this positive focus is entirely in keeping with the recovery agenda and the orientation in practice to focus upon a person's strengths rather than their weaknesses. This approach is in contrast to the more traditionally held view of practice in which the practitioner is the 'expert' in relation to how the service user should overcome their problems. This way of working almost automatically casts service users in a passive mode, much like patients in surgery where they have no option but to lie down and trust that the expert (the surgeon) knows what he or she is doing. Its central weaknesses are twofold:

1. It assumes that a third party (no matter how skilled and professional) can really be the expert on the contents of another person's mind when things go wrong in such a complicated way as they do in depression.

2. Even if it were possible to entirely *sort out* the person's depression and all the complicated life relationships which go with it, there is a risk that the depression will recur and the person will no more be able to deal with it the second time around than they were the first time. In other words, this approach encourages dependency upon services.

The focus on recovery implies an individual journey for each person who experiences mental illness. It may appear a little odd, locating the concept of recovery so early in the process where the service has just been alerted to Mr McBride's condition. However, working with a person on their journey to recovery implies a particular approach that ought to be established from the outset.

Comment

In Figure 6.1, 'doing to' implies the absolute expert/professional/passive patient model discussed above in relation to surgery. 'Doing with' implies a step away from this model, often called *enabling*, whereby the expert supports and imparts expertise to enable the service user to overcome his or her own difficulties. In 'journeys to recovery' a more challenging approach is required. It implies shared expertise, where someone like Mr McBride explores his own path to recovery with the support, facilitation, knowledge and expertise of the professional. While not for discussion in this chapter (indeed it ought to be the subject of another book), one of the greatest challenges is to explore what this might mean in the context of those situations where the person happens to be under compulsion under the terms of the 2003 Act: where a person represents such a risk to health, safety or welfare as to require receipt of care and treatment by compulsion of law, how can 'being alongside' be applied?

Doing to …

Doing with …

Being alongside …

Figure 6.1: A recovery orientation to working with people
Source: Scottish Recovery Network (2001g)

However, this is not to denigrate the value of your expertise in social work or that of your colleagues in other disciplines. For example, a doctor will have a crucial and central role to play if there is any underlying mental illness and modern anti-depressant medication is highly effective in treating depression. Therefore, while it is applied and works away at redressing the biochemical imbalance in the person's brain, you could be working in partnership with the individual to capitalise on strengths and attempt to overcome the cognitive manifestations of depression such as suicidal ideation. Having cautioned you about the risks of focusing on the positives too early on in the relationship when the person may be too depressed to identify them, here are some examples of generally held reasons for living:

- hope that life will change;

- love of family;

- being scared of the act of suicide;

- moral or religious objections about suicide;

- a view that suicide is a sign of weakness (adapted from Linehan, 1985, in Pritchard, 1995.)

Any attempted suicide or parasuicide takes place within a context (Agerbo, Sterne and Gunnell, 2007), and some of these have been broadly referred to above. However, a number of studies have drawn attention to a range of factors which appear to have some association with an increased risk of or causatory role in the act. These include such things as alcohol misuse (Brady, 2006), depression (Scogin and Shah, 2006); personality differences (Useda et al., 2007), attachment relationships (Bostik and Everall, 2007) and self-harm (Styer, 2006) with other research taking a broader perspective in attempting to identify indices of risk factors which could be of assistance in terms of assessing the likelihood of suicide and parasuicide (Borges et al., 2006).

Working with people who have attempted suicide

The most important contribution that you can make as a social worker is to manage to work alongside the service user and your health colleagues to provide a joint approach while retaining the essential and unique features of social work. A major concern when working with people who have attempted suicide is how, or perhaps even if, this event should be discussed.

It is also important to recognise the impact that the attempted suicide or parasuicide (Nock and Kessler, 2006) may have on the professional (Cutliffe et al., 2006; Ting et al., 2006). These considerations (or concerns) should be discussed within supervision and, if necessary, with colleagues. It is important that we do not simply assume that dealing with a situation where suicide has been attempted is 'just another day at the office'; it isn't. Suicide is a very emotive and, to many, a taboo area. It can cut across values and beliefs and leave people, professionals or otherwise, devastated. In some instances, practitioners may well feel a sense of responsibility for the actions of the individual and, where a death occurs, may in fact blame themselves for it.

There are a number of texts which look at the whole issue of suicide and these are worth exploring (Schneidman, 1996; Aldridge, 1998; Joiner, 2005; Pritchard, 2006; Kutcher and Chehil, 2007).

ACTIVITY 6.2

Write down what you would consider to be the reasons for living that would be relevant for you, then write down what you think Mr McBride might say and compare the two.

In our case the psychiatrist at the unit will have carried out an assessment on Mr McBride and this will have been discussed at the care planning meeting that will have taken place before discharge. The type of questions would include the following:

Questions about the incident itself:

- What was his intent?

- What is the relationship between his depression and this attempt?

- What is the risk at the present of a further attempt?

- What kind of help would he be willing to accept?

CASE STUDY *continued*

Mr McBride denies that this was a serious attempt. He has been suffering from mild to moderately severe depression for a number of months but also admitted that he has not been taking his medication regularly. No particular event led to the attempt but he describes it as a build up of events such as the death of his friend and the increased isolation that he feels. He is willing to work with the team to seek ways of improving his life. This would put him in the low risk category.

Questions about the degree of intent:

- Was the attempt planned or impulsive?

- Did he know that he would be found soon after the attempt?

- What drugs were taken? How much alcohol was taken? Were there other drugs that were around but not taken?

- Was a suicide note left?

CASE STUDY *continued*

Mr McBride's attempt at suicide was not thought through and it appears impulsive. He used his prescription medication as the means of trying to 'end it all' and chose a time when his wife was out but also not long before he knew that she was going to return. No arrangements for following his death, suicide notes or update of his will were evident. These put the likelihood of suicide in the low to moderate category.

Assessment of current problems.

- Relationship with family members.

- Financial status.

- Social networks, support and degree of isolation.

- General health.

- Use of alcohol or drugs.

CASE STUDY *continued*

Mr McBride's relationship with his wife has worsened over the last few years and he has no other person in whom to confide. He is struggling to get by financially and in particular is really anxious about living where they do and being without a car. His wife has a strong network of friends but most of his have either died or left the area. He does drink at home by himself from time to time and when he does it is often to excess. He is not very optimistic about the future. This puts him in the moderate risk category.

The above is adapted from a number of guides to assessment (Butler and Pritchard, 1983; Pritchard, 1995, 2006; Barry et al., 2000; Gamble and Brennan, 2000; Deb et al., 2001; Bentley, 2001; Langan and Lindow, 2004; Tolman, 2005; Scottish Executive, 2007f).

The use of such assessment tools should only be undertaken by someone who is skilled and experienced in their application. They are in common use and different clinicians favour different tools.

All research should be treated in a critical manner but also needs to be carefully considered and referred to by professionals. This is how professionals continually develop yet there is evidence that suggests that while medical practitioners may consult the research as a matter of course this is less so with other professionals such as social workers. However, the importance of taking an evidence-based approach to your practice is very current at the moment (Morago, 2006; Pritchard, 2006; Scottish Executive, 2007e, 2007f; Thyer and Wodarski, 2007).

ACTIVITY 6.3

Look back at the developing case of Mr McBride and jot down what you think are the risk factors for suicide. What role could Mrs McBride play in the situation?

Risk assessment

The evaluation of the above risk factors needs to be undertaken by a clinician and all those who form part of the multidisciplinary team who will consider their relevance and likely impact against the available research evidence. In the case of Mr McBride his behaviour appears to be more of a response to the present situation and a general sense of discontent with his social isolation and financial situation rather than total despair. Mrs McBride would seem to be a viable source of support but their relationship is difficult and more likely to be part of the problem than the solution. Mr McBride has only recently seen the doctor about his depression and at the time this was assessed as being mild. Since the initial emergency call out, Mr McBride appears to be less despairing and to have appreciated the opportunity to talk though his worries with someone who is outside the family.

RESEARCH SUMMARY

Effective approaches to risk assessment in social work: an international literature review by Monica Barry, University of Stirling, Scotland (Scottish Executive, 2007f).

This review was commissioned by the Scottish Executive following the publication of its review into social work, Changing Lives *(Scottish Executive, 2006a) in which it was identified that new and different approaches to risk assessment and its subsequent management were required.*

The main findings suggest the following.

- *There continues to be a culture of 'risk aversion' in operation.*

- *There is a tendency to minimise user involvement in decision-making around risk (see Langan and Lindow, 2004).*

- *The (increasingly complex) array of risk assessment tools is in danger of replacing rather than informing professional judgement.*

- *Different organisational cultures and different understandings of what constitutes risk may be acting as a barrier to the development of a common understanding of this phenomenon.*

Given that one of the main emphases within Changing Lives *was the promotion of professional autonomy within a clear framework of personal and professional accountability, these findings should be useful in developing a clearer picture concerning risk and its management.*

(Reports available at: www.scotland.gov.uk/Resource/Doc/194431/0052193.pdf (summary) or www.scotland.gov.uk/Resource/Doc/194419/0052192.pdf (full).)

Care in the community – expanding services to offer choice?

The terms 'care in the community' and 'community care' are often used as a kind of shorthand to refer to the range of legislation, policies and procedures concerned with the development, planning, organisation, funding, delivery and evaluation of services that relate to a number of different client groupings. Most of these services are those delivered within the community, including *domiciliary care* (i.e. within one's own home). This is one area where we see the effect of *UK*-wide legislation (in the form of the NHS and Community Care Act 1990) and *UK*-wide policy initiatives (in the form of the Joint Future Agenda; see www.scotland.gov.uk/Topics/Health/care/JointFuture/Links) as well as specific Scottish legislation and policy (see www.opsi.gov.uk/legislation/scotland/s-acts.htm).

It is particularly relevant for you to be aware that the terms of s 5A of the Social Work (Scotland) Act 1968 (as inserted by s 52 of the NHS and Community Care Act 1990 (UK)) and s 12A of the 1968 Act are important in this context. These relate to local authority plans for community care services (s 5A) and the local authority's *duty* to assess needs (s 12A).

Another point is that the interface between community care services and health services is very prominent. In fact, many of the services which social workers commission and/or co-ordinate in their role as care managers include significant aspects of health-related services. While social workers may co-ordinate and commission such services, they may in fact not *deliver* them. Therefore, when we speak about community care, we must remember that a large element of this is health related. Similarly, a huge amount of the care which goes on in people's own homes and within local communities is *social care* as opposed to *social work*. The social work and social care workforce in Scotland is estimated at 138,000 people, having grown by approximately 33 per cent over recent years and being predominantly female (82 per cent in 2004). Those who are employed in social services in Scotland work in the voluntary sector (25 per cent), the private sector (33 per cent) and in local authorities (42 per cent). Workforce planning, training and development is seen as a priority by the Scottish Executive (Scottish Executive, 2005m). There is also a huge amount of unpaid care which takes place, often by (predominantly female) relatives (Finch and Groves, 1980), and unpaid care is the source of political interest in Scotland (go to www.scotland.gov.uk/Resource/Doc/112273/0027313.pdf for information regarding unpaid care in Scotland).

The role of the social worker in relation to community care clients was redefined as that of 'care manager' in the wake of the 1990 Act and was seen as being pivotal to the achievement of community care objectives in the following ways:

- by encouraging more flexible and sensitive responses to the needs of users and carers;

- by allowing a greater range of options (not choices?);

- by emphasising *minimum intervention* in order to foster increased independence;

- to prevent deterioration;

- to concentrate on those individuals in greatest need.

For a Review of Care Management in Scotland (2002) go to www.scotland.gov.uk/cru/kd01/maroon/rcms-00.asp.

However, it is important to remember that whether you function in the role of a care manager or as a social worker actually delivering services, the core knowledge, skills and values still apply.

The mental health service as it is evolving within the context of community care has the idea of choice as a central and defining feature. By offering service users choice they can be better matched to appropriate services depending upon their need. That some centralised mental health services are unresponsive to service user need is generally accepted but in order to have choice there would need to be an excess of supply over demand which seriously impacts on service efficiency. Thus services continually come up against stark financial realities and it has proved difficult for services that are genuinely user-focused to be developed. To offer genuine choice means starting not with what current and existing services can be matched to what aspect of service user need, but what the service user needs *per se*. It is this which should drive the design and delivery of services. This, however, requires innovation on the part of service providers and the imagination of those charged with assessment and planning (Onyett, 1992; Beresford 2000; Beresford and Croft, 2004; Carpenter et al., 2004; Lester and Glasby, 2006; Tse Fong Leung, 2006). It also means considerable resources need to be poured into making community care a positive *choice* that will enhance the lives of vulnerable people, rather than simply an *option* (Myers and MacDonald, 1996).

However, the use of non-specialist mental health resources is a crucial link in the process of including service users in a partnership of working towards recovery: specialist services have their place. It is undeniable that Mr McBride needed hospital for a short period but there is a risk that if we rely on segregated mental health services too much, we increasingly buy into a mode of practice which makes the service user a passive recipient of expert help. The more one attends specialist mental health services, the harder it is to make the transition to non-specialist services (the sort of everyday services which people use who have no contact with mental health services).

Table 6.1: Relevant community care legislation

Major UK and Scottish community care-related legislation and policy	
Health Services Act 1946	*Modernising Community Care: An Action Plan* (Scottish Office, 1998)
National Assistance Act 1948	*Community Care: A Joint Future* (Scottish Executive, 2000)
Social Work (S) Act 1968	Adults with Incapacity (S) Act 2000
Chronically Sick and Disabled Persons Act 1970	Regulation of Care (S) Act 2001
Chronically Sick and Disabled Persons (S) Act 1972	Community Care and Health (S) Act 2002 (s 7)
National Health Service (S) Act 1978	Mental Health (Care and Treatment) (S) Act 2003
Disabled Persons (Services, Consolidation and Representation) Act 1986	*Mental Health (Care and Treatment) (S) Act 2003: Codes of Practice* (3 vols)
Caring for People: Community Care in the Next Decade and Beyond (DoH, 1989)	*Single Shared Assessment of Community Care Needs* (Scottish Executive, 2001)
NHS and Community Care Act 1990	*Supporting People* (2003)
Carers (Recognition and Services) Act 1995	National Health Service Reform (S) Act 2004
Community Care (Direct Payments) Act 1996	Community Care (Direct Payments) (Scotland) Amendment Regulations 2005 (SSI 114)
Disability Discrimination Act 1995	Adult Support and Protection (S) Act 2007
Sutherland Report (TSO, 1999)	
Care Standards Act 2000	

Remember also that the terms and conditions of the European Convention on Human Rights (1950) and the Human Rights Act 1998 apply.

There is an increasing array of relevant legislation and policy which relates to the delivery of care in the community which is listed in Table 6.1. The key statute relating to care in the community is the National Health Service and Community Care Act 1990 (UK). This Act has since been supplemented by the Carers (Recognition and Services) Act 1995, which introduced the right for carers to have an assessment of their needs made alongside the service user's assessment. The Community Care (Direct Payments) Act 1996, the Community Care and Health (Scotland) Act 2002 and the Community Care (Direct Payments) (Scotland) Amendment Regulations 2005 (SSI 114) have enabled local authorities to provide cash for service users to enable them to purchase the kind of services that they want. Whether this is a good thing or not depends upon individual circumstances. At one level, it can be a means by which service users can be empowered and take some control over their lives. On the other hand, purchasing services can become complex and involve the service user in all sorts of contractual-type relationships which at times can be more trouble than they are worth.

> **CASE STUDY** *continued*
>
> *Mr McBride has returned home and an assessment has been carried out to determine if he is eligible for community care services. It is quite clear that his wife, who cannot drive, is unable and unwilling to take responsibility for her husband's well-being. She is very frightened that he might do something silly to himself.*

Assessing and responding to need

Getting the right help at the right time for the right reasons depends first upon having a thorough assessment of need. Within Scotland, the Joint Future Policy (www.scotland.gov.uk/Topics/Health/care/JointFuture) has been driving the development of a *single shared assessment* process (www.scotland.gov.uk/Topics/Health/care/Joint Future/SSA) which aims to streamline the assessment process and avoid unnecessary duplication of intrusion and effort. In order for this to work effectively, different agencies and professionals have to share information effectively; minimum standards have been designed to assist in this process (www.scotland.gov.uk/Topics/Health/care/JointFuture/minimuminfostandards) and services to older people have piloted these arrangements which are being rolled out across all service user groups.

However, the availability of a single shared assessment format does not mean that all assessments will be the same or simply follow a 'tick-box' approach. Each assessment is in effect a personal narrative concerning another human being's circumstances, and as such it should contain relevant information, agreed with the service user, which *accurately, honestly* and *respectfully* reflects their situation. Its primary function is to identify need. The single shared assessment format is quite simply a tool to serve practitioners and service users; it is a means to an end and not an end in itself. With this in mind it may be the case that this particular format does not provide opportunities to obtain sufficient information, and many agencies have their own, additional assessment tools and formats which can be used to obtain a more comprehensive appreciation of the issues. Whichever tool is used, you must remember what the purpose of the assessment is.

Once an assessment is undertaken, it is then necessary for an analysis of the information to be undertaken, drawing on relevant skills, knowledge and underpinning theories to provide the basis for intelligent and informed service provision.

In real-life situations following assessment, information concerning need is often set against *eligibility criteria*. These levels are used by almost all service providers today as a means of *targeting* (increasingly) scarce resources. All too often assessment can appear to be a routinised administrative task because it is known that the (mainstream) services required are either not available or else are being rationed in some way. These realities are with us and we have to work with these as best we can. This is one clear reason why developing locally based, non-mainstream services can be so productive. Social work in the twenty-first century is complex, demanding and multifaceted with service provision being multi dimensional, multi agency and multiprofessional (see Chapter 8), and as the recent Scottish Review of Social Work pointed out, *social work services don't have all of the answers* (Scottish Executive, 2006a, p8). Therefore utilising the skills, enthusiasm and creativity of service users (ordinary people) to develop services that *they feel will be of use to them* is an exciting and at times inspirational prospect and one which all politicians and professionals, at all levels, should warmly embrace.

The criteria used to inform access to services may vary slightly from area to area but will include some of the following which represent the 'critical need' level:

- significant health problems have developed or will develop;

- inability to carry out vital personal care or domestic routines;

- social support systems and relationships cannot or will not be sustained;

- family and other social roles and responsibilities cannot or will not be undertaken;

- engagement with vital formal support systems is not being maintained;

- serious risk of harm to self or others exists;

- inability to access community facilities.

The extent to which Mr McBride meets the above criteria is largely dependent upon what the assessment reveals. At one extreme, it may be dependent upon how the *assessor* (you in this case) sees the situation. If we adopt the view that the worker is the *expert,* as some approaches to assessment do (Smale, Tuson and Statham, 2000), then it is likely that the services provided will be those currently available with some adaptation for local conditions. If, however, the process of assessment is seen as a *reciprocal* activity, then that increases the likelihood of services being created to suit the current circumstances, not only of Mr McBride, but of the local community as well. Given that Mr McBride lives in a fairly rural location where access to mainstream services is limited anyway, this could offer more of an incentive to be creative and to utilise the resources within the local community. For example, perhaps a self-help or support-type group could be set up which could meet fortnightly at the local community centre. This could provide opportunities for other professionals to attend to offer advice, support and other forms of service on a regular, if relatively infrequent basis. But even if the group were run infrequently, it still establishes a local service which involves local people in running it and its very existence may well determine its future development.

ACTIVITY 6.4

Re-read the case of Mr McBride so far and try to broadly assess how he 'fits' the criteria listed above. Take notes of your answers.

Comment

In the above activity it is likely that Mr McBride would meet most of the criteria to a greater or lesser extent. This is an important point because although the eligibility criteria *appear* to be quite explicit, there is still significant scope for interpretation. For example, what does 'significant' mean? The phrase 'cannot or will not ...' appears numerous times. How do we know? How does anyone know? Is the determination on the balance of probabilities or some other standard? Who determines the standard and how? These are examples of the sorts of issues professionals have to engage with on a regular basis.

In our example Mr McBride may just about meet the eligibility criteria, at least in the short term. But what happens then? Services will generally be provided to people who are unable to perform one or more basic tasks of daily living where:

- informal support (Mrs McBride) cannot be reasonably expected to provide them;

- service users (or their carers) are at significant risk without the provision of such services; or

- services are clearly aimed at increasing independence.

These services will be provided to:

- meet essential personal, social and educational needs;

- ensure that service users and/or carers are not left at significant risk;

- support carers to continue in their caring role;

- support people to continue living in the community through a programme of rehabilitation.

Alternatives to traditional hospital-based services

Acute and crisis services are designed to offer treatment that is less restrictive and less stigmatising than hospitalisation. The development of a range of options, although slow, is happening. Over a decade ago the then Scottish Office launched a partnership funding arrangement with local authorities whereby the government paid upwards of 65 per cent of the cost in order to encourage voluntary organisations to develop a more diverse and responsive range of services under the aegis of the *Specific Mental Health Grant*. This was designed to offset the shrinkage of mainstream services which occurred in the wake of the introduction of more community-based services under the rubric of care in the community (see above) and the current emphasis on a mixed economy of providers, along with the purchaser–provider split, does produce a degree of variety.

Crisis services have become the new policy initiatives as they offer the potential of arresting a difficult situation before it becomes a full-blown emergency and escalates into a hospital admission. A list of these might include:

- crisis intervention teams;

- 24-hour crisis centres that can include short-term residential facilities;

- safe houses that offer less intensive experiences than the crisis centres;

- home treatment services where a multidisciplinary team can support service users in their own homes;

- easier access to psychological or 'talking therapies' (Scottish Executive, 2007e);

- 24-hour telephone support;

- specialist services for people from black and minority ethnic communities.

What do service users want in a crisis?

Most of all what service users want is not to have any more psychiatric emergencies but if they do, they want a service that is responsive to their needs and provides a range of alternatives to hospital admission. Top of the service user list is a feeling of being in control of their crisis. This includes being involved in:

- crisis pre-planning;

- choice of treatments including complementary medicines;

- independent advocates; and

- access to quality information.

In this respect, we must remember that the principles of the 2003 Act endorse the central importance of listening to the present and past wishes of the person (s 1(3)) and obtaining the views of a range of significant others (s 1(4)), as well as having regard to any *advance statement* (s 275 and 276) the individual may have prepared.

They also want to have someone listen to them and to understand their explanation of what their crisis is about. Listening is an active process which social workers need to be skilled at, and they need to be prepared to spend time with them and not simply use the interview to detect signposts that assist with diagnosis (Golightley, 1985).

Some service users who have experienced a number of crises have developed their own checklist of what to do and what not to do when they are experiencing difficulty. This can include how to respond when they say that they do not want to take their medication when it is apparent that they are in distress. Another example is how to respond to them when they say that they are hearing voices. The point that they make is that putting such a list together is relatively easy when they are feeling well and upbeat but when they are distressed they recognise that they can lose their sense of what is best for them. These types of responses can easily be used to form the basis of an advance statement.

Intervention

The advent and underpinning ethos of current legislation was thought to provide the means for an innovative service, which starts from where the service user is rather than from what the available resources are. Thus the social worker or co-ordinator should use their imagination to examine the best way of meeting the needs that have been identified in the assessment.

The most likely successes will come from a treatment approach that embraces a combination of medication and psychosocial supports. Research would suggest that this combination works and is more effective than either psychosocial intervention or medication on its own. The psychosocial intervention could be a form of cognitive behaviour therapy, task-centred work or solution-focused work. This would be in addition to work with the more social aspects such as finances and isolation. With this in mind let us return to our case study and Mr McBride (see Figure 6.2).

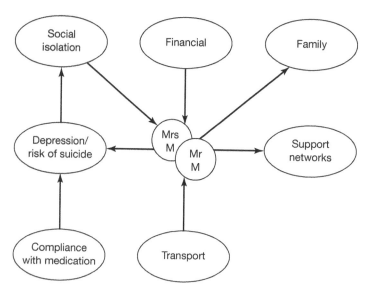

Figure 6.2: Visual note of the anaylsis of Mr McBride's psychosocial needs

On this schematic the main factors are noted. The diagram could be developed further by the use of dotted lines where some aspects are less critical than others or by redrawing connections and relationships as these change over time. It could also be added to by new factors as these develop. This gives a quick and easy picture of the challenges that are facing Mr McBride and his family at any given point in time.

Needs or wants?

One of the long running debates is the choice between what the service user may express as their *want* and what you and other professionals assess as their *need* (see Bradshaw, 1972). Preferences may be expressed for a course of psychoanalysis by a service user but the cost of this may be prohibitive and therefore seldom funded through the NHS. The allocation of scarce resources will always render some decisions difficult and make the realities of empowerment a challenge for social workers to meet. We have discussed some of these issues above.

Empowerment must remain one of the central aims of ethical social work practice along with the promotion of both equal and, we would argue, *equitable* opportunities and anti-oppressive and anti-discriminatory practice. To practise in such a principled manner is also to work in what was called in Chapter 1 a culturally sensitive way.

You may want to consider the idea of 'spiritual healing', which has been developed by John Swinton (2001) in his interesting book *Spirituality and mental health care*. Whatever your views might be about the place of spirituality, it is the case that for many users and carers it is a very important concept. Swinton puts forward a model of social care that includes a spiritual dimension:

> Care that takes seriously the spiritual dimensions of human beings requires an approach that draws carers into the deepest, most mysterious realms of human experience and allows them to function empathetically within a context that is often strange and alien. (Swinton, 2001, p136)

The question which he rightly poses is how this approach can be made accessible to people who have mental health problems. The answer, if indeed there is a single answer, starts with the focus being placed on the people themselves rather than on the implications of their diagnosis. This requires using a different approach and asking of the service user 'What gives the service user's life meaning, and what can be done to enhance their meaning and connectedness?'

Swinton suggests that such a basic refocusing enables the professional to see the situation as the service user sees it and to accept as valid the person's concerns rather than seeing the service user as a diagnostic entity. At its best this is a developed and deep communication with the service user.

Swinton takes this further by arguing that serious attempts to 'walk in the service user's shoes' means that we need to learn a whole new language and ideas. The term 'interpathy' has been coined to describe the entry into the world of the service user and the genuine way of attempting to understand what they are experiencing. This is more than empathy as it has the extra dimension of exploration of the service user's world.

Social workers have an important part to play in this process as one of the few professionals who can interact with the service user, their families and community. The skills that you have learned and are learning should put you in a good position to be able to help others as well as yourself to understand service users and, if you choose to work in this way, to help them to find spiritual meaning in their lives.

Providing for individual need

By now you should be able to see that the most effective intervention will be based upon an accurate and negotiated assessment of needs that has been agreed between the service user, their family (if and as appropriate) and the professionals involved. The actual provision of services will vary depending upon the individual's circumstances and the imagination of the professionals, and of course the assessment of eligibility.

Our plan would be:

- To provide individual work with Mr McBride. This could be in the form of cognitive therapy. The aim is to help him to increase his coping skills.

- To provide information for the family about the nature of depression and suicide.

- To ensure that he has information about his rights, including the right to complain.

- To help him consider using direct payments to provide transport to any of the facilities described below which, in a rural community, will be some distance away.

- To attend a stress reduction class.

- To explore any interests he might like to pursue as leisure activities.

- To encourage him to go the CAB to have a 'financial makeover' as there is a strong possibility that they are under-claiming benefits.

- To provide a short series of 'couple work' sessions to help them to look at their relationship and to respond to some of the anxieties and fears that Mrs McBride has which may be manifesting in her attitude towards her husband.

- To use the Scottish Association for Mental Health (SAMH) to identify social support networks and to put them in touch with the local user group, or maybe even assist them in developing one in their area at some point. Such organisations have a range of groups which cater for different ages and interests as well as a drop-in centre run by the members for the members. This will provide an easy route to helping Mr McBride develop a more expansive social network. *Maintaining* a network is much easier than starting one up from scratch.

- To arrange for a peer-support worker to meet with him and go with him to the shops and get a coffee. This can also be used to encourage him to take his medication. This could be an effective use of direct payments. One of the aims is for him to develop a positive relationship with someone in order that he feels that he always has someone he can call if he needs to. This of course recognises the loss of his close friend.

- To work to encourage and motivate him to want to get better and to continue to do so by continuing to take his medication. As this has been a problem for him in the past, this should be a priority action.

- To work with Mr McBride to help him to write in a diary on a daily basis how he is feeling and what challenges he has faced and how he feels he has coped with them. This will enable him to look back with his social worker and identify any patterns that might exist and find ways of dealing with them.

- To develop with him a contract as the basis for future work. This will specify mutual expectations as well as what he wants people to do if it is noticed that he is becoming withdrawn or talking about it all being too much. This could also include keeping a diary record of his drinking habits.

- To arrange that he visits the crisis centre and makes some contact with them. Now that he has a professional network, he can access services should the need arise and there is a 24-hour helpline. There is a short-stay residential facility at the centre, which can be accessed through a professional referral.

Monitoring and review

Like all plans, they should be regarded as 'work in progress' and subject to modification if and when the situation dictates. The best plans are those that all parties understand and of which they have shared ownership. Mr McBride at present is positive and wanting to develop his coping skills and to improve his relationship with his wife. The plan can facilitate this to happen but may need to be modified as people react differently to change. The Care Programme Approach (CPA) (Scottish Office, 1998b) is of course relevant here.

C H A P T E R   S U M M A R Y

In this chapter you have explored working with service users who need services from time to time. The emerging forms of community care, if used imaginatively and with adequate funding, should offer service users improved services. Effective assessment is crucial to this process and in this chapter the example of an older man who is depressed and potentially suicidal has been used to illustrate some of the key points that social workers must understand in order for them to play a central role in the provision of community-based services.

Imagination and innovation are probably not the first words most people would use to describe the process of assessment and planning, but they are essential attributes that need to be a part of the overall empowering approach. Situations like the case study are often complex and to work effectively you will need to understand not just your role but how that fits in with those of other professionals. You will find it difficult to be empowering of others when you are unsure of yourself.

FURTHER READING

Aldridge, D (1998) *Suicide: the tragedy of hopelessness*. London: Jessica Kingsley. A well-written book.

Pritchard, C (1995) *Suicide: the ultimate rejection*. Buckingham: Open University press. Contains much of relevance regarding the psychosocial aspects of working with suicide. Although published in 1995, it is still worth the effort.

Pritchard, C (2006) *Mental health social work: evidence-based practice*. Abingdon: Routledge.

Tew, J (ed) (2005) *Social perspectives in mental health: developing social models to understand and work with mental distress*.

Other sources can be found in the reference list.

WEBSITES

Useful organisations include:

Depression Alliance: **www.depressionalliance.org/**

Mental Health Foundation: **www.mentalhealth.org.uk**

MIND: **www.mind.org.uk/**

National Self-Harm Network: **www.nshn.co.uk/**

Scottish Association for Mental Health: **www.samh.org.uk**

Survivors Speak Out: **www.gude-informatom.org.uk**

Values into Action: **www.viauk.org**

Chapter 7

Working with vulnerable people: adults who are long-term service users

A C H I E V I N G   A   S O C I A L   W O R K   D E G R E E

This chapter will help you to begin to meet the following (Scottish) Standards in Social Work Education (SiSWE) (Scottish Executive, 2003a), available at www.scotland.gov.uk/library5/social/ffsw.pdf.

Key Role 1: Prepare for, and work with, individuals, families, carers, groups and communities to assess their needs and circumstances.

Learning Focus:

1.1 Preparing for social work contact and involvement.

1.2 Working with individuals, families, carers, groups and communities so they can make informed decisions.

1.3 Assessing needs and options in order to recommend a course of action.

Key Role 2: Plan, carry out, review and evaluate social work practice with individuals, families, carers, groups, communities and other professionals.

Learning Focus:

2.1 Identifying and responding to crisis situations.

2.2 Working with individuals, families, carers, groups and communities to achieve change, promote dignity, realise potential and improve life opportunities.

2.3 Producing, implementing and evaluating plans with individuals, families, carers, groups, communities and colleagues.

2.4 Developing networks to meet assessed needs and planned outcomes.

2.5 Working with groups to promote choice and independent living.

2.6 Tackling behaviour which presents a risk to individuals, families, carers, groups, communities and the wider public.

Key Role 3: Assess and manage risk to individuals, families, carers, groups, communities, self and colleagues.

Learning Focus:

3.1 Assessing and managing risks to individuals, families, carers, groups and communities.

3.2 Assessing and managing risk to self and colleagues.

Key Role 4: Demonstrate professional competence in social work practice.

Learning Focus:

4.1 Evaluating and using up-to-date knowledge of, and research into, social work practice.

4.2 Working within agreed standards of social work practice.

4.3 Understanding and managing complex ethical issues, dilemmas and conflicts.

4.4 Promoting best social work practice, adapting positively to change.

Key Role 5: Manage and be accountable, with supervision and support, for their own social work practice within their organisation.

Learning Focus:

5.1 Managing one's own work in an accountable way.

5.2 Taking responsibility for one's own continuing professional development.

5.3 Contributing to the management of resources and services.

5.4 Managing, presenting and sharing records and reports.

5.5 Preparing for, and taking part in, decision-making forums.

5.6 Working effectively with professionals within integrated, multi-disciplinary and other service settings.

Key Role 6: Support individuals to represent and manage their needs, views and circumstances.

Learning Focus:

6.1 Representing, in partnership with, and on behalf of, individuals, families, carers, groups and communities to help them achieve and maintain greater independence.

Introduction

But he would not go mad. He would shut his eyes; he would see no more. But they beckoned; the leaves were alive; the trees were alive. And the leaves were connected by millions of fibres with his own body ... (Virginia Woolf, Mrs Dalloway, 1925)

This chapter will help you understand the nature of social work in relation to supporting people who are long-term users of 'mental health' services. The example of social work with people who have a diagnosis of schizophrenia is used to illustrate various aspects that are important when engaging with long-term service users. This will help you to understand the role that social workers and other professionals play in the care, support and treatment of people with schizophrenia. Working with long-term users can be a very demanding task and brings to the fore issues about liberty, risk and the value that professionals from various disciplines bring to the management of mental disorder in partnership with the service user.

Social work is an applied subject and:

... is characterised by a distinctive focus on practice in complex social situations to promote and protect individual and collective well-being. At honours degree level the study of social work involves the integrated study of subject-specific knowledge, skills and values and the critical application of research knowledge from the social and human sciences (and closely related domains) to inform understanding and to underpin action, reflection and evaluation. (Subject benchmark statement)

Nowhere is this more relevant than in working with vulnerable people who have long-lasting forms of mental illness, such as schizophrenia. This chapter will bring together some of the learning that has taken place in previous chapters about values and ethics, legal processes and context and understanding about mental disorder and some of the forms of treatment. Unlike the first five chapters in this book the last three start from the world of practice to give you the opportunity of learning about work with specific mental illnesses.

Long-term users who experience schizophrenia

The initial contact

Throughout this chapter we will discuss the case of John, beginning with admission to hospital. As a social worker in a multidisciplinary 'mental health' team you have accepted a referral at a Monday morning meeting. There is a CareFirst report from the out-of-hours duty mental health officer following John's admission to hospital. It appears that he was persuaded to go into hospital on an informal basis following a difficult weekend during which his stepmother, who is his main carer, asserted that she could no longer cope with his shouting and threatening violent behaviour day and night. The available information tells you that John is a recently started mature student, in his early 30s. He has a long-standing diagnosis of schizophrenia and there was some police involvement at the point when he agreed to go into hospital voluntarily last week.

Diversity in Scotland

As first discussed in Chapter 1, effective social work practice is culturally sensitive and appropriate and examines personal, social and structural explanations for mental illness and issues relating to mental health. However, to practise well you need to know about the different impacts that mental illness has on people in relation to attributes of culture, disabilities such as deafness and learning disability and other attributes such as sexual orientation and gender. All the following discussion of practice assumes the principles of culturally sensitive practice which is sensitive to diversity.

Assessment: the first stage

The gathering of information is an essential part of preparing for effective intervention (see Parker and Bradley, 2006). This process will probably be familiar to you and diagrammatically looks like Figure 7.1.

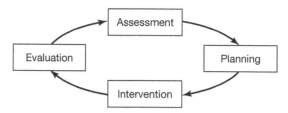

Figure 7.1: Effective intervention

Assessment consists of a number of possibilities. In this case it could include:

- gathering information from the service user's file, which helps to paint a picture of the sort of contact that has gone on and the specific circumstances in which it has occurred;

- meeting with the stakeholders including the service user, their named person and their family or carer;

- discussion with the other professionals who are involved with the service user.

With this in mind the case file shows that similar incidents have occurred three times over the last couple of years and John has been detained on two of those occasions. He is a mature student who has been in and out of employment and decided this year that he would start at university with a view to a career in the health and social care professions. John has had several social workers including a student social worker over this period and the file has some major gaps. Unfortunately the compilation of records can be treated as low priority by some social workers and it is at times like this that it becomes obvious that this means a certain degree of starting over again. However, when a CTO application is made, proposing detention in hospital or measures of compulsion in the community, there is a statutory requirement that a care plan should be completed by the MHO and this ought to involve those people significant in the care and social environment of the patient. During his last admission, 18 months ago, John was subject to detention under a CTO and such a report exists in the CTO application, offering valuable information including the views of his named person – his father – and his main carer – his stepmother. This will provide some of the full cycle of assessment, planning, intervention and evaluation of work up to the point that it was considered that John no longer required this level of intervention.

The picture that is emerging is of a young man who has few friends and continues to live with his father and stepmother. He has few outside interests and the file shows that the relationships at home are not very supportive. Past crises in John's *mental health* have been surrounded by moments of family stress and argument, when his stepmother has threatened to leave his father if his father did not do something about his heavy use of alcohol.

This stage is still about gathering information about John and trying to determine what the current episode means for him and his family. You have the opportunity to visit the family and, once you have got as much information as you are able to get, the next step is to determine what to do with the information.

In Chapter 4 we discussed risk assessment in the heightened context of services for mentally disordered offenders. While we acknowledged that the proportion of people affected by mental disorder who pose a serious risk to others is low, the information so far about John does raise issues about threatened violence. This has to be quantified in some way. What you find from the information you have available is the following.

- John has threatened his stepmother with violence in the past and he punched a hole in his bedroom wall last year, out of frustration with his voices.

- John has discontinued medication in the past, against medical advice.

- John occasionally drinks very heavily in order to cope with his mental confusion but he has never used any other drugs which might exacerbate his condition.

- As in the past, there have been arguments in the family home on this occasion and this has placed John under stress of late.

To place this in context, we do not need the formal structure of HCR20 (see Chapter 4). If you recall, HCR20 uses three focuses: Historical, Clinical and Risk Management factors (giving it the H, C and R of its acronym).

ACTIVITY **7.1**

While HCR20 is a risk assessment tool for use with seriously dangerous mentally disordered people, we can still draw from its basic structure here. Can you apply the H, C and R to the information about John, above? Take some notes of your response.

Comment

- **H** Did you list John's history of threatened violence, his history of drinking and the family history of marital stress? Note here that because *violence* is such an emotive issue, it is important to be precise as it will otherwise be open to misinterpretation. Nothing so far says that John is violent other than that he punched a hole in a wall. He has only *threatened violence*, and even then, it has only been directed at one person (none of which means that it ought not be taken seriously).

- **C** The most obvious factor to note is John's diagnosis of schizophrenia. Did you also note the relationships between his illness and family stress and his use of alcohol?

- **R** Did you note that John's discontinuation of medication is a factor which appears to have been poorly managed in the past?

If you put all of this together, John comes off his medication although clinical indicators suggest that, in conjunction with supports to enable the person to understand and manage their condition, long-term maintenance on medication can be the best way of managing schizophrenia. Then he becomes plagued by the auditory hallucinations (his voices) and he becomes frustrated and drinks to self-medicate. Then he is extremely vulnerable and the breaking point is the stress of family arguments, for which he blames his stepmother rather than his father. (We could read lots into this last point in terms of relationships within a reconstituted family.)

In the discussion of risk in Chapter 4, we were rightly preoccupied with public protection and the risk to others. However, were you to carefully re-read that discussion, you would see that we reiterated an important point. While the small minority of people affected by mental disorder present a risk to others, the overwhelming risk for this vulnerable group is the risk they pose to themselves, to which we ought to have added *and the risk that they are abused or exposed to neglect by others.*

ACTIVITY **7.2**

Review the information you have on John so far. What risks can you list that John might pose to himself and what are the risks of abuse or neglect from those who support him?

Comment

Were you able to note that there is a risk to John in that he is allowing his medical condition to deteriorate? Did you note that there are medical, relationship and psychological risks in drinking too much? Did you note that he risks losing home and family if his behaviour cannot be brought back into the realm where his stepmother can act as his main carer (assuming John agrees that remaining within the home is in his best long-term interests)?

The hospital visit

Shortly after the family has been interviewed, John is visited on the ward. An initial and brief conversation with the nurse in charge reveals that John is in quite a distressed state and is receiving anti-psychotic medications. He is hearing voices and can exhibit challenging behaviour from time to time. The initial diagnosis has been confirmed as paranoid schizophrenia. This is also an important time for you to discuss with the nurse your safety when meeting with John. Very much in line with our assessment that his threatening behaviour is directed at his stepmother, in this instance the on-ward risk assessment is that despite his level of distress, John presents very low risk while in hospital.

Understanding the impact of schizophrenia

In Chapter 1 we described some of the characteristics of schizophrenia. This is information that you would need to know prior to your meeting with John, to enable you to discuss the treatment and care plan as far as you can with him and in detail with the other professionals. The model that is used in this chapter suggests that even with disorders that have a physiological or genetic component to them, stress plays an important part. People with schizophrenia have a high sensitivity to stressful events which can trigger the onset of an episode of schizophrenia. Such instances of stress can be located in life events such as divorce or loss of someone close to them, but could also include the loss of work or other events outside of their personal or family domain.

One of the features of some forms of schizophrenia is the experience of auditory hallucinations, commonly known as 'hearing voices'. Some people who have schizophrenia also have feelings of thoughts being inserted into their minds or have visual hallucinations. It is also common to hold fixed beliefs which seem to have no bearing on any physical, social or cultural shared reality.

This latter point is an interesting and complicated issue. We all experience the world in different ways. Some of that difference is dictated by our cultural beliefs. It is always easier to see this difference in others, because our own beliefs are invisible to us. We simply pass them off as *this is how the world is*.

It is not important to our social functioning that we all see what we call reality in slightly different ways. What is important is that the gulf between my perception of reality and yours does not become too wide and that any gap can be explained by social or cultural factors or some other causes. For example, we all know that crossing the road is a dangerous and potentially fatal activity. However, we cross so many roads (especially if you live in a city) that we all become rather blasé about it. Now, supposing you meet an adult who is seriously terrified of crossing the road. This would represent a gulf in experience of reality. And yet the gulf might be bridged if you then heard that this person has just got out of hospital after being badly run over, or if this person had just arrived from their home in a rural country where there are very few cars.

Where the thought that crossing the road appears to become delusional is when it rests on a fixed belief which cannot be explained by such social, cultural or historical factors. Suppose this traffic-phobic person explained to you that drivers do not drive cars, but cars in fact *drive their drivers*. In other words, cars are independently-willed beings which control their drivers rather than the other way around. The idea is so strange and has so little logic to it that we cannot understand it. Neither can we understand how someone could believe it. If reasoned argument could not convince the person out of their belief, we would begin to say that he or she is suffering from a delusion.

Interestingly both hallucinations and delusions are usually culturally specific, with people in the West hearing voices and believing things from the familiar realms of the technology that surrounds modern life: from things like television, space or computers. People from less developed countries may report hearing voices that are more to do with religion or demonic possession.

Working with people who are hearing voices and experiencing delusions

Katie Glover (2000) has written a very practical guide for communicating with people who have problems in relation to mental illness and there are some other guides that will help you to understand the best way of working with people who experience delusions or hallucinations.

There are some very practical steps including:

- recognition that the service user is experiencing voices instead of ignoring them and trying to carry on as if nothing was happening: *Are you having difficulty following what I am saying? Are you hearing voices*?

- acknowledgement of the difficulty and distress that are caused by hearing voices: *It must be very hard for you to continue with this conversation, thank you for sticking with it* (Glover, 2000, p157).

If John has said that he is experiencing too much distress to speak to you, you need to acknowledge that you understand and then be prepared to wait for a while or to postpone your interview. What you should not do is be dismissive of John's voices. They are real for him and you are starting from where he is.

Experience of delusions can mean that the person is confused about who you are, who they are or often where they are. This can be disturbing for the family and disconcerting even for professionals. In John's case, the diagnosis of *paranoid schizophrenia* suggests the presence of *paranoid delusions*. Paranoid is a word used to indicate the experience of thoughts of *persecution*. By *persecution*, we mean that someone, some organisation or some thing is hostile towards the person. For example, in the troubled international climate of post–9/11, it is sadly common for people to hold paranoid delusions about the CIA or an Islamic terrorist organisation. That is not to deny that both such organisations do really persecute a large number of people. Just as with our crossing-the-road example, one would not be paranoid if one felt persecuted by the CIA while being held captive in Guantanamo Bay.

By and large the work that you would do with people who are experiencing delusions is simply a mixture of empathy and honesty. Consequently, faced with someone who says that they are a secret agent from MI5, you might suggest that, *while this experience must be very real and frustrating for you, now you are in this hospital and I want to work out with you how we can best help you.* This approach acknowledges the presence of the delusion but avoids collusion with it and tries to establish a foothold in reality.

Admission to hospital

John is in hospital on an informal basis. This means that he can discharge himself at any time, subject to potential use of the Mental Health (Care and Treatment) (Scotland) Act 2003 (Scottish Executive, 2003f). For example, in certain clearly defined circumstances, powers may be invoked to detain John on the ward under emergency or short-term orders (Chapter 2 covers this aspect). He is on an acute admission ward that specialises in the assessment of a patient's disorder. John is known to the services. Consequently the assessment will not be to determine if he has schizophrenia, but to try to stabilise his current situation to the point where John can return home or move into some other appropriate facility and a community treatment plan can be agreed between John, his carer and those responsible for his care and treatment.

Regardless of the powers discussed in Chapter 2, informal patients can refuse treatment in line with common law. This is strengthened by the principles of the 2003 Act, which stipulate that treatment must be given in the least restrictive way possible. This right to refuse can be overridden by use of compulsion if the patient is assessed as not having the capacity to make such decisions and if certain risks to welfare or health or safety are present. Questions around capacity or lack of capacity are ones that medical practitioners have to address, often consulting with other professionals and, most notably, the MHO.

John is reasonably content to take his medication which the RMO has prescribed and which includes anti-psychotic medication. This follows, you have learnt, a typical pattern for John. He will take his medication when in hospital and for a short while after discharge back to the community but he then stops his medication or becomes erratic in his self-administration. Changing this into a more reliable pattern becomes one of the goals for his maintenance in the community.

If John had been detained on a section of the 2003 Act, the mental health officer and the hospital managers would be obliged to ensure that John was given specific information as soon as practicable about his admission and other information including rights about treatment, detention, renewal and discharge and his rights to independent advocacy (s 37, 38, 45 and 46 of the 2003 Act) (see Chapter 2). This is required by law, but similar information should be made available to John as an informal patient.

Because he has experienced lengthy admissions in the past, life on the ward is a return to the familiar for John, but even so his experiences have not been overwhelmingly positive. This fits with evaluations of many service users who report concerns about:

- feelings of being unsafe on the ward;
- lack of meaningful activities to keep them occupied;

- insufficient information about their disorder and expectations of the ward staff;

- low levels of one-to-one interaction with the professional staff; and

- lack of involvement with planning their treatment and return to the community.

This has a bearing on the discussion in Chapter 1 about Individual Care Pathways in the Delivering for Mental Health Policy (Scottish Executive, 2006c). ICPs are documents which outline what any patient is entitled to expect at key stages throughout their stay in hospital. There is currently a draft ICP for patients with schizophrenia.

Many service users report the importance to them of one or two individuals with whom they made a significant relationship or the importance of the other service users who helped them to get through the difficulties that they were in. But others feel that they were largely ignored and saw their RMO insufficiently for it to be a major factor in their recovery.

Following the publication of *Rights, relationships and recovery: the National Review of Mental Health Nursing in Scotland* (Scottish Executive, 2006l) the nursing profession is rising to the challenge of addressing some of these issues.

Planning for successful intervention: working across agencies

The Care Programme Approach (CPA) has meant that the planning for John's discharge has already got underway and an initial plan has been developed in conjunction with John and using information from the family. This is put alongside the diagnosis, the previous notes and the views of the medical practitioner and the nursing team.

Working across agencies and between professionals from different disciplines has long presented a challenge for professionals who are trying to deliver a community-based service that is effective. The policy of CPA was introduced in Scotland in 1992 to make sure that people with serious mental illness and complex social care needs received co-ordinated care. Scottish Office Circular SWSG16/96 (Scottish Office, 1996) gave revised guidance to local authorities, health boards and Trusts on how they should implement the CPA. A further revision is currently underway of CPA for patients subject to restriction under criminal procedures (see Chapter 4). The CPA should be a system that ensures that service users are supported in the community and that this reduces the chances of them drifting out of contact with the services. The CPA should produce a holistic service that is co-ordinated and uses a key worker or care-coordinator system that takes the lead in all aspects of the involvement with the service user. One of the key aspects of this is an assumed common vision of how the service might work. In one study in the North of England, all the professionals thought that they had clear objectives and a commitment to involving service users. Central to this is the attitude of the workers who are involved and the few evaluations of this tend to show that among nurses, social workers and support workers there is a shared view and a desire to change practices to be more user-focused (Carpenter et al., 2003). Joint Futures is the name of the policy launched in 2000 to encourage health boards and their local authority partners to work closely together in providing comprehensive health and social care services. (visit www.scotland.gov.uk/Topics/Health/care/JointFuture).

The Deputy Minister for Health and Community Care in 2006, Lewis Macdonald suggested a step beyond this in the introduction to the Mental Health Delivery Plan when he wrote: *Service Users are central to their own care, treatment and recovery* (Scottish Executive, 2006c).

The recovery agenda (Chapters 1 and 6) suggests more than just partnerships of doctors, nurses, social workers, occupational therapists (OTs) and other professionals. It also suggests real partnerships with those who use the services: a new direction built upon the back of policies like CPA and Joint Futures. When teams come together this creates a common approach which is strengthened by the differing perspectives each discipline brings to the holistic view of care and treatment. However, it would be a mistake to think that there is no abrasion in bringing together social work, with its roots in eclectic social, legal and psychological knowledge and psychiatrists and nurses with their more medical orientation.

Historically, doctors have been at the centre of the process in which the patient is passive and the hospital the hub of care. A thoughtful reader of these pages may even note how difficult it is for us not to be pulled into this dynamic where 'the patient' is a passive pawn in the system. When this is put alongside research it shows, not surprisingly, the acquiescence of the service user to medical practitioners. Low (2004) writes that what has been missing is the concept of the active interest and involvement of lay people or, in our terms, service users. The effect of this was to create a hierarchy in which the service user remained at the bottom, the professionals, other than doctors, were in agreement with each other while doctors sat at the top. We emphasise that this is a *historical* perspective. If you are a careful and thoughtful reader you may also have noticed that this picture is entirely out of step with current policy with its focus on Recovery, ICPs and the law which both articulates the human rights of the service user through the principles of the 2003 Act and gives autonomous roles and duties to other professionals like MHOs.

Things never change overnight, and there is more than a 100-year-old tradition of the dominance of the psychiatrist in this field, but with Joint Futures and modern law and policy, the few backward-looking professionals increasingly seem like dinosaurs when they fail to embrace their partnership with each other and the service users for whom they work.

We trust that we have represented the complexity of mental disorder to you in such a way that you can understand that it has both social and medical causal factors and that the mixed solution of care, treatment and involvement of the service user at the heart of management of the condition is the way forward. In this picture it would be foolish indeed to say that the medical is more important than the social, or vice versa. As you read further in this chapter, you will come across specific psychosocial interventions which underpin this.

Service users on top

It is increasingly the recognition that service users needed to be at the centre of reforms that led the government to embark on a comprehensive listening process to enable the service user voice to be heard. The national 'mental health' service users' organisation VOX, 'Voices of Experience' was set up *to make our voices heard, to assist people in speaking out and to maximise the impact of our message while seeking recovery and taking our role in society as active citizens* (www.Voxscotland.org.uk). It works closely with other national movements which support 'mental health' service users, such as the

Scottish Association for Mental Health (SAMH) and local organisations like the Highland Users Group (HUG), to give weight to individual voices and raise a collective voice that is difficult to ignore or marginalise.

As far as John is concerned you are lucky to be working for one of the newly formed Community Mental Health Teams, a multidisciplinary venture run under Joint Futures by a partnership of the local authority and health board, with a shared management structure. It is in this context that you are trying to plan with John a course of treatment and care that will help him to stabilise while in the hospital and eventually to make the important move into the community.

Even after recovery from an acute phase, most people leaving hospital struggle to reintegrate into the community. In John's case, there were few community links prior to hospitalisation so the task of reintegration is even more difficult. Where home life is difficult the importance of work and outside activities increases and part of your task may be to identify what is available in the community. This could include sheltered workshops, day centres, hostel or user groups. A good supportive environment is often to be found at voluntary organisations like the Scottish Association of Mental Health (known as SAMH – the Scottish version of the English charity MIND) or other active 'mental health' groups.

The 2003 Act places duties on local authorities to provide, or *secure provision of*, a wide range of services from care and support services to services to promote well-being and social development for people suffering from mental disorder (s 25 and 26). The term 'secure provision' above means that the local authority need not provide these services itself, as long as it funds other organisations to do so for it. Therefore, a range of local voluntary service provision has been encouraged in all areas of Scotland for people like John.

Early intervention

The frequent contact with services interspersed with periods of low or no contact is sometimes also referred to as the *revolving door* and presents a challenge to services. These patterns seem to be entrenched in John's case, which is unfortunate as research suggests that a key determinant in a person's career as a 'mental health' patient is the speedy and effective response to the initial episode (Frangou and Bryne, 2000).

First episodes of schizophrenia happen typically in the late teenage years or early twenties and probably like John the behaviour can go undetected for several months or even longer. This is largely because of the contextual factors that include:

- erratic behaviour that is also a characteristic of late teenage years;
- the known use of recreational drugs like cannabis which confuse the symptoms of psychosis;
- the first signs may be negative ones such as withdrawal, social isolation and emotional flattening, none of which on their own may cause significant concern; and
- people who hear voices are often reluctant to tell people of this partly because they feel that people will think of them as being mad!

Trigger events

The models used in Chapter 1 help to conceptualise the onset and some of the factors that can result in mental illness such as schizophrenia. Whether the occurrence of an episode is as a result of some event which effectively triggers this or whether it is inside the person is unclear. However, the likelihood is that it is as a result of key events that produce considerable stress for the user.

Trigger events could be the result of some unresolved issue for John which has left him conflicted; this might be something hugely significant like emotional or other abuse while growing up. It could also be as a result of a stressful event that he has been unable to resolve – this could be starting at university and not being able to make social contacts, exacerbated by living at home. It might also be a combination of these.

Although the lifetime prevalence of schizophrenia is about 1 per cent, the impact of schizophrenia brings with it huge social and personal costs. People who are diagnosed with this severe disorder often have difficulty in engaging with others. They experience high levels of discrimination (which can be very confusing on top of paranoid delusions of persecution) and it is easy to become excluded and isolated. The impact of the disability can be understood in the same way that Oliver (1996) writes about the social model of disability. The disorder itself can have a significant impact upon the person and their family but this is magnified by the association in the public's mind with dangerousness and the difficulties that the public has in dealing with unusual and unpredictable behaviour.

Consequently it really is in everyone's interest that early recognition and an appropriate response are made. The use of medication in the first episode is reported as being more likely to succeed because, in the initial phase, the user may be more responsive to treatment (Frangou and Bryne, 2000). This can take the edge off the psychotic symptoms and be an effective maintenance tool but on its own is probably insufficient.

The prognosis for people diagnosed with schizophrenia is that about 80 per cent will recover but over 70 per cent will have a second episode within a five- to seven-year period (Frangou and Bryne, 2000). This suggests that treatment should be considered longer term than the initial episode and that long-term maintenance courses of anti-psychotic medication may be advised. However, the most likely successful recovery or maintenance is to be found when the medication is a part of the overall treatment plan and a more holistic approach is used. This fits in with the model that was covered in Chapter 1 that brought together the different components that may impact on and lead to a mental illness such as schizophrenia.

Although the dominant paradigm is medical the evidence that supports the primacy of an unidirectional approach is hard to find. As a social worker you need to assert you own views and be proactive in bringing a social perspective to the discussion. Using a more holistic assessment approach has many advantages. For example, it brings understanding to the question of why more Afro-Caribbean young men are diagnosed with schizophrenia than their equivalent white male counterparts. It also helps you to understand the role that families can play in the onset of florid episodes of schizophrenia and, more positively, in care and treatment.

Intervention

It is generally considered that family circumstances are important determinants of future success or relapse with people who have schizophrenia. The research shows that relapse is more likely for users who have a diagnosis of schizophrenia if, after a period of hospitalisation, they return to a family that is overly critical or is emotionally over-involved and controlling (Brown, in Butler and Pritchard, 1983, p90). This results in the development of a concept called expressed emotion (EE) and the rather surprising finding that users may fare better in the community if they do not return to their families.

More recently Pharoah, Mari and Steiner (2000) conducted an evaluation of the effectiveness of family interventions for people with schizophrenia in line with the drive towards increasing the evidence base for a variety of interventions. This evaluation took Brown's work as the starting point and has produced strong evidence that confirmed their work. Even so the use of this approach in a practice setting is limited and it has by and large been left to one or two researchers to 'promote' it. The work of Leff, Kuipers and Lam (2002) is an example of this approach being slowly spread to other practitioners (nurses and social workers) through the Thorn Initiative.[1]

Expressed emotion is a clinical concept and the presence of high expressed emotion has a high predictive value. EE is actually a research technique and measures things like critical comments, hostility and over-involvement that in turn produce emotions of various strengths. Experiencing high EE can cause considerable stress for some people and, it seems, especially for people with schizophrenia. Work with families involves trying to get families to move from expressing the negative side of emotions to developing techniques and mechanisms that demonstrate the positive aspect of emotions.

Measuring expressed emotion can be carried out using a standardised assessment schedule such as the Camberwell Family Interview (CFI) that was developed in the 1960s. This is usually completed by the user's family and because the user has been admitted to hospital the completion of the schedule occurs soon thereafter. Interviews are usually taped and then subjected to analysis or scoring over three dimensions:

- criticism – which is measured by scoring the number of overtly critical and specific comments that have been made;

- hostility – which is scored when there is rejection of the patient as a person or a combination of general criticism and rejection;

- over-involvement – which includes exaggerated emotional responses, usually self-sacrifice and overly devoted behaviour, over-protection that is inappropriate to the patient's age and difficulties in maintaining boundaries.

We will now review some of the information that you already have about John, in order to allow you to engage with it in case study format.

This requires practice and training as the tone and content of the interview are also taken as measures of the expressed emotion.

The model of intervention as expressed by Leff et al. (2002) is underpinned by a view that can be summarised as follows.

- Schizophrenia has a biological basis but people who are diagnosed are particularly sensitive to stressful events which makes them vulnerable to relapse.

- Family members need to join in with therapeutic work as they are both affected by the arrival of schizophrenia and may have contributed unwittingly to the relapse and possible onset.

- Honesty, openness and clear communication are important in order to share information about the nature of the disorder and to recognise the limitations of this knowledge.

- Families have positive as well as negative features and it is important to build on the strengths.

- This form of work needs to be carried out together with other forms of intervention and supervision.

As you can see, this is, in reality, a psychosocial education form of intervention in which your role as a social worker is to take the part of educator with the family. While social workers need to be aware of the medical side of mental illness it is important that they retain their own skill base and capacity to work in an empowering way. Do you remember how in Chapter 1 we carefully separated out mental health from mental illness, and as a consequence, were able to say that it is possible to improve the mental health of someone who is mentally ill? This approach is empowering as the family is encouraged to learn more about schizophrenia and to work with the therapists to determine their own solutions to the problems as they see them. As such, it is targeted on improving self-esteem through gaining a sense of control and achievement; it is a socially inclusive approach in that it develops skills and participation in partnership and it may undermine some of the more stigmatising aspects of mental illness by being factual and by encouraging the view that schizophrenia is a condition much like less stigmatised illnesses such as asthma. There are great similarities.

- They are both conditions which have biochemical bases but can be greatly improved with careful self-management.

- They are both conditions which are potentially life-long but only manifest their symptoms under certain circumstances.

- They are both conditions which respond to medical treatment but effective management requires a mixture of social, personal, interpersonal and psychological factors.

Therefore it is an approach which may improve poor mental health generated by the social consequences of the illness.

Evidence is being gathered from other countries which shows similar results to those achieved in the UK. Kalfi and Torabi (1996) carried out a study in Iran that included a cross-cultural comparison. This revealed that expressed emotion is an important factor in predicting relapse among users who have schizophrenia who lived in Iran. In a similar vein studies about the impact of high EE in families that contain a user with bipolar or unipolar affective disorders also look promising.

While to become fully competent in this type of intervention does require additional training the general principles of these approaches can be usefully applied to many situations. As a social worker you could be the champion of an approach that is empowering of the service user while retaining the treatment ethos of a unidirectional approach. This approach encapsulates social factors such as unemployment, substance misuse, poor social networks and high expressed emotions and puts them alongside the diagnosis of mental illness as equal partners rather than as subsidiary parts (Tew, 2002).

Working with John and his parents in a holistic manner puts them centre stage and offers them the opportunity to learn about schizophrenia and to understand the effect that their communication patterns may have upon John. In some cases it may be advisable for John to leave his parents' home and to live in other accommodation and 'manage' his relationship with his parents in this way. This enables him to escape the 'trapping' patterns of communication while not placing the blame for his disorder on the parents. After all, it is very unlikely that parents consciously choose to relate to their children in ways that create problems.

Caring for the carers

Carers of people with long-term mental illness may find the process challenging and debilitating. Informal and unpaid carers are slowly becoming recognised as a mainstay of support for 'mental health' service users. The policy of CPA directs professionals to bring carers as well as the service user into the planning process for meeting the needs of the user. Carers are now entitled to independent assessment of their own needs to enable them to continue in the supporting role (Carers (Recognition and Services) Act 1995) and, were John subject to compulsion under the 2003 Act, his main carer would have specific rights in the process.

The plan

Your work with John will be informed by your own understanding of the challenges that he faces and your assessment of the trigger events. This nearly always means achieving a balance between what the service user wants, what you and other professionals think that the service user needs and the reality of what is actually available. The process should begin early and have the service user at the front of the deliberations about treatment options. The CPA assumes that the care plan will be drawn tighter with the active involvement of the service user and that they will have agreed and signed the action plan.

Your three plans would of course be drawn up following discussion with other professionals, John and his family. They might include (but not be limited to) the following.

Plan one

Do nothing and let John leave hospital and return home taking anti-psychotic medication. Everyone involved has your telephone number and if the situation worsens they can contact you. The justification for this is that it's the least invasive plan and of course uses the least direct resources. This assumes that you have all decided that John is not a risk to either himself or to others.

Plan two

John returns home taking anti-psychotic medication, and with the offer of family work to reduce the level of expressed emotion in the family and with your support he will eventually return to university.

Plan three

John moves to supported living accommodation in town, his family are offered a number of sessions to help them to understand how they can change some of their behaviours to help his recovery, he starts going to the local SAMH drop-in support centre and takes part in a support group run by service users for people hearing voices. The local Community Mental Health Team offers him a package of comprehensive services including monitoring his medication.

Several themes should be evident in this chapter, not least of which is working in partnership with service users. Because of the debilitating nature of schizophrenia and the low level of public knowledge about the condition you will have to move at a slow pace and act as both therapist and psychosocial educator. The use of a holistic assessment and psychosocial methods of working is likely to be the most effective social work intervention with people who have long-term schizophrenia (like John).

As a social worker you have a crucial role to play in holistic assessment and in order to fulfil this role you need to be a professionally competent worker who has sufficient knowledge to be able to hold your own with medical practitioners without unnecessary acquiescence to them. Your work should be characterised by empowerment and a high level of specific knowledge about the resources that you have available in your area and about what works.

RESEARCH SUMMARY

Priebe and Slade's (2002) book Evidence in mental health care *has some very useful chapters about what works and with whom. See the chapter on the user perspective about what counts as evidence.*

For help and advice about benefits consult The big book of benefits and mental health *from Neath Mind, 32 Victoria Gardens, Neath SA11 3BH. A ten-page proforma is available online from www.rightsnet.orguk/pdfs/AA.*

Subject benchmark statements are best accessed through the Quality Assurance Agency (QAA) website: www.QAA.ac.uk, and then into subject benchmarks.

See also Joseph Rowntree Foundation, York: www.jrf.org.uk.

> ### CASE STUDY
>
> *As stated at the beginning of this chapter, John is a mature student at university who lives with his father and his stepmother in an inner city area. He was admitted to the local psychiatric hospital on Saturday evening following an incident in which the police were involved. The events surrounding the admission are unclear, but it seems that John's stepmother had called the social services duty team when his behaviour became extreme and she felt threatened.*

> ### ACTIVITY 7.3
>
> *No mention has been made of whether John was from a minority ethnic group. What assumptions, if any, did you make about this? What difference would it make if John were Afro-Caribbean? Can you recall the impact of mental illness in the black and minority ethnic communities?*

Comment

Did you perceive that John may have experienced racism in the past and may, in his confused state, misunderstand the police intervention as some form of racial harassment? Did you remember the importance of culturally sensitive practice? For example, were we to replace *Afro-Caribbean* with *Islamic*, there might be gender issues with him relating to a female worker.

There is also the need to understand how mental disorder is differently understood and how it manifests itself differently in different cultures.

> ### CASE STUDY continued
>
> *John's mother and stepfather felt that John needed 'sorting out' and that the services repeatedly let them down. They said that he was a danger to others when 'ill' and yet no one seemed to be interested in their view.*
>
> The next steps taken were to read John's file and to begin to refine an understanding of what had happened. The files make interesting reading and tell the story of a person who has been diagnosed as having paranoid schizophrenia and has been drifting in and out of contact with the services over the last five or so years. As a strong man he can present a rather threatening manner to people who annoy him and there is documented evidence of his articulated threats to his stepmother.
>
> The visit to the home is quite illuminating as both John's father and his stepmother initially present themselves as well educated, caring people. However, as the interview progresses, it becomes clear that while they may be caring, they are very critical of John and his social attitude and general behaviour. His father regards it as a failure that John is unable to live up to his brother's example. He went to St Andrews University, lives and works in Edinburgh and is a bright person with a lot of friends. When his father divorced and remarried, John's stepmother thought that John had not got used to the idea of being in a new family and sometimes she felt his behaviour was intended simply to wreck her relationship with his father. All of this is complicated by John's stepmother's view that his father drinks too much and the fact that it is clearly a source of tension between them.

Comment

Understanding what the arrival of schizophrenia must mean to people is crucial for you as a social worker. We talk about walking in the other person's shoes and you should find whatever source you can in order to do this. Given the high prevalence of both seriously poor mental health in Scotland and rates of mental illness, it is likely that either you yourself, one of your friends or of a member of your family has first-hand experience to draw on. It may well be that, on your course, there is input from service users who have had experiences of mental illness. However, the most useful resource available in Scotland is the 'Narratives and Research' page of the Recovery Network at www.scottishrecovery.net.

The narratives web page is a place where people can post their own stories and experiences of recovery from mental illness. It contains a wide range of interesting and sometimes very moving accounts.

Understanding visual hallucinations is a feature of the movie *A Beautiful Mind* that shows the life of the brilliant professor John Nash who works at an Ivy League University in the USA and has been a lifetime sufferer from schizophrenia that includes visual hallucinations. If possible try to see this film.

CASE STUDY continued

During your first interview with John he begins to act rather distanced and when you check with him he tells you that he is hearing voices. This poses a real challenge because you have never come across this before and you are not sure what to do.

On subsequent visits John has responded well to treatment and after ten days is already being considered for the next step of returning to the community. You begin to feel that you are developing a relationship with John. You have also made more visits to the family and begin to understand that there are anxieties that John is a danger to others as a result of the way in which he openly expresses his frustrations through aggression in the home.

ACTIVITY 7.4

Think about the realities of working together in one multidisciplinary team and the rather out-of-date notion that service users and workers might be in acquiescence to medical practitioners. What benefits would your perspective on John's difficulties bring to a multidisciplinary discussion? How might the medical perspective enhance your understanding of John's situation?

Comment

Multidisciplinary practice ought to enhance an all-round, holistic view of how service-users may be helped. In this melting pot of views were you able to ascertain that you now have a clear picture of dynamics in the family and how they act as triggers to John's bouts of illness? Were you able to see that, in reviewing the various plans for John's care as outlined above, your specific social knowledge will assist in evaluating the pros and cons of a return home versus a move to supported accommodation?

Did you note that someone with medical training is able to identify and prescribe the appropriate drugs in their appropriate amounts to help overcome John's florid symptoms? Furthermore, a good knowledge of effects and side effects of prescribed drugs may inform why it is that John so readily comes off his medication. It may be that he has been on drugs that needlessly give him adverse and uncomfortable side effects and that there are better ones available.

ACTIVITY **7.5**

Imagine that John lived in your area. Try to find out what resources would be available for him.

Comment

The exercise of trying to find out what resources are available can be very telling in itself. More and more service users use the internet these days. If you undertook this task through your computer, how easy was it? Your experience is bound to mirror the attempts by local service users, their friends, families and informal carers. If you had less success, here are some pointers. If you have a local SAMH or other 'mental health' charity resource, they usually have a list of all the resources that are in your area and sometimes Community Mental Health Teams have similar information. Most areas of Scotland have an umbrella charity network like Aberdeen Council of Voluntary Organisations (ACVO) or the Edinburgh Voluntary Organisations Council (EVOC). These keep a directory of local organisations.

Identifying service-based resources is just one part of the solution. As we have indicated above, John himself, with all his wealth of experience of mental illness, is a resource. To tap this experience, you may need to help him to see it as a resource and therefore you may need to help him to redefine and structure it.

ACTIVITY **7.6**

Take a moment to speculate upon what might be the triggers that precipitate John's illness.

Comment

As with all chronic conditions, schizophrenia requires management not just by doctors at the level of medical intervention, but by the person him or herself. Just as a person with asthma ought to take responsibility for their condition and not smoke or sit in smoky environments, so someone like John should be encouraged to explore positive management of his illness. Therefore it is vital that not just you, the worker, but also John, the service user, recognise the triggers.

We have already mentioned many of them at various points in the discussion above. Did you make a link between the work of Leff and others on high expressed emotions above and John's recent situation? You would need to talk to John in great detail to understand (and help him to understand) how EE affects his life. Other triggers may be boredom and lack of structure to his day, poor social contacts and lack of purpose. For these reasons, local supports and resources are literally a lifeline.

On the other hand, it now sounds as if John's father is over-ambitious for him and that this may place him under stress. Just as too little stimulation is stressful, so is too much!

ACTIVITY 7.7

As a final exercise in this chapter, take a few minutes to get an idea of how your local statutory services are organised for mental health care. Make some inquiries, if you do not already know, about local Community Mental Health Teams in the area in which you live. They should be traceable through your local authority social work services. Get their information for service users which should help you to understand more about this specialised multidisciplinary service.

With the information from Activities 7.4 to 7.7, you should have enough basic knowledge to begin to formulate a plan which, in reality, you would be drawing up with John and others involved in his care. The plan for John could take on a number of different shapes depending on resources and his preferences (for example, should he wish to return home or move into supported accommodation). At this point with the little information that you have, you might wish to round off this chapter by making some notes of possible plans. This would be useful as it is an activity which begins to trace the care planning exercise used by practitioners.

CHAPTER SUMMARY

This chapter has focused upon practice with people who have long-term mental illness. In particular it has tracked one case study of a man with schizophrenia through a hospital admission and your role with him as his social worker. By reading this you should now be aware of the following:

- the process of assessment, including consideration of risk;

- the process of planning beyond hospital admission;

- greater awareness of schizophrenia and its impact upon individuals and families;

- specifically, the concept of high expressed emotion in relation to triggers of illness;

- the value of multidisciplinary working;

- the value of involving service users in the maintenance of their own health.

Note

1   The Thorn Initiative is an extensive course in psycho-education approaches pioneered by the Maudsley NHS Trust and the University of Manchester.

Chapter 8

Working across organisational and professional boundaries

A C H I E V I N G   A   S O C I A L   W O R K   D E G R E E

This chapter will help you to begin to meet the following (Scottish) Standards in Social Work Education (SiSWE) (Scottish Executive, 2003a), available at www.scotland.gov.uk/library5/social/ffsw.pdf.

Key Role 1: Prepare for, and work with, individuals, families, carers, groups and communities to assess their needs and circumstances.

Learning Focus:

1.1 Preparing for social work contact and involvement.

1.2 Working with individuals, families, carers, groups and communities so they can make informed decisions.

1.3 Assessing needs and options in order to recommend a course of action.

Key Role 2: Plan, carry out, review and evaluate social work practice with individuals, families, carers, groups, communities and other professionals.

Learning Focus:

2.2 Working with individuals, families, carers, groups and communities to achieve change, promote dignity, realise potential and improve life opportunities.

2.3 Producing, implementing and evaluating plans with individuals, families, carers, groups, communities and colleagues.

2.4 Developing networks to meet assessed needs and planned outcomes.

Key Role 4: Demonstrate professional competence in social work practice.

Learning Focus:

4.1 Evaluating and using up-to-date knowledge of, and research into, social work practice.

4.2 Working within agreed standards of social work practice.

4.3 Understanding and managing complex ethical issues, dilemmas and conflicts.

4.4 Promoting best social work practice, adapting positively to change.

Key Role 5: Manage and be accountable, with supervision and support, for their own social work practice within their organisation.

Learning Focus:

5.1 Managing one's own work in an accountable way.

5.2 Taking responsibility for one's own continuing professional development.

5.3 Contributing to the management of resources and services.

5.4 Managing, presenting and sharing records and reports.

5.5 Preparing for, and taking part in, decision-making forums.

5.6 Working effectively with professionals within integrated, multidisciplinary and other service settings.

Key Role 6: Support individuals to represent and manage their needs, views and circumstances.
Learning Focus:
6.1 Representing, in partnership with, and on behalf of, individuals, families, carers, groups and
    communities to help them achieve and maintain greater independence.

Introduction

This chapter looks at the whole issue of working together with other professionals, agencies and organisations in the pursuit of ethically sound and effective practice with and for people with mental health problems and their families. Social work with this and any other group is a very complex task and it is just not possible nowadays for one professional, or indeed one agency or organisation, to meet all aspects of need. This is because notions of need (Bradshaw, 1972) and societal expectations as to what it is that service delivery agents should provide have become much more sophisticated. In part, this reflects the developments that have taken place in terms of societal attitudes towards mental health and illness; the closure of long-stay institutions (Wolfenberger, 1972) and the development of community care practices have signalled a shift in mental health policy and these have evolved into the arrangements we now have.

In this chapter we look at some of the underpinning themes and issues central to any consideration of collaboration and partnership working before going on to look at some specific issues regarding the importance of effective collaboration in terms of mental health and mental illness.

Working together

Within all areas of social work there is an acknowledgement that working together with other professionals is the right way to deliver services. Within the area of mental health social work, policy documents are predicated upon the need for inter-professional collaboration (Scottish Executive, 2001b, 2002a, 2002b, 2003b, 2003c, 2003d, 2003e, 2004b, 2005g, 2005i, 2006c). However, although policy statements and legislation make the case for collaboration and in some instances insist that this occurs, in our view collaboration with others is the *only effective way to do the job properly*. Do not develop the mindset which thinks that we collaborate because we are told to. Think it through – reflect upon any of the situations you are involved in and ask how things would work if you were to do it on your own. You couldn't. We will look at collaboration now and consider what it means (see Quinney, 2006).

What is collaboration all about anyway?

What does collaboration mean? Dictionary definitions talk about working jointly, co-operation, the joining of forces, working as a team, liaison, even collusion, conniving and behaving conspiratorially. We use the word here to include the notion of a partnership between people, agencies and organisations who are working towards a shared goal, however broadly defined, which involves the sharing of a range of resources in order to achieve a desired outcome. Whittington (2003) is emphatic in his view that partnerships need to exist in order that the objectives of care services can be met. Pollard, Sellman and Senior (2005) talk of *inter-professional working to mean collaborative practice: that is, the process whereby members of different professions and/or agencies work together to provide integrated health and/or social care for the benefit of service users* (p10). In this regard, we would say that it is just not possible to provide an effective service for people with mental health problems *without* collaborating with a range of other people, including the person themselves and their family. In this way we can aim to develop empowering practice which Payne (2005) reminds us is about helping people *to gain power of decision and action over their lives* (p295). In the area of mental health practice, this is very important but it needs to be done thoughtfully; for example, empowerment does not necessarily mean always agreeing with what the service user feels they want or need. There will be times when professional views will be in opposition to what the service user wants and you may have to 'enforce' certain courses of action through the use of compulsory powers. This may look like anathema to the notion of empowerment but the reality can be very different. Look at the case study below.

CASE STUDY

Hamish is 42 years old, married with two children aged 11 and 14. He works as a departmental manager at the local superstore. For the past five years, Hamish has suffered from recurrent episodes of bipolar affective disorder which were thought to have worsened in the wake of his mother's sudden death. His wife and family have managed to support Hamish at home when he has become unwell, but find this increasingly difficult as each episode appears slightly worse than the previous one. His employer has been sympathetic to Hamish's illness but there is a sense in which this is wearing a little thin; during his last illness, Hamish's behaviour while at work caused some colleagues to feel intimidated by his behaviour, particularly during the manic phases.

Hamish has become unwell again. His wife is insisting that she can manage and despite the fact that this episode appears to be quite severe, the family maintain that everything is under control. The GP has expressed his concern to both yourself and the psychiatrist feeling that the family is beginning to break apart under the strain, despite assurances to the contrary from both Hamish and his wife. The school has been in touch with the social work department expressing some concern for the children who are reported as being anxious and withdrawn.

On investigation (s 33, 2003 Act) you learn that Hamish has been taking his prescribed medication only intermittently although both he and his wife would deny this. During discussions you make it clear that Hamish's treatment does not appear to be as effective as it might be and suggest that this be reviewed. Hamish and his wife are adamant that things are fine and refuse to engage in further discussion with either yourself or the GP.

Should the matter be referred to the mental health officer?

Comment

How do you empower someone in such a situation? The easy answer is to allow Hamish and the family to 'get on with it' and accept their version of events. In this way, they appear to have power in relation to decision and action, but we could argue that on the basis of available evidence and in the context of professional opinion, this power in relation to the decisions and actions being taken (or not) could compromise the well-being of a number of people. It is important that Hamish and his wife are fully aware of the possible consequences of the current course of (in)action and that this is set alongside the range of other options that may be necessary and under what circumstances these may need to be considered. The professionals involved should encourage Hamish to engage with his treatment and provide all means possible for this to happen. Information should be offered regarding possible scenarios should this not be acted upon; a compulsory treatment order may become necessary (s 57) or even detention in hospital under an emergency (s 36) or short-term detention certificate (s 44). It is always the case that the least restrictive alternative should be worked towards but empowerment does not mean doing nothing if such a course of action on the basis of all available evidence suggests that this would be detrimental. By providing John with as much information as possible he is better able to make an informed decision even though subsequent events may run counter to this choice.

RESEARCH SUMMARY

Regulating practice and delivering services

In terms of working together, each professional, agency and organisation is largely responsible for regulating its own practice. All professionals deliver services in line with their own professional, agency and organisational standards, rules and protocols and regulate their practice by reference to their own particular ethical codes of conduct and practice standards. Such codes are integral to the professional identity of each grouping and to some extent inevitably reflect professional self-interest (Homan, 1991) but they are the means through which professions formally articulate those distinctive attitudes which characterise the culture of a professional group (Häring, 1972, p24, in Butler, 2002, p239). Practice standards act as a benchmark against which performance and quality can be assessed and (hopefully) assured and they also operate as a means by which levels of accountability can be identified. The Scottish Social Services Council's Codes of practice for social service workers and employers (SSSC, 2005) describe what is expected of social workers and others involved in social care as do the British Association of Social Workers' codes (BASW, 2002). These codes have implications for everyone in terms of their conduct, both professionally and personally. Since the introduction of the Regulation of Care (Scotland) Act 2001 and the subsequent creation of the Scottish Social Services Council (SSSC), social workers and social care workers have to register in order to continue to practice. This process of registration is designed to afford a measure of protection to service users by ensuring that workers are safe to practice. Similar codes exist for nurses and midwives (NMC, 2002; Semple and Cable, 2003), doctors (BMA, 2004), psychologists (BPS, 2000), teachers (GTCS, 2002) and other professionals, although there are differing requirements in terms of continuous professional development or a means of allowing a professional to re-register in order to practice.

One of the difficulties professionals face in relation to working together is how to do it effectively. There have been a number of inquiries in situations where service users have been harmed or have died and professionals have been criticised for not working together effectively in a way which could/should have prevented such a situation from arising. Each of these reports has produced a list of recommendations, many of which focus on issues of collaboration and *communication* (Hammond, 2001; O'Brien, Hammond and MacKinnon, 2003; Mental Welfare Commission, 2003; SWSI, 2004; Scottish Executive, 2006l; see also Reder, Duncan and Gray, 1993; Reder and Duncan, 1999, 2003; Thompson, 2003; Koprowska, 2005).

One of the things social workers and other professionals must do is to understand what collaboration is all about. Too often people assume that it 'just happens' but there is a range of factors which influence whether collaboration is effective or not and below we look at some of these from Hothersall (2006).

Analysing collaboration

It can be helpful to distinguish between the *organisational* or *agency* aspects of collaboration and the *professional* or *disciplinary* aspects. The former refers to aspects of collaboration which involve organisations and agencies within which professional and discipline-related practice takes place. Thus the impact of the organisation, its policies, procedures, administrative practices and its general culture (Alvesson, 2003) cannot and should not be overlooked. The professional or discipline aspects of collaboration are those which relate to the activities of social workers, psychiatrists, nurses, occupational therapists and psychologists and others either individually or as members of a team. These have more of a focus upon the *intra-* and the *interpersonal* dimensions of collaboration.

A second and related distinction is that which refers to the level of integration, interaction, adaptation and flexibility between the organisational and professional dimensions. In the language of collaboration, there are two main prefixes in use; 'multi' and 'inter'. We have multi-agency practice/teams/collaboration, multidisciplinary meetings, multi professional forums, etc; we also have inter-agency practice, inter agency collaboration, inter-disciplinary teamwork and so on. The prefix 'multi' tends to represent situations and arrangements where the agencies, teams and professionals tend to work alongside and in parallel to each other without dismantling professional boundaries or professional identities. The prefix 'inter' tends to denote a more integrative, interactive and adaptive arrangement which (theoretically) allows for a much easier partnership where organisations and individual professionals are (more) comfortable with the transfer of knowledge, values and skills between organisational and professional boundaries thus maximising the free-flow of ideas, skill mix and the development of creative practices (Payne, 2000). In reality these two terms are often used interchangeably and within any team or organisational setting there are likely to be variations on the theme and many shades of grey.

Influences upon collaborative practice

The following sections consider a number of interrelated contexts which influence the nature of collaboration. These are:

- the legal and policy context;

- the organisational and agency context;

- the personal and professional context;

- the practice context;

- the higher education and learning context (Whittington, 2003);

- service user and carer context.

To some extent these categorisations are artificial in that they may appear to draw distinctions which do not exist in pure form and there will be overlap between them. However, it is useful to consider these areas separately in order that the main themes and issues of each can be highlighted.

The legal and policy context

The current legislative and policy context is one which has collaboration as a key theme. This emphasis on collaborative practice recognises that no one organisation or agency or any one professional group or discipline is able to successfully deliver the range of services required in the twenty-first century. Legislation and policy is now designed to facilitate collaborative working and this has been influenced by a number of factors including:

- the changing nature of need and the way it is defined, and by whom (Scottish Executive, 2006a);

- changing and ever increasing demands upon human services and increasing specialisation;

- the impact of 'near misses', child fatalities and the subsequent inquiries into these (Reder, Duncan and Gray, 1993; Reder and Duncan, 1999; Sinclair and Bullock, 2002; Mental Welfare Commission, 2003; O'Brien, Hammond and MacKinnon, 2003; SWSI, 2004; Bostock et al., 2005; Scottish Executive, 2006l);

- an increasing recognition of the need to address the whole person in terms of how services are designed and delivered (Bronfenbrenner, 1979; Scottish Executive, 2005g, 2005i, 2006c);

- service user perspectives (Cleaver and Freeman, 1995; Beresford, 2002a; Statham, 2004);

- accountability issues (OPM/CIPFA, 2004);

- issues concerning the nature of professional identity, training and development (Miller, Freeman and Ross, 2001; Barr, 2003);

- issues concerning the boundaries between individuals, professionals, agencies and organisations, including communication issues (Woodhouse and Pengelly, 1991; Reder and Duncan, 2003; Tietze, Cohen and Musson, 2003);

- awareness of organisational influences (Hudson, 1987, 2002; Alvesson, 2003);

- the nature of working in groups (teams) (Øvretveit, Mathias and Thompson, 1997; Payne, 2000).

Legislation, policy and guidance therefore offer a framework within which collaboration can take place. For example, the 2003 Act makes specific reference to this in terms of local authority functions and related matters (s 25–35).

Collaboration takes place at a number of different levels including:

- *The policy level* Policy-makers from different government directorates collaborate with other agencies and organisations to develop policies which reflect the optimum way of meeting social need.

- *The strategic level* Agencies and organisations collaborate to design, develop and finance services from joint resources in order to implement the policies.

- *The organisational/managerial level* Agencies and organisations collaborate to determine how the strategy for service delivery should be implemented and who should be accountable and responsible for this.

- *The operational level* Professionals, agencies and organisations collaborate to implement services 'on the ground', looking at the practicalities of making things happen. This includes thinking about how long it takes to do a particular piece of work and who is best placed to do it in the here and now.

- *The practice level* This is where practitioners collaborate with colleagues both in their own and other teams to provide those services so designed directly to the people they are working with.

These levels represent the broad spread of activity within the service arena; there are other ways of representing this (Whittington, 2003) but these offer a straightforward way of appreciating that collaboration takes place in a range of contexts at a number of different levels and is very much a necessity.

RESEARCH SUMMARY

Legislation and policy for collaboration

Social Work (S) Act 1968	Community Care and Health (S) Act 2002
Education (S) Act 1980	Community Care (Joint Working, etc.) (S) Regulations 2002
NHS and Community Care Act 1990 (UK)	*It's Everyone's Job to Make Sure I'm Alright* (2002)
Children (S) Act 1995	*Getting Our Priorities Right* (2003)
Criminal Procedure (S) Act 1995	*Integrated Strategy for Early Years* (2003)
New Community Schools (1998)	*The Laming Inquiry* (2003)
Sure Start (1998)	*Caleb Ness Inquiry* (2003)
Protecting Children – A Shared Responsibility (1998)	*Borders Inquiry* (2003)

RESEARCH SUMMARY *continued*

Social Inclusion Strategy (1999)

Towards a Healthier Scotland (2000)

Joint Future (2000)

Adults with Incapacity (S) Act 2000

For Scotland's Children (2001)

Changing Children's Services Fund (2001)

Promoting Children's Mental Health within Early Years Settings (2001)

Regulation of Care (S) Act 2001

Mental Health (Care and Treatment) (Scotland) Act (2003)

21st Century Review of Social Work (2004)

Hidden Harm (2004)

Integrated Children's Services Plans (2004)

Delivering for Health (2005)

Delivering for Mental Health (2006)

Inquiry into Care of Mr L and Mr M (2006)

Children's Services (S) Bill (2007)

Adult Support and Protection (S) Act 2007

All of the statutes and policy documents listed in the Research Summary above make provision for collaboration, cooperation and partnership at a number of different levels. This provision can be both prescriptive, as in statute, and facilitative, as in the provisions of many of those policy documents referred to.

However, the many exhortations to work together, as exemplified by many of the recommendations contained within inquiry reports, do not always bring about the desired results (Hudson, 2002). Below we shall look at some of those factors which make collaboration a reality or not. If we ignore the broader contextual factors which relate to collaboration, then we are very likely to continue to wonder why it doesn't work, because sometimes it doesn't. Therefore being alive to those factors which may help or hinder the collaborative process is a necessary part of the collaborative endeavour itself.

The organisational and agency context

As a social worker (or MHO, psychiatrist, CPN, nurse, psychologist, etc.) we work within an organisational context. Organisations have their own rules, regulations, language (Tietze, Cohen and Musson, 2003) and culture (Alvesson, 2003) which govern their functioning and are designed primarily to ensure their continued existence. Social work exists within an organisational context which may or may not be fully aligned to the same value base. For example, as a social worker you may be employed by an organisation which is profit-driven. A situation may arise where you feel, as a professional social worker, that a particular course of action is necessary. The organisation on the other hand believes that this will be too costly and affect profits. You are therefore prevented from undertaking this piece of work. In a local authority social work department, you may similarly believe that a person requires a particular resource but are told that this is not available as the budget is overspent. These are the kinds of conflicts which can arise when the organisational and professional contexts appear to clash.

In a similar way, there are situations which arise where the agency may adopt particular administrative or operational requirements which appear to constrain professional judgement and practice. It may be the case that in order for you as a member of one organisation to obtain a resource from another (let's say in the form of staff time from another professional), you have to make numerous formal requests, in writing, via your manager who correspondingly requests this from your colleague's manager. This can take time and it can be frustrating, particularly in those situations where the time you require is minimal and the professional whose time you would like is happy to oblige and yet cannot because their organisational and related administrative systems prohibit this in the absence of signed authorisations which are sent to the finance department for cost-analysis in relation to unit costs per head for inter-agency collaboration. Here again, at the organisational level such practices are completely understandable, but from the professional perspective absolutely maddening.

What effect might these kinds of organisational issues have upon effective collaboration? Both intra- and inter-organisational collaboration depends upon the degree of fit between organisational and professional goals. These are not always in perfect accord and the resultant tensions can at times be debilitating, particularly in high-stress situations where professionals simply want to get on with the job in hand rather than become embroiled in administrative processes which at times appear to have little or nothing to do with supporting people. It may be that in response to these tensions, professionals adopt a particular approach to practice which may be defensive, routinised, defeatist or otherwise dangerous (Thompson, 2005). However, if the organisation is sensitive enough and good quality supervision is available to the worker, then these issues can be discussed and effectively dealt with.

The issue to recognise is that organisations have their own 'rules of engagement' and these may not always appear to be synchronous with the values of the profession in terms of ongoing practice. The social worker in these situations will have to utilise their own communication and interpersonal skills to the full and engage with the organisation on behalf of their client in an advocacy role. Thompson (2005) makes the point that most social workers have as their practice focus direct work with individuals (Thompson, 2002). What is not so readily acknowledged, nor indeed readily attended to, particularly in qualifying training, is that an increasing amount of time is spent in direct work with organisations, agencies and other professionals. These skills we shall consider below. However, what does need to be acknowledged is that the organisational context has a pervasive influence on the practice of professionals and as such must be accounted for in relation to conceptions of day-to-day social work practice.

These factors are often to the fore in today's social work arena because of the tendency for services to 'reorganise' on a regular basis. In the drive to integrate services for the benefit of users, services have had to realign themselves with different partners and stakeholders as the requirement for increasingly specialised, responsive and accountable services has taken hold. Policy initiatives, different funding options and new categories of need all conspire to place demands upon existing services to be more effective and efficient. Competition, once the watchword of private, 'for-profit' organisations is now a central feature of the human service lexicon, particularly insofar as third-sector (voluntary) organisations are concerned. While these organisations are 'not-for-profit', their very existence can often be threatened by other organisations competing for core and short-term funding to provide services from both central government and local authorities. These economic drivers mean that when a service reconfigures or otherwise reinvents itself, fragmentation can occur, leaving both service users and professionals confused and bewildered. Many funding streams are relatively short term, often for three years at which point the new service has to be self-funding or otherwise financed through core funding. The effect on professionals can be quite debilitating, especially if your job is on the line at the end of a funding period.

These issues are very much to the fore in terms of current social work practice in all parts of the UK. While policy would endeavour to generate a climate within which collaboration and co-operation can flourish to the advantage of service users, the interface between policy intent, organisational *raison d'être* and professional obligation is often blurred and somewhat jagged at the edges. Hudson (1987) notes that there are two main difficulties for organisations when faced with the need to collaborate, as most health and social welfare organisations these days are expected to. Firstly, the organisation faces the loss of its freedom to act independently, having to relinquish control over its own domain. Secondly, and very importantly in relation to the current welfare climate, it has to invest scarce resources into developing and maintaining collaborative relationships. From an organisational perspective, the investment in collaboration may in fact not yield any benefits. However, it is also the case that just such an investment may in fact increase the capacity for it to achieve its goals because it can then utilise the resources of the other organisation(s) and thereby achieve a state of *inter*dependence.

The personal and professional context

At the individual level there are a number of issues to consider which relate to the whole area of collaborative activity. Motivation is a key factor in terms of how well people work, both alone and as part of a team (Herzberg, 1968). Being part of a team implies many things, not the least of which is that the team will function effectively. Notions of teams and teamworking are contested issues (Øvretveit, 1997; Øvretveit, Mathias and Thompson, 1997; Payne, 2000) and some of these have been referred to above. Payne and others refer to teams and to work groups, the former having some sense of identity, a shared vision, clarity concerning role, task and function and a range of shared policy statements on key service areas while the 'work group' is seen as being more diffuse, less focused and formed for a very short period to undertake a specific piece of work before being disbanded. Both of these arrangements exist within the context of collaborative working in social work, as do variations on this theme and groupings which may lie somewhere in between.

Whatever the particular arrangement it is important to realise that both teams and work groups are subject to particular dynamics and go through a number of processes in their development. These processes reflect human capabilities and issues and can determine whether the group will function effectively or not. Tuckman and Jensen (1977) describe a four stage process.

Forming (socialisation)

During this stage of coming together, the key issues will relate to the communication of team objectives, orientation and socialisation. This 'forming' stage is likely to be very unproductive in terms of task-related activity although this stage is crucial to the overall process. In fact, the 'forming' stage is best accomplished without there being too many task demands made upon the team. It is important to note that if this stage is not given enough time, then the next stage, that of 'storming', may last longer than it should which could be detrimental to the whole team process and the achievement of its objectives.

Essentially the 'forming' stage is concerned with the development of social relations, the exchange of professional and personal information and the breaking down of barriers. It is in many respects characterised by 'sizing up' the other members and of getting a sense of the knowledge, skills and values of others which allows for people to judge their position within the group.

It is also important to note that the presence of a team leader is important at this stage otherwise there may well be no movement forward and the 'self-selection' of a leader may create difficulties.

Storming (conflict)

This is the stage where team members are beginning to get to know each other. This can be the most difficult and worrying time in the life of the group. In some cases it may seem that the team is rife with internal conflict, disagreement and discord and may in fact give the impression of being on the verge of collapse. The team leader is crucial here, for if these differences and tensions are well managed, with a clear focus on why the group is in existence, then it is likely that the group will emerge strong and well developed with a very clear sense of its collective identity.

Norming (rule setting)

In this stage, the group develops its working structures and clarifies its internal and external relationships. Roles are established and clarified with everyone being expected to sign up to these. Agreement is reached on how conflicts will be dealt with and the theme is one of a search for consensus. It is this phase which allows for people to relax and begin to focus upon the task at hand, bringing to bear on the situation the very things they brought to the group: their unique contribution of knowledge, values and skills.

Performing (doing)

Once the rules have been set and the task defined, the team can get on with the work. This stage is characterised by high task orientation.

These four phases are adequate to explain most aspects of team formation and performance. However, some writers feel that this typology is somewhat limited and have added other stages (Cartwright, 2002).

Dorming (plateau)

In this stage, the team has been working well but suddenly reaches a plateau where performance levels fall off. This may represent nothing more than a team functioning at its maximum level. If there is no more potential to be had from the team, then there is, arguably, not a problem. However, if it appears to be the case that the team is not achieving its objectives, despite what appears to be maximum performance, then there is a problem. It might be that some team members have given up on the team and feel they have no more to contribute or perhaps internal conflicts and tensions are compromising the productivity of the team. Whatever the cause, it has to be dealt with. If, however, the team is performing at its maximum and running smoothly, it is important not to perceive the apparent lack of energy and the dynamism of earlier periods as problematic. If it isn't broken, don't try to fix it.

Re-forming

This stage recognises that most groups will change their membership at some time for a number of reasons. Some of these will relate to personal reasons, some will relate to the wider needs of the parent organisation(s) or a change in task orientation. Whatever the case, and it is very likely that every team in the UK has altered its membership at some time during its existence, new members alter the established dynamic. As a result, there is a period where the group needs to re-establish itself because of the new member(s) who bring with them different characteristics, knowledge, values and skills which need to be worked into the fabric of the group. Mini phases of forming, storming and norming can be seen to occur. These can be perceived as being indicative of problems within the group but they are nothing more than the team re-establishing social relations, positions and rules in respect of the new members. It has to be remembered that in these situations, a drop in team performance is likely until equilibrium is restored.

Adjourning

Some teams are permanent; an area social work team is likely to be there for a long time. However, some teams are not permanent, either by design or default. If a team is established on the basis that it is *not* going to be permanent, then this needs to be stated at the outset so that people can concentrate on achieving the task rather than on diversionary activities designed to prolong something which has to end. These kinds of activities are fully understandable but much energy and effort can be wasted and hopes built up only to be shattered. When a team adjourns, this is likely to be difficult for some people as the relationships they have developed may be very significant to them and so they may be grieving for these losses as they can have an impact upon one's sense of self and both personal and professional identity. This phase has to be managed effectively; endings must be recognised and feelings of loss acknowledged.

In the face of political pressure to collaborate, more and more groups or teams are formed on a frequent basis. Group dynamics play a central role in determining how likely effective collaboration will be so it is important that attention is paid to these aspects of collaborative practice.

Professional identity and collaboration

Having a clear sense of professional identity is generally regarded as a vital ingredient to effective practice, irrespective of the discipline concerned or the location of that within a particular agency or organisational context. Knowing what it is you do as a social worker, an MHO, a CPN, a nurse or a psychiatrist is pretty important to service users. This identity will reflect differing knowledge bases, theoretical orientations, value bases, skill levels and a range of other factors often unique to that professional role. These differences must be seen constructively and recognition given to the value of diversity.

ACTIVITY **8.1**

Make a list of what it is you think a social worker working in the field of mental health actually does. Next to this, make a list of what you think a community psychiatric nurse might do and then a list for a psychiatrist.

If you are not sure, make contact with a CPN and/or a psychiatrist. Ask them what they think they do.

Once you have drawn up your lists, put them side by side and compare them. Are there any core skills *which all three do? Are there any* common skills *which any/either could do? Are there any* complementary skills *which are specific to any one of the three roles?*

Comment

You may have found that there were quite a lot of *core skills*, those which each person undertakes as a necessary part of their role. A good example might be interviewing and assessment. The *common skills* might be undertaking some type of groupwork or therapy with someone. Anyone *could* do it, but a decision would taken as to who *should* at a particular time, often for particular reasons. *Complementary skills* might be making a diagnosis (psychiatrist), consenting to detention under the 2003 Act (MHO) and administering depot injections within the community (CPN).

The practice context

By far the most important aspect of collaboration is that between the worker(s) and the service user(s) and their families with whom they have contact. It is important to recognise that the very nature of the intervention itself may help or hinder the sense of collaboration, co-operation and partnership experienced. For example, in cases where the client is in some respects involuntary, for example where compulsory detention has taken place, there may well be resistance to intervention and levels of co-operation and collaboration may be lower than hoped for (Trotter, 1999). In these situations partnership, co-operation and collaboration may well be principles furthest from people's minds and as a result the demands upon the worker's communication and interpersonal skills become that much greater.

From the perspective of what inquiries and reports have told us, there are a number of issues which appear to emerge time after time which relate to the whole issue of collaboration and why at times it appears to be problematic. When we speak of collaboration, we imply that its many facets are operating seamlessly. If collaboration is to happen then its constituent elements need to be evident. Some of these are:

- effective communication;
- adequate sharing of information;
- accurate recording of information;
- understanding of roles and responsibilities;
- clarity of purpose;
- clear time-frames;
- effective decision-making;
- easy access to and effective use of resources.

The nature of practice has therefore to include these things as well as the human elements referred to above.

The educational context

In relation to the educational context, I refer specifically to the need for those institutions of higher education which provide qualifying and post-qualifying training for social work and social care staff, as well as continuous professional and employee development courses to actively include reference to collaborative working within the curriculum. The Standards in Social Work Education in Scotland (Scottish Executive, 2003a) make reference to the need for students of social work to be able to work effectively within organisations and to work collaboratively. These are addressed by all institutions but there is a need for the explicit juxtaposition of those transferable skills to the notions referred to above concerning social workers spending significant amounts of time in direct work with *organisations*.

A further development is that relating to *inter-professional* education (Miller, Freeman and Ross, 2001; Barr, 2003) which recognises the need for students in a range of professions to learn together with other professionals from the very start of their careers, and also while in practice.

At the practice level, many groups (for example the forensic school, child protection committees, etc.) are concerned to offer training to staff from different professions, agencies and organisations who contribute in some way to service provision. This endeavour extends not only to a range of different and diverse professional groups, but also to the social care community and the community at large.

What is clear is that the need to work together has never been more acute than it is today. It is therefore essential that policy-makers, managers, practitioners and educators appreciate what collaboration actually entails and approach it systematically, applying theory and critical analysis to it rather than assuming that effective collaboration just happens. Like most things in life, it has to be worked at and not taken for granted.

The service user and carer context

As noted in Chapter 7, there has been an increasing recognition of the need to *actively* involve those who use mental health services and their carers in discussions concerning the quality of those services and their experiences of them. This is something which has been developing over a number of years and continues to actively and effectively engage many people at a number of levels. The main principle is that those who experience the service have something valuable to say and these views need to be considered (Macdonald, et al., 2002; Blenkiron, et al., 2003; Brandon et al., 2003; Longo and Scio, 2004; Beck, 2006; Bowl, 2007) as do the views of service users' and carers in relation to the education and training of social work and other healthcare professionals (Faddon, Holsgrove and Shooter, 2005; Basset, Campbell and Anderson, 2006; Repper and Breeze, 2007).

It is important for professionals to actively listen to what people have to say about what happens to them and about what they feel would make things better. This is nowadays as much a part of the professional task as delivering a service. (Go to www.voxscotland.org.uk; www.scottishrecovery.net; www.hug.uk.net)

Areas of particular concern regarding collaboration

In this section we will consider two areas which require our attention. The first relates to what we can learn from inquiries and a consideration of the *dynamics of collaboration* (see Woodhouse and Pengelly, 1991) while the second relates to those areas of practice which require that special attention be given to issues of effective collaboration because of increased risk and vulnerability.

Learning from inquiries

There have been a number of inquiries in which people have either harmed or killed others or have themselves not been adequately protected by those services which should have done so. Sadly, these situations occur across a range of service user groupings including children, people with mental illness, those with learning difficulties and older people.

All of these inquiries seek to identify the reasons why such incidents occurred and they all make recommendations which aim to further our understanding of what appears to have gone 'wrong' and to equip everyone with the benefit of hindsight.

Each of these inquiries is in many respects unique; in other ways they highlight what appear to be 'common' errors – of judgement, practice and procedure. While each needs to be read as a stand-alone report, there are some common themes across all of them which can be identified:

- a lack of communication between professionals, agencies and others involved in the care, treatment, protection, management and/or supervision of a person;

- a lack of *understanding* between those referred to above about the *nature* of the information being communicated (see Reder and Duncan, 2003);

- a lack of effective (risk) assessment and (risk) management;

- poor record-keeping;

- a lack of clarity regarding the role and function of individuals involved in a case;

- a lack of understanding concerning policy and procedure;

- a reliance on assumptions.

(See earlier chapters regarding the Mental Welfare Commission and the Social Work Inspection Agency.)

It is vitally important that case planning, recording and management *is seen as being everyone's business*. Where there is a care plan in place, a nominated lead-person must take the responsibility for ensuring that all parties involved fulfil their obligations. This places quite a responsibility upon you if that is you; however, as a professional, you are accountable for your actions (and inactions). This is not to say that it is all down to you, the individual practitioner; it isn't. However, clear frameworks exist within which practice must take place. An important part of case planning and management is ensuring that these are evident, that procedures are in place for clear lines of communication and that everyone is clear about what they are (and are not) responsible for. It is important that all professionals take heed of issues relating to the *dynamics of collaboration* referred to above.

For more information go to: www.mwcscot.org.uk/GoodPractice/Publications/Inquiry_reports.asp, and www.victoria-climbie.org.uk/index.php, and see Reder, Duncan and Gray, (1993) and Reder and Duncan (1999).

The whole issue of the protection of vulnerable adults is a policy and practice area which is quite sophisticated in Scotland and the recent addition of the Adult Support and Protection (Scotland) Act 2007 to the statute books adds another dimension to this (see Chapter 2).

Areas of increased vulnerability and risk

As we can see from the above scenarios, there are some situations where there are increased levels of vulnerability and risk in evidence as well as involvement from a range of different professionals and agencies. Where people are deemed to be *particularly* vulnerable, professionals need to ensure that the mechanisms for fast, efficient and effective collaboration, communication and *action* are in place and regularly reviewed.

One area where such issues need to be carefully considered is that of the effect of parental mental illness upon children.

Children whose parents have mental disorders
The effect on children who have at least one parent with a mental disorder is worthy of consideration. If we go back to the importance of stress as an intervening variable it is possible to appreciate the impact that the mental disorder of a parent can have on a child and the family as whole. A substantial body of research and evaluation exists in relation to this issue(Rutter and Quinton, 1994; Reder and Lucey, 1995; Cogill et al., 1996; Falkov, 1996; Rutter, 1966, 1985, 1990; Weir and Douglas, 1999; Reder, McClure and Jolley, 2000;

Sheppard and Kelly, 2001; Walker, 2003b; Tunnard, 2004; Göpfert, Webster and Seeman, 2004; Somers, 2006) and although complex, the major issues appear to be as follows:

- *Impact upon the child/ren* – developmental delays, conduct disorders, poor self-esteem, attention-related problems, high levels of self-blame, sleep disorders, psychosomatic problems, anxiety and depression.

- *Impact upon the unwell parent (in relation to parenting capacity)* – an inability to regulate and display appropriate affect, potential threats to continuity of care because of hospitalisation, lack of capacity to offer appropriate guidance and control, lowered levels of basic care. Many of these issues can be a function of the severity of the parent's illness at any given time.

- *Key variables* – the seriousness of the parent's illness and its chronicity; the level of discord evident, within the household (either as a direct *or* indirect result of the illness); the quality of the relationship between the adults in the household; the presence or absence of a 'well' parent with whom the child had a positive relationship; the age and resilience level of the child and associated protective factors (refer back to Chapter 5). According to the (seminal) paper by Rutter and Quinton (1984):

  ... family discord and hostility constitute the chief mediating variable in the association between parental mental disorder and psychiatric disturbance in the children. (p877)

Many interventions focus upon supporting the 'well' parent in order that they in turn may support the unwell parent and the family.

A major concern in this area is the extent to which children act as carers for parents who are unwell. There has been much debate regarding the role of adult psychiatrists in this area where they are diagnosing mental disorders in adults who have parental responsibilities. Good practice and the principles of the 2003 Act should ensure that medical practitioners are alert to the issues parental mental disorder brings with it from the child and family perspective. Under the terms of s 29(2) b) of the 2003 Act local authorities are obliged to have regard to the provisions of s 22(1) of the Children (Scotland) Act 1995.

C H A P T E R   S U M M A R Y

This chapter has looked at the issues relating to working together and illustrated not only how important it is, but how complex. The chapter has also introduced you to some of the wider issues relating to the *dynamics* of collaboration which, in our view, are sometimes ignored. We have also looked at some of the influences on collaboration and at the legal and policy frameworks which, in conjunction with sound professional practice, can facilitate effective partnerships. We have also looked at some areas of concern, including inquiries and the effect of parental mental illness on children.

FURTHER READING

Tunnard, J (2004) *Parental mental health problems: key messages from research, policy and practice*. Dartington: Research in Practice. Available at: **www.rip.org.uk/publications/researchreviews.asp**.

WEBITES

For more information concerning relevant public inquiries see
www.mwcscot.org.uk/GoodPractice/Publications/Inquiry_reports.asp.

Mental Welfare Commission for Scotland: **www.mwcscot.org.uk/home/home.asp**

Conclusion

It would just not be possible to provide comprehensive coverage for all aspects of mental health social work in a book of this size, particularly at a time of such rapid growth. Indeed, if you take the message of recovery to heart you might say that it is hardly possible to provide such coverage in any book because it would mean telling the stories and getting the opinions of every individual in Scotland who has personal experience of the struggle to maintain good mental health. We have therefore had to make choices about which key issues to relate to and we have chosen to draw focus on values and ethics, the differentiation of mental health from mental illness and related terms, some of the key perspectives on what we call mental illness, diagnosis, treatment and assessment, mental health law (both civil and in relation to the criminal law), the law relating to incapacity and adult protection, issues of support for children and young people and people with short-term and long-term problems and, finally, commentary on the importance of understanding the organisational context and collaborative working.

Throughout this we have threaded important themes for modern social work practice in Scotland: working alongside service users in a recovery oriented way; taking account of the service user's perspective and balancing it against the professional knowledge bases of doctors and social workers; and taking account of policy directives and shifts in emphasis.

In this list of the core contents of the text, there are many tensions which have to be resolved in practice. For example, the biochemical treatment orientation of the medical perspective is nowadays to be viewed less and less as the antithesis of the social perspective on mental health. However, there are undeniable tensions in that a doctor will always have a strong view based upon systematic medical knowledge of what a patient ought to do for his or her own good, while a social perspective might suggest that self-determination is what is best for any marginalised person in order for them to work towards inclusion. Buried somewhere in this conundrum is the problem of how to uphold the individual rights of the service user while sometimes having to enforce protective measures upon him or her. These tensions are evident in the two wings of policy: the one which encourages social inclusion, self-determination, anti-oppression and mental well-being, and the other which expands the powers to restrict the liberty of mentally disordered people who are vulnerable and at risk of harm by the imposition of compulsion.

We have highlighted these tensions and, in case studies and exercises, have encouraged you to think about how you might manage them in practice. What we cannot do in this or any book, is to resolve these tensions for you. You will need to do that yourself, by reference to your own knowledge and skills and to that of others around you. And we hope that this book will provide you with some assistance in that challenging but nonetheless rewarding task.

Glossary

Adults with Incapacity (Scotland) Act 2000 (the 2000 Act) The 2000 Act gives powers to manage the finances, property and welfare of adults who lack capacity to determine their own choices in these matters because of mental disorder or physical disability which amounts to an inability to communicate. It contains major roles for the mental health officer (see below).

Adult (the adult) The term used by the 2000 Act for a person over the age of 16 years who requires the use of powers of the Act.

Approved medical practitioner (AMP) Under s 22(1) of the Mental Health (Care and Treatment) (Scotland) Act 2003 doctor is approved by Direction from the Scottish Ministers. Currently the Direction on Approval of Medical Practitioners states that they must have four years of experience working in psychiatric services and have undertaken special AMP training. They may then be subsequently approved by their employing health board as 'having special experience in the diagnosis and treatment of mental disorder' (s 22(1), 2003 Act).

Behaviour modification Based on the idea of learning theory and conditioning. Intervention focuses on the relearning of behaviour.

BNF Stands for the British National Formulary reference text, which is published twice a year and contains up-to-date information about the maximum dosage of medication for patients. Hospital wards should always have the latest copy available.

Bolam test Where a health care professional is not considered to be negligent if s/he adopts the practice which a responsible body of professionals (e.g. psychiatrists, nurses or social workers) accept as appropriate.

CAMHS Child and Adolescent Mental Health Services.

CMHT Community Mental Health Team.

Cognitive therapy A treatment intervention, available on the NHS, that focuses on maladaptive patterns of thinking that affect the person's behaviour.

CPN Community psychiatric nurses are qualified and experienced psychiatric nurses who play a major role in the supervision and treatment of patients in the community. Along with MHOs, psychiatrists and others, they have a pivotal role in community mental health and outreach teams.

Criminal Procedure (Scotland) Act 1995 (the 1995 Act) The 1995 Act provides the framework in which criminal courts make their decisions in Scotland. As such, it interfaces with the 2003 Act to make decisions about the disposal of mentally disordered offenders who require care and treatment within the mental health services.

CSIP NIMHE (National Institute of Mental Health for England) has now been absorbed into a successor body, the Care Services Improvement Partnership (CSIP). CSIP embraces eight programmes. They are the National Child and Adolescent Mental Health Services (CAMHS) Support Service, Health in Criminal Justice, the Integrated Care Network, Integrating Community Equipment and Support, the National

Institute for Mental Health in England, the Health and Social Care Change Agent Team, the Valuing People Support Team and Children for Change. It has an annual budget of more than £30 million. Website: www.csip.org.uk

Diagnosis Forms part of the assessment process and the identification of specific mental disorder in which reference is made to either the DSM-IV or to the ICD–10 reference texts both of which classify mental disorder.

Direction of the Scottish Ministers Directions are written requirements which are allowed by law. The principle Directions for the purposes of mental health law are those for the appointment of MHOs (s 32, 2003 Act) and AMPs (s 22, 2003 Act). They allow the Ministers to change or add to the requirements for appointment without having to change the law itself.

Expressed emotion This term is used usually in the sense that the family may have 'high expressed emotion' that is having an adverse effect on the service user. This includes over-involved parents and a highly critical atmosphere.

Family therapy The focus is on working with the family to restore the family system to a more functioning unit.

LA (local authority) Any one of the 32 Scottish local councils which provide a range of statutory local services including social work services

Levels of security There are three levels of security designated by policy for the in-patient management of mentally disordered offenders (high, medium and low security). There is one high secure unit and three medium secure units, shared by all health boards.

Mentally disordered offender (MDO) An MDO is a person who has committed or appears to have committed a criminal offence and suffers from a mental disorder.

Mental health officer (MHO) A registered social worker who has undergone a Scottish Social Services Council approved additional training course and meets the other requirements set out by Directions of the Scottish Minister under s 32 of the 2003 Act. In order to comply with the 2003 Act and ensure independence of role, the MHO must be appointed and employed by the local authority.

Mental Health (Care and Treatment) (Scotland) Act 2003 (the 2003 Act) The primary legislation in this area. It is primarily about the compulsory measures of care and treatment of people who are diagnosed as having a mental disorder.

Mental Welfare Commission for Scotland (MWC) An independent body the commissioners of which are appointed by Royal Appointment for a set period to undertake this statutory role. The MWC monitors the operation of the 2003 Act in respect of patients subject to compulsion. The MWC publishes an Annual Report and a list of Inquiries into Deficiencies of Care and Treatment. Commissioners and their officers regularly visit all hospitals in Scotland and meet with detained patients, those subject to compulsion or restriction in the community and adults subject to guardianship under the Adults with Incapacity (Scotland) Act 2000.

Mental Health Tribunal for Scotland (MHTS) The MHTS is an autonomous body the purpose of which is to hear applications for measures of compulsion and patients' appeals against compulsory treatment orders, compulsion orders and other orders. It also reviews orders where there is no appeal. A Tribunal comprises three people: a legal member (chair), a lay member and a medical member.

Named person Clearly defined under s 250 to 254 of the 2003 Act. Named persons are nominated by people who are at risk of being subject to powers under the Act. They exercise protecting functions such as a right to be heard at Tribunal hearings.

National Institute for Clinical Excellence (NICE) Conducts research and evaluations of various treatments and publishes guidance and advice.

Office of the Public Guardian (OPG) The independent agency which registers, regulates and monitors financial powers under the 2000 Act.

NES NHS Education for Scotland

NHS National Health Service.

Patient The term used throughout the 2003 Act using the male pronoun. Social workers use the term 'service user', implying that more of a partnership exists between themselves and the *user* of the service, but 'patient' is still used as the term of reference in proximity to the Act.

PHCT Primary health care team or GP surgery.

Principles In the legal context, *principles* are those fundamental and overarching principles which must guide any action taken by those given powers and duties under that particular piece of legislation. They are *statutory duties* (see below) and, as such, any action performed by an agent of the legislation without regard to the principles will risk being unlawful.

Prognosis The medical assessment of the future course of events and probable outcome of the patient's mental disorder.

Psychoanalysis Based on Freudian thinking, the aim is that through the client/therapist relationship, people can resolve conflicted states of mind. Not (usually) available on the NHS.

Recovery Recovery is the term of preference to acknowledge that everyone who has a mental illness may and should be assisted to recover from the experience.

Responsible medical officer (RMO) The psychiatrist who has full clinical legal responsibility for a patient detained under the 2003 Act. They will usually be a consultant psychiatrist and approved under s 22 of the Act as having a special experience in the diagnosis and treatment of mental disorder.

Restricted patient The legal term used to describe a mentally disordered offender who has been placed under a restriction order with a compulsion order (a CORO) by the court. This means that the person cannot be discharged from the orders, nor can the measures of care and treatment be altered without consultation with the First Minister. Restricted patients will be mentally disordered offenders who have committed crimes of a serious violent or sexual nature.

Second opinion appointed doctor (designated medical practitioner) A registered medical practitioner (experienced psychiatrist) appointed by the MWC to provide an independent opinion in respect of consent to treatment under s 233 of the 2003 Act.

State Hospital The State Hospital is Scotland's only high security hospital for the care and treatment of mentally disordered offenders. It is located near the village of Carstairs in South Lanarkshire and is sometimes referred to as *Carstairs*.

Statutory A requirement dictated by Act of Parliament, e.g. the 2000 Act or the 2003 Act.

Statutory duty A duty that must be complied with, if contained within an Act of Parliament.

Statutory instrument Relates to delegated legislation drafted by the relevant department under powers attributed by an Act of Parliament. Statutory regulations are most commonly drafted as Statutory Instruments and laid before Parliament.

References

Abela, J R Z and Hankin, B L (eds) (2008) *Handbook of depression in children and adolescents*. Hove: Guilford Press.

Achenbach, T M and Rescola, L A (2006) *Multicultural understanding of child and adolescent psychopathology*. Hove: Guilford Press.

Adams, J R and Drake, R E (2006) Shared decision-making and evidence-based practice. *Community Mental Health Journal*, 42 (1), 87–105.

Agerbo, E, Sterne, J and Gunnell, D (2007) Combining individual and ecological data to determine compositional and contextual socio-economic risk factors for suicide. *Social Science and Medicine*, 64 (2), 451–61.

Akhurst, S, Allnock, D, Garbers, C and Tunstill, J (2005) Sure-Start Local Programmes: implications of case study data from the national evaluation of Sure Start. *Children & Society*, 19 (2), 158–71.

Aldridge, D (1998) *Suicide: the tragedy of hopelessness*. London: Jessica Kingsley.

Alvesson, M (2003) *Understanding organisational culture*. London: Sage.

American Psychiatric Association (1994) *Diagnostic and Statistical Manual of Mental Disorders (DSM–IV)*. Washington, DC: American Psychiatric Association.

Angold, A and Egger, H L (2007) Pre-school psychopathology: lessons for the lifespan. *Journal of Child Psychology and Psychiatry*, 48 (10), 961–6.

Banks, S (2006) *Ethics and values in social work*. 3rd edition. Basingstoke: Macmillan.

Bannerjee, S, Clancy, C and Crome, I (eds) (2002) *Co-existing problems of mental disorder and substance misuse ('dual diagnosis'): an information manual*. London: Royal College of Psychiatrists.

Barkley, R A (2006) *Attention-deficit hyperactivity disorder: a handbook for diagnosis and treatment*. 3rd edition. Hove: Guilford Press.

Barkley, R A and Murphy, K R (2006) *Attention-deficit hyperactivity disorder: a clinical workbook*. 3rd edition. Hove: Guilford Press.

Barnes, C and Mercer, G (eds) (2005) *Disability policy and practice: applying the social model of disability*. London: Disability Press.

Barnes, J (2003) Interventions addressing infant mental health problems. *Children & Society*, 17, 386–95.

Barr, H (2003) *Interprofessional education: today, yesterday and tomorrow: a review*. Available at: **www.health.ltsn.ac.uk/miniprojects/HughBarrFinal.htm**.

Barrowclough, C, Haddock, G, Fitzsimmons, M and Johnson, R (2006) Treatment development for psychosis and co-occuring substance misuse: a descriptive review. *Journal of Mental Health*, 15 (6), 619–32.

Barry, A M and Yuill, C (2007) *Understanding the sociology of health: an introduction*. London: Sage.

Barry, M M, Doherty, A, Hope, A, Sixsmith, J and Kelleher, C C (2000) A community needs assessment for rural mental health promotion. *Health Education Research*, 15 (3), 293–304.

Basset, T, Campbell, P and Anderson, J (2006) Service users survivors' involvement in mental health training and education. *Social Work Education*, 25 (4), 393–402.

Beck, A (2006) Users' views of looked after children's mental health services. *Adoption and Fostering*, 30 (2), 53–63.

Becker, H (1963) *Outsiders: studies in the sociology of deviance*. New York: Free Press.

Bee, H and Boyd, D (2004) *The developing child*. Harlow: Pearson.

Bellis, M D D (2005) The psychobiology of neglect. *Child Maltreatment*, 10 (2), 150–72.

Bentall, R P, Fernyhough, C, Morrison, A P, Lewis, S and Corcoran, R (2007) Prospects for a cognitive-developmental account of psychotic experiences. *British Journal of Clinical Psychology*, 46 (2) 155–73.

Bentley, K J (2001) *Social work practice in mental health: contemporary roles, tasks and techniques*. New York: Wadsworth.

Beresford, P (2000) Service users' knowledge and social work theory: conflict or collaboration? *British Journal of Social Work*, 30, 489–503.

Beresford, P (2002a) Thinking about 'mental health': towards a social model. *Journal of Mental Health*, 11 (6), 581–4.

Beresford, P (2002b) Making user involvement real. *Professional Social Work*, June, 16–17.

Beresford, P and Croft, S (2004) Service users and practitioners reunited: the key component for social work reform. *British Journal of Social Work*, 34, 53–68.

Biglan, A, Brennan, P A, Foster, S L and Holder, H D (eds) (2005) *Helping adolescents at risk*. Hove: Guilford Press.

Bisman, C (2004) Social work values: the moral core of the profession. *British Journal of Social Work*, 34 (1), 109–23.

Blackburn, D and Golightley, M (2004) European Sociological Conference paper. University of Lincoln.

Blackstock, K, Cox, S, Mason, A and Smith, A (2005) Dementia care provision in rural Scotland: service users' and carers' experiences. *Health and Social Care in the Community*, 13 (4), 354–65.

Blenkiron, P, Cuzen, I, Hammill, A C and Kwai-Hong, M (2003) Involving service users in their mental health care: The CUES project. *Psychiatric Bulletin*, 27 (9), 334–38.

Bonynge, E R, Lee, R G and Thurber, S (2005) A profile of mental health crisis response in a rural setting. *Community Mental Health Journal* 41 (6), 675–85.

Borges, G, Angst, J, Nock, M K, Ruscio, A M, Walters, E E and Kessler, R C (2006) A risk index for 12 month suicide attempts in the National Co-Morbidity Survey Replication (NCS-R). *Psychological Medicine*, 36 (12), 1747–57.

Borsay, A (2004) *Disability and social policy in Britain since 1750*. Basingstoke: Palgrave Macmillan.

Bostik, K E and Everall, R D (2007) Healing from suicide: adolescent perceptions of attachment relationships. *British Journal of Guidance and Counselling*, 35 (1), 79–96.

Bostock, L, Bairstow, S, Fish, S and Macleod, F (2005) *Managing risk and minimising mistakes in services to children and families.* London: SCIE.

Bowl, R (2007) The need for change in UK mental health services: South Asian service users' views. *Ethnicity and Health*, 12 (1), 1–19.

Bradshaw, J (1972) The concept of social need. *New Society*, 19 (496), 640–3.

Bradshaw, T, Harris, N and Lovell, K (2005) Healthy living interventions and schizophrenia: a systematic review. *Journal of Advanced Nursing*, 49 (6), 634–54.

Brady, J (2006) The association between alcohol misuse and suicidal behaviour. *Alcohol and Alcoholism*, 41 (5), 473–8.

Briggs, S (2002) Working with the risk of suicide in young people. *Journal of Social Work Practice*, 16 (2), 135–48.

British Association of Social Workers (2002) *The code of ethics for social work.* Birmingham: BASW.

British Medical Association (2004) *Handbook of ethics and law.* 2nd edition. London: BMA.

British National Formulary (2007a) *British national formulary for children.* London: Pharmaceutical Press.

British National Formulary (2007b) *British national formulary vol. 54.* London: Pharmaceutical Press.

British Psychological Society (2000) *Code of conduct, ethical principles and guidelines.* London: BPS.

Bromley, C and Curtice, J (2003) *Attitudes to discrimination in Scotland.* NatCen/Edinburgh: Scottish Executive.

Brondon, T, Carpenter, J, Schneider, J and Wooff, D (2003) Correlates of stress in carers. *Journal of Mental Health*, 12 (1), 29–40.

Bronfenbrenner, U (1979) *The ecology of human development.* Cambridge, MA: Harvard University Press.

Bronfenbrenner, U (1986) Ecology of the family as a context for human development: research perspectives. *Developmental Psychology*, 22 (6), 723–42.

Brown, G W and Harris, T O (1978) *The social origins of depression.* London: Tavistock.

Buckley, P F and Brown, E S (2006) Prevalence and consequences of dual diagnosis. *Journal of Clinical Psychiatry*, 67 (7), 5–9..

Bürk, F, Kurz, A and Möller, K-J (1985) Suicide risk scales: do they help predict suicidal behaviour? *European Archives of Psychiatry and Clinical Neuroscience*, 235 (3), 153–7.

Burroughs, H, Lovell, K, Morley, M, Baldwin, R, Burns, A and Chew-Graham, C (2006) 'Justifiable depression': how primary care professionals and patients view late-life depression: a qualitative study. *Family Practice*, 23 (3), 369–77.

Butcher, J N, Mineka, S, Hooley, J M and Carson, R C (2004) *Abnormal psychology.* 12th edition. Boston, MA: Pearson.

Butler, A and Pritchard, C (1983) *Social work and mental illness.* Basingstoke: Macmillan.

Butler, I (2002) A code of ethics for social work and social care research. *British Journal of Social Work*, 32, 239–48.

Campbell, P (1999) *Training for mental health 3: exploring key areas*. Brighton: Pavilion Publishing.

Campbell, S P (2006) *Behaviour problems in preschool children*. 2nd edition. Hove: Guilford Press.

Carpendale, J and Lewis, C (2006) *How children develop social understanding*. Oxford: Blackwell.

Carpenter, J, Schneider, J, Brandon, T and Wooff, D (2003) Working in multidisciplinary mental health teams: the impact on social workers and health professionals of integrated mental health care. *British Journal of Social Work*, 33, 1081–103.

Carpenter, J, Schneider, J, McNiven, F, Brandon, T, Stevens, R and Wooff, D (2004) Integration and targeting of community care for people with severe and enduring mental health problems: users' experiences of the care programme approach and care management. *British Journal of Social Work*, 34, 313–33.

Carr, A (2006) *The handbook of child and adolescent clinical psychology: a contextual approach*. 2nd edition. Abingdon: Brunner-Routledge.

Cartwright, R (2002) *Mastering team leadership*. Basingstoke: Palgrave Macmillan.

Cassidy, J and Shaver, P R (eds) (1999) *Handbook of attachment: theory, research, and clinical applications*. New York: Guilford Press.

Cheers, B and Pugh, R (2008) *Rural social work: international perspectives*. Bristol: Policy Press.

Clark, C (2000) *Social work ethics*. Basingstoke: Macmillan.

Clark, T and Rowe, R (2006) Violence, stigma and psychiatric diagnosis: the effects of a history of violence on psychiatric diagnosis. *Psychiatric Bulletin*, 30 (7), 254–6.

Cleaver, H and Freeman, P (1995) *Parental perspectives in cases of suspected child abuse*. London: HMSO.

Cochrane, R (1983) *The social creation of mental illness*. Harlow: Longman Applied Psychology.

Cochrane-Brink, K A, Lofchy, J S and Sakinofsky, I (2000) Clinical rating scales in suicide risk assessment. *General Hospital Psychiatry*, 22 (6), 445–51.

Cogill, S R, Caplan, H L, Alexandra, H, Robson, K M and Kumar, R (1996) Impact of maternal depression on cognitive development of young children. *British Medical Journal*, 292, 1165–7.

Coid, J W (1996) Dangerous patients with mental illness: increased risks warrant new policies, adequate resources, and appropriate legislation. *British Medical Journal*, 312, 965–6.

Conrod, P J and Stewart, S H (2006) New advances in the treatment of co-occurring substance use and psychiatric disorders. *Journal of Mental Health*, 15 (6), 615–18.

Coppock, V (2005) 'Mad', 'bad' or misunderstood? In Hendrick, H (ed), *Child welfare and social policy*. Bristol: Policy Press.

Cratsley, K, Regan, J, McAllister, V, Simic, M and Aitchison, K J (2007) Duration of untreated psychosis, referral route and age of onset in an early intervention in psychosis service and a local CAMHS. *Child and Adolescent Mental Health* (Online Early Access). DOI: 10.1111/j.1475-3588.2007.00467.x.

Crawford, K and Walker, J (2007) *Social work and human development*. 2nd edition. Exeter: Learning Matters.

Crittenden, P (1992) Children's strategies for coping with adverse home environments: an interpretation using attachment theory. *Child Abuse and Neglect*, 16 (3), 329–43.

Crittenden, P M (2006) A dynamic-maturational model of attachment. *Australia and New Zealand Journal of Family Therapy*, 27, 105–15.

Crome, I B (1999) The trouble with training: substance misuse education in British medical schools revisited. What are the issues? *Drugs: Education, Prevention and Policy*, 6, 111–23.

Crone, D, Smith, A and Gough, B (2005) 'I feel totally alive and totally happy'. A psycho-social explanation of the physical activity and mental health relationship. *Health Education Research*, 20 (5), 600–11.

Cunningham-Burley, S, Carty, A, Martin, C and Birch, A (2006) *Sure-Start mapping exercise*. Edinburgh: Scottish Executive. Available at: www.scotland.gov.uk/Resource/Doc/89238/0021346.pdf.

Cutliffe, J R, Stevenson, C, Jackson, S and Smith, P (2006) A modified grounded theory study of how psychiatric nurses work with suicidal people. *International Journal of Nursing Studies*, 43 (7), 791–802.

Daniel, B and Wassell, S (2002) *Assessing and promoting resilience in vulnerable children: Vol. 1 – The early years; Vol. 2 – The school years; Vol. 3 – Adolescence.* London: Jessica Kingsley.

Deb, S, Matthews, T, Holt, G and Bouras, N (2001) *Practice guidelines for the assessment and diagnosis of mental health problems in adults with intellectual disability*. Brighton: Pavilion Press.

Department for Constitutional Affairs (1998) *The Human Rights Act 1998*. London: DoCA.

Department of Health (1999) *The Disability Discrimination Act 1999*. London: DoH.

Department of Health (2001) *Treatment choice in psychological therapies and counselling: evidence-based clinical practice guideline*. London: DoH.

Department of Health (2007) *Promoting mental health for children held in secure settings*. London: DoH.

Dogra, N, Parkin, A, Gale, F and Frake, C (2002) *A multidisciplinary handbook of child and adolescent mental health for front-line professionals*. London: Jessica Kingsley.

Double, D (2006) *Critical psychiatry: limits of madness*. New York: Palgrave Macmillan.

Durkheim, E (1897/2006) *On suicide*. London: Penguin Classics.

Eisen, A R (ed) (2007) *Treating childhood behavioural and emotional problems: a step-by-step evidence-based approach*. Abingdon: Routledge.

EMCDDA (2004) Selected issue 3: Co-morbidity. In European Monitoring Centre for Drugs and Drug Addiction, *Annual Report 2004: The state of the drugs problem in the European Union and Norway*. Luxembourg: Office for Official Publications of the European Communities, pp94–102. Available at: **http://annualreporTemcddAeu.int**.

Epstein, S (1983) Natural healing processes of the mind. In Newton, J (1988), *Preventing mental illness*. Abingdon: Routledge.

European Commission (2005) Green Paper – *Improving the mental health of the population: towards a strategy on mental health for the European Union*.

European Commission on Human Rights (1950) *Convention for the protection of human rights and fundamental freedoms* (as amended by Protocol No. 11, Rome, 4.XI). Brussels: European Commision Health and Consumer Protection Directorate. Available at: **http://ec.europa.eu/health/ph_determinants/ life_style/mental_green_paper/mental-gp-en.pdf**.

Fadden, G, Holsgrove, G and Shooter, M (2005) Involving carers and service users in the training of psychiatrists. *Psychiatric Bulletin*, 29 (7), 270–74.

Falkov, A (1996) *Study of 'Working Together' Part 8 Reports. Fatal child abuse and parental psychiatric disorder.* London: DoH.

Farrell, M, Howes, S, Taylor, C, Lewis, G, Jenkins, R, Bebbington, P, Jarvis, M, Brugha, T, Gill, B and Meltzer, H (2003) Substance misuse and psychiatric comorbidity: an overview of the OPCS National Psychiatric Morbidity Survey. *International Review of Psychiatry*, 15, 43–9.

Fernado, S (1999) Ethnicity and mental health. In Ulas, M and Connor, A (eds), *Mental health and social work.* London: Jessica Kingsley.

Fernando, S (2003) *Cultural diversity, mental health and psychiatry: the struggle against racism.* Abingdon: Brunner-Routledge.

Finch, J and Groves, D (1980) Community care and the family: a case for equal opportunities. *Journal of Social Policy*, 9 (4), 487–511.

Fonagy, P, Steele, M, Steele, H, Higgitt, A and Target, M (1994) The theory and practice of resilience. *Journal of Child Psychology and Psychiatry*, 35 (2), 231–55.

Foucault, M (1964) *Madness and civilisation.* New York: Random House.

Frangou, S and Bryne, P (2000) How to manage the first episode of schizophrenia. *British Medical Journal*, 321 (7260), 522.

Frankenberger, W and Cannon, C (1999) Effects of Ritalin on academic achievement from first to fifth grade. *International Journal of Disability, Development and Education*, 46 (2), 199–221.

Galilee, J (2005) *Learning from failure: a review of major social care/health inquiry recommendations.* Edinburgh: Scottish Executive.

Gamble, C and Brennan, G (eds) (2000) *Working with serious mental illness: a manual for clinical practice.* Oxford: Ballière Tindall.

Geller, B and DelBello, M P (eds) (2006) *Bipolar disorder in childhood and early adolescence.* Hove: Guilford Press.

General Teaching Council for Scotland (2002) *General code of practice.* Edinburgh: GTCS.

Gilbert, P (2003) *The value of everything: social work and its importance in the field of mental health.* Lyme Regis: Russell House.

Gilligan, R (1999) Working with social networks: key resources in helping children at risk. In Hill, M (ed.), *Effective ways of working with children and families.* London: Jessica Kingsley.

Gilligan, R (2000) Promoting resilience in children in foster care. In Gilligan, R and Kelly, G (eds), *Issues in foster care.* London: Jessica Kingsley.

Glaser, D (2001) Child abuse and neglect and the brain: a review. *Journal of Child Psychology and Psychiatry and Allied Disciplines*, 41 (1), 97–116.

Glover, K, in Bassett, T and Cuthbert, S (2000) Certificate in Community Mental Health. *Student's workbook*. Southampton: Ashford Press.

Goffman, E (1961) *Asylums*. London: Penguin.

Golightley, T M (1985) *If only they would listen: the case for a community-orientated mental health service*. Lincoln: University of Lincoln.

Golightley, M (2006) *Social work and mental health*. 2nd edition. Exeter. Learning Matters.

Göpfert, M, Webster, J and Seeman, M V (eds) (2004) *Parental psychiatric disorder: distressed parents and their families*. 2nd edition. Cambridge: Cambridge University Press.

Green, H, McGinnity, A, Meltzer, H, Ford, T and Goodman, R (2005) *Mental health of children and young people in Great Britain 2004*. Basingstoke: Palgrave Macmillan.

Griffiths, R (1988) *Community care: agenda for action*. London: HMSO.

Hammersley, P, Read, J, Woodall, S and Dillon, J (2007). Childhood trauma and psychosis: The genie is out of the bottle. *Journal of Psychological Trauma*. 6 (2/3), 7–20.

Hammond, H (2001) *Child protection inquiry into the circumstances surrounding the death of Kennedy McFarlane (17/4/97)*. Dumfries and Galloway: Child Protection Committee.

Hankin, B L and Abela, J R Z (eds) (2005) *Development of psychopathology: a vulnerability-stress perspective*. London: Sage.

Häring, B (1972) *Medical ethics*. Slough: St Paul. Cited in Butler, I (2002) A code of ethics for social work and social care research. *British Journal of Social Work*, 32, 239–48

Hawton, K and van Heeringen, K (eds) (2000) *The international handbook of suicide and attempted suicide*. Chichester: Wiley.

Heads Up Scotland (2007) *Infant mental health: a guide for practitioners*. Edinburgh: Heads Up Scotland.

Healy, K (2005) *Social work theories in context: creating frameworks for practice*. Basingstoke: Palgrave Macmillan.

Helliwell, J F (2007) Well-being and social capital: does suicide pose a puzzle? *Social Indicators Research*, 81 (3), 455–96.

Herzberg, F (1968) One more time: how do you motivate employees? *Harvard Business Review*, 46, 53–62.

Hewitt, D (2005) An inconvenient mirror – do we already have the next Mental Health Act? *Journal of Mental Health Law*, November, 138–49.

Hoghughi, M and Long, N (eds) (2004) *Handbook of parenting: theory and research for practice*. London: Sage.

Homan, R (1991) *The ethics of social research*. Harlow: Longman.

Horner, N (2006) *What is social work? Context and perspectives*. 2nd edition. Exeter: Learning Matters.

Hothersall, S J (2006) *Social work with children, young people and their families in Scotland.* Exeter: Learning Matters.

Hothersall, S J (2007) Parental psychiatric disorder: its impact upon children. Unpublished paper. Aberdeen: Robert Gordon University.

Hudson, B (1987) Collaboration in social welfare: a framework for analysis. *Policy and Politics*, 15 (3), 175–82.

Hudson, B (2002) Interprofessionality in health and social care. *Journal of Interprofessional Care*, 16 (1), 7–17.

Huxley, P (2002) Evidence in social care. In Priebe, S and Slade, M (eds), *Evidence in mental health care.* Abingdon: Brunner-Routledge.

Innes, A, Cox, S, Smith, A and Mason, A (2006) Service provision for people with dementia in rural Scotland. *Dementia*, 5 (2), 249–70.

James, A and Prout, A (eds) (2003) *Constructing and reconstructing childhood.* 2nd edition. Abingdon: Routledge Falmer.

Jamison, K R (2001) *Night falls fast: understanding suicide.* London: Vintage Books.

Jobes, D A (2006) *Managing suicidal risk: a collaborative approach.* Hove: Guilford Press.

Joiner, T E (2005) *Why people die by suicide.* Cambridge, MA: President and Fellows of Harvard.

Jones, K (1993) *Asylums and after: a revised history of the mental health services from the early 18th century to the 1900s.* London: Athlone Press.

Joseph Rowntree Foundation (2004a) *Mental health service users and their involvement in risk assessment and management.* York: JRF.

Joseph Rowntree Foundation (2004b) *Understanding what children say about living with domestic violence, parental substance misuse or parental health problems.* York: JRF.

Kalfi, Y and Torabi, M (1996) The role of parental 'expressed emotion' in relapse of schizophrenia. *Iran Journal of Medicine*, 21 (172), 46.

Kant, I (1785/1964) *Grundlegung zur Metaphysik der Sitten/Groundwork of the metaphysics of morals.* London: Harper & Row.

Karr-Morse, R and Wiley, M S (2000) *Ghosts from the nursery: tracing the roots of violence.* New York: Atlantic Monthly Press.

Keating, F and Robertson, D (2002) Breaking the circles of fear: a review of mental health services to African and Caribbean communities. *Your Shout: Mental Health Promotion*, 4, 18–19.

Kermode, F and Kermode, A (eds) (1995) *Oxford book of letters.* Oxford: Oxford University Press.

Killen, M and Smetana, J G (eds) (2005) *Handbook of moral development.* New York: Lawrence Erlbaum Associates.

Kirk, S (2005) *Mental disorders in the social environment: critical perspectives.* New York: Columbia University Press.

Kohli, R K S (2007) *Social work with unaccompanied asylum seeking children*. Basingstoke: Palgrave Macmillan.

Koprowska, J (2005) *Communication and interpersonal skills in social work*. Exeter: Learning Matters.

Kutcher, S and Chehil, S (2007) *Suicide risk management: a manual for health professionals*. Oxford: Blackwell.

Laing, R D (1985) *Wisdom, madness and folly. The making of a psychiatrist*. Basingstoke: Macmillan.

Laker, C (2006) How successful is the dual-diagnosis good practice guide? *British Journal of Nursing*, 15 (14), 787–90.

Langan, J and Lindow, V (2004) *Living with risk: mental health service user involvement in risk assessment and management*. Bristol: Policy Press.

Leason, K (2003) Ritalin nation. *Community Care*. 4–10 December, 26–8.

Le Grange, D and Lock, J (2007) *Treating bulimia in adolescents: a family-based approach*. Hove: Guilford Press.

Leff, J, Kuipers, K and Lam, D (2002) *Family work for schizophrenia*. 2nd edition. London: Royal College of Psychiatrists.

Lehmann, J (2005) Human services management in rural contexts. *British Journal of Social Work*, 35, 355–71.

Lerner, R M (2002) *Adolescence: development, diversity, context and application*. Englewood Cliffs, NJ: Prentice Hall.

Lerner, R M and Spanier, G B (1980) A dymanic interactional view of child and family development. In Lerner, R M and Spanier G B, (eds), *Child influences on marital and family interaction: a lifespan perspective*. New York: Academic Press, ppl–20

Lester, H and Glasby, J (2006) *Mental health policy and practice*. Basingstoke: Palgrave Macmillan.

Lewin, K (1997) Behaviour and development as a function of the total situation. In Lewin, G and Cartwright, D (eds), *Resolving social conflicts and field theory in social science*. Washington, DC: American Psychological Association.

Littlewood, R and Lipsedge, M (1997) *Aliens and alienists: ethnic minorities and psychiatry*. 3rd edition. Abingdon: Routledge.

Lock, J and Le Grange, D (2004) *Help your teenager beat an eating disorder*. Hove: Guilford Press.

Lohmann, N and Lohmann, R A (eds) (2005) *Rural social work practice*. New York: Columbia University Press.

Longo, S and Scior, K (2004) In-patient psychiatric care for individuals with intellectual disabilities: The service user and carer perspectives. *Journal of Mental Health*. 13 (2), 211–21.

Low, J (2004) *Lay acquiescence to medical dominance in assessing the efficacy of alternative and complementary therapies: reflections on the active citizenship thesis*. Paper presented to the European Sociological Association Symposium on Professions, Social Inclusion and Citizenship. Lincoln: University of Lincoln.

Maas-Lowit, M (2002a) *Adults with Incapacity (Scotland) Act 2000. Pack 1: Workbook and guidance for social and health care staff.* Edinburgh: Scottish Executive.

Maas-Lowit, M (2002b) *Adults with Incapacity (Scotland) Act 2000. Pack 2: Workbook and guidance for assessment and care management staff.* Edinburgh: Scottish Executive.

Macdonald, E, Hermann, H, Hinds, P, Crowe, J and McDonald, P (2002) Beyond interdisciplinary boundaries: Views of consumers, carers and NGOs on teamwork. *Australasion Psychiatry*, 10 (2), 125–29.

McBeath, G and Webb, S (2002) Virtue, ethics and social work: being lucky, realistic and not doing one's duty. *British Journal of Social Work*, 32, 1015–36.

McNorrie, K (1998) *The Children (Scotland) Act 1995: Green's annotated acts.* Edinburgh: W Green & Son.

McKinney, C, Donnelly, R and Renk, K (2007) Perceived parenting, positive and negative perceptions and late adolescent emotional adjustment. *Child and Adolescent Mental Health* (Online Early Articles). DOI: 10.1111/j.1475-3588.2007.00452.x.

Malacrida, C (2002) Alternative therapies and attention deficit disorder: Discourses of maternal responsibility and risk. *Gender and Society*, 16 (3), 366–85.

Manley, D (2005) Dual diagnosis: co-existence of drug, alcohol and mental health problems. *British Journal of Nursing*, 14 (2), 100–6.

Martin, A, Volkmar, F R and Lewis, M (2007) *Lewis's child and adolescent psychiatry: a comprehensive textbook.* 4th edition. Philadelphia, PA: Lippincott Williams & Wilkins.

Martin, J K, Pescosolido, B A and Tuch, S A (2000) Of fear and loathing: the role of 'disturbing behaviour', labels and causal attributions in shaping public attitudes towards people with mental illness. *Journal of Health and Social Behaviour*, 41 (2), 208–23.

Mash, E J and Barkley, R A (eds) (2007) *Assessment of childhood disorders.* 4th edition. Hove: Guilford Press.

Maslow, A (1987) *Motivation and personality.* 3rd edition. New York: Addison-Wesley.

May, R (2006) Resisting the diagnostic gaze. *Journal of Critical Psychology, Counselling and Psychotherapy*, 6 (3), 155–8.

Meltzer, H, Gatward, R, Goodman, R and Ford, T (2000) *Mental health of children and adolescents in Great Britain.* London: TSO.

Meltzer, H, Lader, D, Corbin, T, Goodman, R and Ford, T (2004) *The mental health of young people looked after by local authorities in Scotland: summary report.* Norwich: HMSO.

Menninger, K (1963) *The vital balance: the life process in mental health and illness.* London: Viking Press.

Mental Health Foundation (1999) *The big picture: promoting children and young people's mental health.* London: Mental Health Foundation.

Mental Welfare Commission (2003) *Investigations into the Scottish Borders Council and NHS Borders Services for people with learning disability.* Edinburgh: Mental Welfare Commission for Scotland.

Mental Welfare Commission (2006) *Report of the inquiry into the care and treatment of Mr L and Mr M.* Edinburgh: Mental Welfare Commission for Scotland.

Miklowitz, D J (2002) *The bipolar disorder survival guide.* Hove: Guilford Press.

Miller, C, Freeman, M and Ross, N (2001) *Interprofessional practice in health and social care.* London: Arnold.

Mischon, J (200) *Report of the independent inquiry team into the care and treatment of Daniel Joseph.* London: Sutton and Wandsworth Health Authority and Southwark and Lewisham Health Authority.

Morago, P (2006) Evidence-based practice: from medicine to social work. *European Journal of Social Work*, 9 (4), 461–77.

Moss, S, Emerson, E, Kiernan, C, Turner, C, Hatton, C and Alborz, A (2000) Psychiatric symptoms in adults with learning disability and challenging behaviour. *British Journal of Psychiatry*, 177, 452–6.

Mulvany, J (2000) Disability, impairment or illness? The relevance of the social model of disability to the study of mental disorder. *Sociology of Health and Illness*, 22 (5), 582–601.

Myatt, H, Rostill, H and Wheeldon, S (2004) Alternatives to Ritalin for looked after children: A culture shift. *Clinical Psychology*, 40, 34–7.

Myers, F and MacDonald, C (1996) 'I was given options not choices': involving older users and carers in assessment and care planning. In Bland, R (ed.), *Developing services for older people and their families.* London: Jessica Kingsley.

Nelson, T D, Steele, R G and Mize, J A (2006) Practitioner attitudes toward evidence-based practice: themes and challenges. *Administration and Policy in Mental Health*, 33 (3), 398–409.

Newman, B M and Newman, P R (2007) *Theories of human development.* London: Lawrence Erlbaum Associates.

Newman, T and Blackburn, S (2002) *Transitions in the lives of children and young people: resilience factors.* Barnardo's Policy, Research and Influencing Unit, Scottish Executive Education Department.

Newton, J (1988) *Preventing mental illness.* Abingdon: Routledge.

Nock, M K and Kessler, R C (2006) Prevalence of and risk factors for suicide attempts versus suicide gestures: analysis of the National Co-Morbidity Survey. *Journal of Abnormal Psychology*, 115 (3), 616–23.

Nursing and Midwifery Council (2002) *Code of professional conduct.* London: NMC.

O'Brien, S, Hammond, H and McKinnon, M (2003) *Report of the Caleb Ness inquiry.* Edinburgh and Lothians Child Protection Committee.

O'Connor, T G and Byrne, J G (2007) Attachment measures for research and practice. *Child and Adolescent Mental Health* (Advanced Access: DOI: 10.1111/j. 1475-3588.2007.00444.x).

O'Sullivan, T (1999) *Decision making in social work.* Basingstoke: Macmillan.

Oakley, A (1976) *Housewife.* London: Penquin.

Office of Public Management/Chartered Institute of Public Finance and Accountancy (2004) *The good governance standard for public services.* London: OPM/CIPFA.

Oliver, M (1996) *Understanding disability: from theory to practice.* Basingstoke: Macmillan.

Onyett, S (1992) *Case management in mental health.* Cheltenham: Stanley Thornes.

Øvretveit, J (1997) How to describe interprofessional working. In Øvretveit, J, Mathias, P and Thompson, T (eds), *Interprofessional working for health and social care.* Basingstoke: Macmillan, pp9–33.

Øvretveit, J, Mathias, P and Thompson, T (eds) (1997) *Interprofessional working for health and social care.* Basingstoke: Macmillan.

Parker, J and Bradley, G (2006) *Social work practice: assessment, planning, intervention and review.* 2nd edition. Exeter: Learning Matters.

Patel, B, Winters, M and Bashford, J (2003) *Engaging and changing: developing effective policy for the care and treatment of black and minority ethnic detained patients.* London: DoH.

Patrick, H (2006) *Mental health, incapacity and the law in Scotland.* Edinburgh: Tottel Publishing.

Patrick, H (2007) *Adult Support and Protection Bill: an update,* MHO Newsletter 14. Edinburgh: Scottish Executive.

Paudras, F (1998) *Dance of the infidels – a portrait of Bud Powell.* New York: Da Capo.

Payne, J (2006a) *Adult Support and Protection (Scotland) Bill: Part 1 – Protection of Adults at Risk of Abuse,* SPiCE Briefing 06/31. Edinburgh: Scottish Parliament. Available at: **www.scottish.parliament uk/business/research/briefings-06/SB06-31.pdf**.

Payne, J (2006b) *Adult Support and Protection (Scotland) Bill: Adults with Incapacity and Other Measures,* SPiCE Briefing 06/32. Edinburgh: Scottish Parliament. Available at: **www.scottish. parliamentuk/business/research/briefings-06/SB06-32.pdf**.

Payne, M (2000) *Teamwork in multiprofessional care.* Basingstoke: Palgrave Macmillan.

Payne, M (2005) *Modern Social Work Theory.* 3rd edition. Basingstoke: Palgrave Macmillan.

Petersen, A C (1988) Adolescent development. In M R Rosenzweig (ed.), *Annual review of psychology,* Vol 39. Palo Alto, CA: Annual Reviews, pp583–607.

Pharoah, F M, Mari, J J and Steiner, D (2000) *American Journal of Psychiatry,* 153, 607–17, in the *Cochrane Library,* issue 3, 2002, Oxford update software.

Philo, G (ed.) (1996) *Media and mental distress.* London: Glasgow Media Group and Longman.

Pilgrim, D and Rogers, A (1999) *A sociology of mental health and illness.* 2nd edition. Buckingham: Open University Press.

Platt, L (2007) *Poverty and ethnicity in the UK.* Bristol: Policy Press.

Pollack, W (1999) *Real boys.* New York: Henry Holt.

Pollard, K, Sellman, D and Senior, B (2005) The need for interprofessional working. In Barrett, G, Sellman, D and Thomas, J (eds), *Interprofessional working in health and social care: professional perspectives.* Basingstoke: Palgrave Macmillan, pp7–17.

Priebe, S and Slade, M (2002) *Evidence in mental health care.* Abingdon: Brunner-Routledge.

Prior, V and Glaser, D (2006) *Understanding attachment and attachment disorders: theory, evidence and practice*. London: Jessica Kingsley.

Pritchard, C (1995) *Suicide – the ultimate rejection*. Buckingham: Open University Press.

Pritchard, C (2006) *Mental health social work: evidence-based practice*. Abingdon: Routledge.

Public Health Institute of Scotland (2003) *Needs assessment report on child and adolescent mental health*. Glasgow: PHIS. Available at: www.phis.org.uk/pdf.pl?file=publications/CAMH1.pdf.

Pugh, R (2000) *Rural social work*. Lyme Regis: Russell House.

Pugh, R (2003) Considering the countryside: is there a case for rural social work? *British Journal of Social Work*, 33, 67–85.

Quinney, A (2006) *Collaborative social work practice*. Exeter: Learning Matters.

Ramon, S (2001) Opinions and dilemmas facing British mental health social work Cited, in Tew, J, (2001) Going social: championing a holistic model of mental distress within professional education. *Social Work Education*, 21 (2), 43–55.

Reamer, F G (1998) The evolution of social work ethics. *Social Work*, 43 (6), 488–500.

Reder, P and Duncan, S (1999) *Lost innocents: a follow-up study of fatal child abuse*. Abingdon: Routledge.

Reder, P and Duncan, S (2003) Understanding communication in child protection networks. *Child Abuse Review*, 12, 82–100.

Reder, P and Lucey, C (eds) (1995) *Assessment of parenting: psychiatric and psychological contributions*. Abingdon: Routledge.

Reder, P, Duncan, S and Gray, M (1993) *Beyond blame: child abuse tragedies revisited*. Abingdon: Routledge.

Reder, P, McClure, M and Jolley, A (eds) (2000) *Family matters: interfaces between child and adult mental health*. Abingdon: Routledge.

Repper, J and Breeze, J (2007) User and carer involvement in the training and education of health professionals: A review of the literature. *International Journal of Nursing Studies*, 44 (3), 511–19.

Ridgeway, S M (1997) Deaf people and psychological health – some preliminary findings. *Deaf Worlds*, 1 (13): 9–17.

Risk Management Authority (2006) *Annual report and accounts*. Edinburgh: RMA.

Ritchie, E C, Watson, P J and Friedman, M J (eds) (2006) *Interventions following mass violence and disaster*. New York: Guilford Press.

Ritchie, J H, Dick, D and Lingham, R (1994) *The report of the inquiry into the care and treatment of Christopher Clunis*. London: HMSO.

Rutherford, R B, Quinn, M M and Mathur, S R (eds) (2007) *Handbook of research in emotional and behavioural disorders*. Hove: Guilford Press.

Rutter, M (1966) *Children of sick parents: an environmental and psychiatric study*, Institute of Psychiatry, Maudsley Monographs 16. Oxford: Oxford University Press.

Rutter, M (1985) Resilience in the face of adversity. *British Journal of Psychiatry*, 147, 598–611.

Rutter, M (1990) Commentary: some focus and process considerations regarding the effects of parental depression on children. *Developmental Psychology*, 26, 60–7.

Rutter, M (1995) Psychosocial adversity: risk, resilience and recovery. *Southern African Journal of Child and Adolescent Psychiatry*, 7 (2), 75–88.

Rutter, M and Quinton, D (1984) Parental psychiatric disorder: effects on children. *Psychological medicine*, 14, 853–80.

Rutter, M and Taylor, E (eds) (2005) *Child and adolescent psychiatry*. 4th edition. Oxford: Blackwell.

Saxena, S, Van Ommeren, M, Tang, K C and Armstrong, T P (2005) Mental health benefits of physical activity. *Journal of Mental Health*, 14 (5), 445–51.

Scheyett, A, McCarthy, E and Rausch, C (2006) Consumer and family views on evidence-based practices and adult mental health services. *Community Mental Health Journal*, 42 (3), 243–57.

Schneidman, E S (1996) *The suicidal mind*. Oxford: Oxford University Press.

Scogin, F and Shah, A (2006) Screening older adults for depression in primary care settings. *Health Psychology*, 25 (6), 665–74.

Scottish Executive (2000a) *Adults with Incapacity (Scotland) Act 2000*. Edinburgh: Scottish Executive.

Scottish Executive (2000b) *Serious violent and sexual offenders* (The McLean Report). Edinburgh: Scottish Executive.

Scottish Executive (2000c) *Our national health*. Edinburgh: Scottish Executive.

Scottish Executive (2001a) *The same as you? A review of services for people with learning disability in Scotland*. Edinburgh: Scottish Executive.

Scottish Executive (2001b) *For Scotland's children: better integrated children's services*. Edinburgh: Scottish Executive.

Scottish Executive (2001c) *New Directions: report on the review of the Mental Health (Scotland) Act 1984* (Millan Report). Edinburgh: Scottish Executive.

Scottish Executive (2002a) *Choose Life: a national strategy and action plan to prevent suicide in Scotland*. Edinburgh: Scottish Executive. Available at **www.scotland.gov.uk/Resource/Doc/46932/0013932.pdf**.

Scottish Executive (2002b) *'It's everyone's job to make sure I'm alright': report of the Child Protection Audit and Review*. Edinburgh: Scottish Executive.

Scottish Executive (2003a) *The framework for social work education in Scotland*. Edinburgh: Scottish Executive.

Scottish Executive (2003b) *'Mind the Gaps': meeting the needs of people with co-occurring substance misuse and mental health problems*. Edinburgh: Scottish Executive.

Scottish Executive (2003c) *Getting our priorities right: good practice guidance for working with children and families affected by substance misuse.* Edinburgh: Scottish Executive.

Scottish Executive (2003d) *National programme for improving mental health and well-being. action plan 2003–2006.* Edinburgh: Scottish Executive.

Scottish Executive (2003e) *Integrated care pathways: Guide 1 – Definitions and concepts.* Edinburgh: Scottish Executive.

Scottish Executive (2003f) *Mental Health (Care and Treatment) (Scotland) Act 2003.* Edinburgh: Scottish Executive.

Scottish Executive (2003g) *Criminal Justice (Scotland) Act 2003.* Edinburgh: Scottish Executive.

Scottish Executive (2004a) *Sharing information about children at risk: a brief guide to good practice.* Edinburgh: Scottish Executive. Available at: **www.scotland.gov.uk/library5/social/sicar.pdf**.

Scottish Executive (2004b) *Getting it right for every child: report on the responses to the phase one consultation on the review of the children's hearing system.* Edinburgh: Scottish Executive.

Scottish Executive (2005a) *The new Mental Health Act – what's it all about? A short introduction.* Edinburgh: Scottish Executive

Scottish Executive (2005b) *Reserved functions of the social worker.* Edinburgh: Scottish Executive.

Scottish Executive (2005c) *The need for social work intervention.* Edinburgh: Scottish Executive.

Scottish Executive (2005d) *The role of the social worker in the 21st century: a literature review.* Edinburgh: Scottish Executive.

Scottish Executive (2005e) *The statutory social worker's role in prevention and early intervention with children.* Edinburgh: Scottish Executive.

Scottish Executive (2005f) *Equal minds: addressing mental health inequalities in Scotland.* Edinburgh: Scottish Executive.

Scottish Executive (2005g) *The mental health of children and young people: a framework for promotion, prevention and care.* Edinburgh: Scottish Executive. Available at: **www.scotland.gov.uk/Resource/Doc/77843/0018686.pdf**.

Scottish Executive (2005h) *Getting it right for every child: Supporting paper 1: The process and content of an integrated framework and the implications for implementation.* Edinburgh: Scottish Executive.

Scottish Executive (2005i) *Mental Health (Care and Treatment) (Scotland) Act 2003: Code of Practice* (Vols 1–3). Edinburgh: Scottish Executive.

Scottish Executive (2005j) *The Mental Health (Care and Treatment) (Scotland) Act 2003 (Modification of Enactments Order) 2005.* Edinburgh: Scottish Executive.

Scottish Executive (2005k) *Building a health service fit for the future* (The Kerr Report). Edinburgh: Scottish Executive.

Scottish Executive (2005l) *Child Health Support Group: inpatient working group-psychiatric inpatient services.* Edinburgh: Scottish Executive.

Scottish Executive (2005m) *National strategy for the development of the social service workforce in Scotland: a plan for action 2005–2010.* Edinburgh: Scottish Executive.

Scottish Executive (2005n) *Delivering for health.* Edinburgh: Scottish Executive.

Scottish Executive (2006a) *Changing Lives: report of the 21st century social work review.* Edinburgh: Scottish Executive.

Scottish Executive (2006b) *Co-morbid mental health and substance misuse in Scotland.* Edinburgh: Scottish Executive.

Scottish Executive (2006c) *Delivering for mental health.* Edinburgh: Scottish Executive.

Scottish Executive (2006d) *Evaluation of the first phase of 'Choose Life': the national strategy and action plan to prevent suicide in Scotland: research findings (52/2006).* Edinburgh: Scottish Executive.

Scottish Executive (2006e) *Hidden Harm: Next Steps: supporting children – working with parents.* Edinburgh: Scottish Executive.

Scottish Executive (2006f) *National quality standards for substance misuse services.* Edinburgh: Scottish Executive.

Scottish Executive (2006g) *Key capabilities in child care and protection.* Edinburgh: Scottish Executive.

Scottish Executive (2006h) *Getting it right for every child: draft Children's Services (Scotland) Bill Consultation.* Edinburgh: Scottish Executive.

Scottish Executive (2006i) *Emergency care framework for children and young people in Scotland.* Edinburgh: Scottish Executive.

Scottish Executive (2006j) *Delivering for mental health: National mental health delivery plan, National standards for crisis services.* Edinburgh: Scottish Executive.

Scottish Executive (2006k) *Joint response by the Scottish Executive, NHS Greater Glasgow and Glasgow City Council Social Work Department to the report of the inquiry into the care and treatment of Mr L and Mr M by the Mental Welfare Commission.* Edinburgh: Scottish Executive.

Scottish Executive (2006l) *Rights, relationships and recovery: the National Review of Mental Health Nursing in Scotland.* Edinburgh: Scottish Executive.

Scottish Executive (2006m) *Memorandum of procedure on restricted patients.* Edinburgh: Scottish Executive.

Scottish Executive (2007a) *The epidemiology of suicide in Scotland 1989–2004: an examination of temporal trends and risk factors at national and local levels.* Edinburgh: Scottish Executive.

Scottish Executive (2007b) *Delivering for mental health: mental health and substance misuse: consultation draft.* Edinburgh: Scottish Executive.

Scottish Executive (2007c) *Delivering a healthy future: an action framework for children and young people's health in Scotland.* Edinburgh: Scottish Executive. Available at: **www.scotland.gov.uk/Publications/2007/02/14154246/0**.

Scottish Executive (2007d) *Child and adolescent mental health services: primary mental health work. Guidance Note for NHS Boards/Community Health (and Social Care) Partnerships and other partners.* Edinburgh: Scottish Executive. Available at: **www.scotland.gov.uk/Publications/2007/02/26111857/0**.

Scottish Executive (2007e) *Increasing the availability of evidence-based psychological therapies in Scotland.* Edinburgh: Scottish Executive. Available at: **www.scotland.gov.uk/Topics/Health/health/mental-health/servicespolicy/DFMH/psychtherapies/**.

Scottish Executive (2007f) *Effective approaches to risk assessment in social work: an international literature review.* Edinburgh: Scottish Executive. Available at: **www.scotland.gov.uk/Resource/Doc/194419/0052192.pdf**. Summary report at: **www.scotland.gov.uk/Resource/Doc/194431/0052193.pdf**.

Scottish Executive (2007g) *National evaluation of 'Doing Well by People with Depression' Programme.* Edinburgh: Scottish Executive.

Scottish Executive (2007h) *Multi-agency public protection arrangement.* Edinburgh: Scottish Executive.

Scottish Executive (2007i) *Revised care programme approach for restricted patients.* Edinburgh: Scottish Executive.

Scottish Executive (2007j) *Adult Support and Protection (Scotland) Act 2007.* Edinburgh: Scottish Executive.

Scottish Executive (2007k) *Circular No. JD/15/2006 (updated March 2007). Implementation of the multi-agency public protection arrangements in Scotland.* Edinburgh: Scottish Executive.

Scottish Executive Education Department (2002) *National evaluation of the New Community Schools Pilot Programme in Scotland Phase 1 (1999–2002).* Edinburgh: SEED.

Scottish Executive/HMIe (2006) *Improving outcomes for children and young people: the role of schools in delivering integrated children's services.* Edinburgh: Scottish Executive/HMIe. Available at: **www.scotland.gov.uk/Resource/Doc/92327/0022073.pdf**.

Scottish Office (1995) *Criminal Procedures (Scotland) Act 1995.* Edinburgh: HMSO.

Scottish Office (1996) *Scottish Office Circular SWSG16/9.* Edinburgh: Scottish Office

Scottish Office (1997a) *Scotland's children: the Children (Scotland) Act 1995 Regulations and Guidance* (Vols 1–4). Edinburgh: Scottish Office.

Scottish Office (1997b) *Framework for mental health services in Scotland.* Edinburgh: Scottish Office.

Scottish Office (1998a) *New community schools: the prospectus.* Edinburgh: Scottish Office.

Scottish Office (1998b) *Implementing the care programme approach.* Edinburgh: Scottish Office.

Scottish Recovery Network (2007a) *National conference report 2007.* Glasgow: Scottish Recovery Network.

Scottish Recovery Network (2007b) *Realising Recovery: a national framework for learning and training in recovery focused practice.* Edinburgh: NHS Education for Scotland.

Scottish Social Services Council (2005) *Code of practice for social services workers and employers*. Dundee: SSSC.

Searle, J R (1995) *The construction of social reality*. London: Penguin.

Semple, M and Cable, S (2003) The new code of professional conduct. *Nursing Standard*, 17 (23), 40–8.

Shaw, P and Rapoport, J L (2006) Decision making about children with psychotic symptoms: Using the best evidence in choosing a treatment. *Journal of the American Academy of Child and Adolescent Psychiatry*, 45 (11), 1381–86.

Shea, S C (2002) *The practical art of suicide assessment: a guide for mental health professionals and substance abuse counsellors*. New Jersey: John Wiley & Sons.

Sheppard, M and Kelly, N (2001) *Social work practice with depressed mothers in child and family care*. London: TSO.

Shillington, A M, Reed, M B, Lange, J E, Clapp, J D and Henry, S (2006) College undergraduate Ritalin abusers in south western California: Protective and risk factors. *Journal of Drug Issues*, 36 (4), 999–1014.

Sinclair, R and Bullock, R (2002) *Learning from past experience: a review of serious case reviews*. London: DoH.

Singh, I (2004) Doing their jobs: Mothering with Ritalin in a culture of mother-blame. *Social Science and Medicine*, 59 (6), 1193–1205.

Smale, G, Tuson, G and Statham, D (2000) *Social work and social problems*. Basingstoke: Palgrave Macmillan.

Smalley, N, Scourfield, J and Greenland, K (2005) Young people, gender and suicide. *Journal of Social Work*, 5 (2), 133–54.

Smith, P K, Cowie, H and Blades, M (2003) *Understanding children's development*. 4th edition. Oxford: Blackwell.

Social Work Services Inspectorate (2004) *Investigations into Scottish Borders Council and NHS Borders services for people with learning disabilities: joint statement from the Mental Welfare Commission and the Social Work Services Inspectorate*. Edinburgh: Scottish Executive.

Somers, V (2006) Schizophrenia: the impact of parental illness on children. *British Journal of Social Work*. Advanced Access DOI:10.1093/bjsw/bc1083.

Sroufe, L A, Egeland, B, Carlson, E A and Collins, W A (2005) *The development of the person: the Minnesota Study of Risk and Adaptation from Birth to Adulthood*. Hove: Guilford Press.

Statham, D (ed) (2004) *Managing front-line practice in social care*. London: Jessica Kingsley.

Styer, D M (2006) An understanding of self-injury and suicide. *Prevention Researcher*, 13, 10–12.

Swain, J, French, S and Cameron, C (2003) *Controversial issues in a disabling society*. Buckingham: Open University Press.

Swinton, J (2001) *Spirituality and mental health care*. London: Jessica Kingsley.

Szasz, T S (1972) *The myth of mental illness*. London: Paladin.

Szasz, T S (2003) Psychiatry and the control of dangerousness: on the apotropaic function of the term 'mental illness'. *Journal of Social Work Education*, 39 (3), 375–81.

Tew, J (2002) Going social: championing a holistic model of mental distress within professional education. *Social Work Education*, 21 (2), 143–55.

Thompson, M, Cooper, M and Hooper, C M (2005) *Child and adolescent mental health: theory and practice*. London: Hodder Arnold.

Thompson, N (2002) *People skills*. 2nd edition. Basingstoke: Palgrave Macmillan.

Thompson, N (2003) *Communication and language*. Basingstoke: Palgrave Macmillan.

Thompson, N (2005) *Understanding social work: preparing for practice*. 2nd edition. Basingstoke: Palgrave Macmillan.

Thyer, B A and Wodarski, J S (eds) (2007) *Social work in mental health: an evidence based approach*. New Jersey: John Wiley & Sons.

Tietze, S, Cohen, L and Musson, G (2003) *Understanding organisations through language*. London: Sage.

Tiffin, P A (2006) Managing psychotic illness in young people: a practical overview. *Child and Adolescent Mental Health* (Online Early Articles DOI: 10.1111/j.1475-3588.2006.00418.x).

Ting, L, Sanders, S, Jacobson, J M and Power, J R (2006) Dealing with the aftermath: a qualitative analysis of mental health social workers' reactions after a client suicide. *Social Work*, 51 (4), 329–41.

Titterton, M (2004) *Risk and risk taking in health and social welfare*. London: Jessica Kingsley.

Tolman, A O (2005) *Depression in adults: the latest treatment and assessment strategies*. New York: Compact Clinicals.

Trotter, C (1999) *Working with involuntary clients*. London: Sage.

Tse Fong Leung, T (2006) Accountability to welfare service users: challenges and responses of service providers. *British Journal of Social Work* (Advanced Access DOI:10.1093/bjsw/bcl351).

Tuckman, B W and Jensen, M C (1977) Stages of small group development revisited. *Group and Organisational Studies*, 2, 419–27.

Tudor, K (1996) *Mental health: paradigms and practice*. Abingdon: Routledge.

Tunnard, J (2004) *Parental mental health problems: key messages from research, policy and practice*. Dartington: Research in Practice.

Turner, B (2002) Mad, bad or dangerous to know? *New Scientist*, 173, 30 March, 46–7.

Ulas, M and Connor, A (1999) *Mental health and social work: research highlights in social work 28*. London: Jessica Kingsley.

Useda, J D, Duberstein, P R, Connor, K R, Beckman, A, Franus, N, Tu, X and Conwell, Y (2007) Personality differences in attempted suicide versus suicide in adults 50 years of age or older. *Journal of Consulting and Clinical Psychology*, 75 (1), 126–33.

Vonnegut, M (1998) *The Eden express: a memoir of insanity*. London: Random House.

Vostanis, P (ed) (2007) Mental health interventions and services for vulnerable children and young people. London: Jessica Kingsley.

Vygotsky, L (1978) *Mind and society. The development of higher mental processes.* Cambridge, MA: Harvard University Press.

Walker, S (2003a) Social work and child mental health: psychosocial principles in community practice. *British Journal of Social Work*, 33, 673–87.

Walker, S (2003b) *Working together for healthy young minds.* Lyme Regis: Russell House.

Walker, S (2003c) *Social work and child and adolescent mental health.* Lyme Regis: Russell House.

Walker, S and Beckett, C (2003) *Social work assessment and intervention.* Lyme Regis: Russell House.

Wallwork, A (2007) Attention deficit discourse: Social and individual constructions. *Journal of Critical Psychology, Counselling and Psychotherapy*, 7 (2), 69–84.

Walsh, B W (2005) *Treating self-injury: a practical guide.* Hove: Guilford Press.

Wanigaratne, S, Davis, P, Pryce,K and Brotchie, J (2005) *The effectiveness of psychological therapies on drug misusing clients.* London: National Treatment Agency.

Warnock, M (1998) *An intelligent person's guide to ethics.* London: Gerald Duckworth.

Webb, S (2006) *Social work in a risk society.* New York: Palgrave Macmillan.

Webster, C D, Douglas, K S, Eaves, D and Hart, S D (1997) *HCR-20: Assessing risk for violence* (Version 2). Burnaby, British Columbia: Mental Health, Law, & Policy Institute, Simon Fraser University.

Weir, A and Douglas, A (1999) *Child protection and adult mental health: conflict of interest?* Oxford: Reed.

Westwood, S (2007) *Suicide junkie.* London: Chipmuna Publishing.

Whittington, C (2003) *Learning for collaborative practice with other professions and agencies.* London: DoH.

Wolfe, D A and Mash, E J (eds) (2006) *Behavioural and emotional disorders in adolescents.* Hove: Guilford Press.

Wolfensberger, W (1972) *The principle of normalisation in human services.* New York: NIMR.

Woodhouse, D and Pengelly, P (1991) *Anxiety and the dynamics of collaboration.* Aberdeen: Aberdeen University Press.

Woods, P and Kettles, A (eds) (2008) *Risk assessment and management in mental health nursing.* Oxford. Blackwell.

Woolf, V (1925) *Mrs Dalloway.* London: Hogarth.

Woolfson, R C, Mooney, L and Bryce, D (2007) *Young people's views on mental health education provided in schools*, National Programme for Improving Mental Health and Well-Being. Edinburgh: Scottish Executive. Available at: **www.scotland.gov.uk/Publications/2007/03/27152013/0**.

World Health Organisation (1992) *The ICD-10 classification of mental and behavioural disorders.* Geneva: WHO.

World Health Organisation (1998) *1997/1998 health behaviour in school-aged children: collaborative cross-national survey*. Available at: **www.euro.who.int/document/e82923_part_1.pdf**.

World Health Organisation (2001) *World health report*, p11. Available at: www.who.int/whr/2001.

World Health Organisation (2004) *Lexicon of alcohol and drug terms*. Geneva: WHO. Available at: **www.who.int/substanceabuse/terminology/wholexicon/en/**.

YoungMinds (2003) *Mental health services for adolescents and young adults*. London: YoungMinds.

YoungMinds (2004) *Mental health in infancy*. London: YoungMinds.

Index

Added to the page reference 'f' denotes a figure, 'g' denotes glossary and 't' denotes a table.